FREEDOM READERS

THE WILLIAM AND KATHERINE DEVERS SERIES

IN DANTE AND MEDIEVAL ITALIAN LITERATURE

Zygmunt G. Barański, Theodore J. Cachey, Jr., and Christian Moevs, editors

FREEDOM
READERS

The African American
Reception of Dante Alighieri
and the *Divine Comedy*

DENNIS LOONEY

University of Notre Dame Press

Notre Dame, Indiana

Manufactured in the United States of America

Manuscript page of the prologue to *Invisible Man* by Ralph Ellison.
Copyright © Ralph Ellison, used with permission of The Wylie Agency.

The author and publisher are grateful for permission to publish poetry from:

Black Anima by N. J. Loftis. Copyright © 1973 by N. J. Loftis.
Used by permission of Liveright Publishing Corporation.

"Detroit Renaissance" by Dudley Randall, in *A Litany of Friends,* 2d edition.
By permission of Lotus Press, Inc.

"One sees pictures of Dante" by Carl Phillips, from *Cortège.*
Copyright © 1995 by Carl Phillips. Reprinted with the permission of
Graywolf Press, Minneapolis, Minnesota, www.graywolfpress.org.

"Erudition" by Al Young. Copyright © 1992 and 2001 by Al Young.
Reprinted with permission of the author.

Library of Congress Cataloging-in-Publication Data

Looney, Dennis.
Freedom readers : the African American reception of Dante Alighieri
and The Divine Comedy / Dennis Looney.
p.   cm. — (The William and Katherine Devers series in Dante
and Medieval Italian literature ; v. 12)
Includes bibliographical references and index.
ISBN-13: 978-0-268-03386-6 (pbk. : alk. paper)
ISBN-10: 0-268-03386-2 (pbk. : alk. paper)
1. Dante Alighieri, 1265–1321—Appreciation—United States.
2. African Americans—Intellectual life.   3. Dante Alighieri, 1265–1321.
Divina commedia.   4. Dante Alighieri, 1265–1321—Influence.   I. Title.
PQ4385.U5L66   2011
851'.1—dc22

2010049951

For Rosamund and Virgil

I was glad to find him black, I have no prejudice against his color.

——Frederick Douglass on the statue of St. Peter in the Vatican

"I had some curiosity in seeing devout people going up to the black statue of St. Peter—
I was glad to find him black, I have no prejudice against his color—and kissing the old fellow's
big toe, one side of which has been nearly worn away by these devout and tender salutes of
which it has been the cold subject" (*Life and Times of Frederick Douglass* 577). For images of the
bronze statue, and a discussion of its color and material, as well as its attribution to Arnolfo
di Cambio (1232?–1302), see Calvesi, *Treasures of the Vatican* 28–31.

CONTENTS

ABOUT THE WILLIAM AND KATHERINE DEVERS SERIES IN DANTE AND MEDIEVAL ITALIAN LITERATURE

The William and Katherine Devers Program in Dante Studies at the University of Notre Dame supports rare book acquisitions in the university's John A. Zahm Dante collections, funds visiting professorships, and supports electronic and print publication of scholarly research in the field. In collaboration with the Medieval Institute at the university, the Devers program initiated a series dedicated to the publication of the most significant current scholarship in the field of Dante studies. In 2011, the scope of the series was expanded to encompass thirteenth- and fourteenth-century Italian literature.

In keeping with the spirit that inspired the creation of the Devers program, the series takes Dante and medieval Italian literature as focal points that draw together the many disciplines and lines of inquiry that constitute a cultural tradition without fixed boundaries. Accordingly, the series hopes to illuminate this cultural tradition within contemporary critical debates in the humanities by reflecting both the highest quality of scholarly achievement and the greatest diversity of critical perspectives.

The series publishes works from a wide variety of disciplinary viewpoints and in diverse scholarly genres, including critical studies, commentaries, editions, reception studies, translations, and conference proceedings of exceptional importance. The series enjoys the support of an international advisory board composed of distinguished scholars and is published regularly by the University of Notre Dame Press. The Dolphin and Anchor device that appears on publications of the Devers series was used by the great humanist, grammarian, editor, and typographer Aldus Manutius (1449 –1515), in whose 1502 edition of Dante (second issue) and all subsequent editions it appeared. The device illustrates the ancient proverb *Festina lente,* "Hurry up slowly."

Zygmunt G. Barański, Theodore J. Cachey, Jr.,
and Christian Moevs, *editors*

ACKNOWLEDGMENTS

I have incurred many debts in the process of envisioning and writing *Freedom Readers*, beginning with colleagues, past and present, at the University of Pittsburgh, who responded generously to my questions at one time or another: Walter Albert, Jonathan Arac, Renate Blumenfeld-Kosinski, Paul Bové, Yves Citton, Larry Davis, Seymour Drescher, Lucy Fischer, Larry Glasco, Ann Sutherland Harris, Roberta Hatcher, Lina Insana, Paula Kane, Marcia Landy, Mark Possanza, Francesca Savoia, Phil Smith, Susan Smith, Phil Watts, and David Wilkins. Jean Carr, Marianne Novy, and Ogle Duff planted a seed at the Chancellor's Diversity Seminar in 1998. I am indebted to the generosity of administrators too. N. John Cooper, Dean of Arts & Sciences, the late Alec Stewart, Dean of the University Honors College, William Brustein and Lawrence Feick, the former and current Directors of the University Center for International Studies, Alberta Sbragia, Director of the European Union Center for Excellence and European Studies Center, and Nancy Washington, former Assistant to the Chancellor, supported this project at various points over the past decade.

Colleagues at colleges, universities, and conferences hosted me and/or responded to my research as it developed, prompting me to articulate *Freedom Readers* in its final shape: Luigi Ballerini, Roberto Buranello, Maria Cristina Cabani, Alberto Casadei, Gary Cestaro, Massimo Ciavolella, Sylvie Davidson, M. Giulia Fabi, Guido Fink, William Francke, Laura Giannetti, Manuele Gragnolati, the late Amilcare Iannucci, Tim Kircher, Victoria Kirkham, Joseph Luzzi, Giuseppe Mazzotta, Ty Miller, Karen Pinkus, Lawrence F. Rhu, Guido Ruggiero, Arielle Saiber, Deanna Shemek, Michael Sherberg, Meile Steele, Michael Syrimis, Patricia Ward, Elissa Weaver, John Welle, Rebecca West, and Sergio Zatti.

The anonymous readers for the University of Notre Dame Press, internal and external, were helpful at every step, and their attention enabled me to turn a rough manuscript into a much better book. I owe special thanks to Nick Havely, who read the penultimate draft with great care; my notes make clear, I hope, how much I have learned from his expertise in these matters. From start to finish, Barbara Hanrahan and her staff at the University of Notre Dame Press, especially Rebecca R. DeBoer, have been a real pleasure to work with in producing the book. *Freedom Readers* would not have come into being without the support of the William and Katherine Devers Program in Dante Studies at Notre Dame, whose series editors, Ted Cachey and Christian Moevs, hosted me at the beginnings of this project and stayed in touch as the vague idea transformed into a book. The intellectual camaraderie they foster and share is inspiring.

The following librarians and libraries have been solicitous when I was on site and/or in response to my queries from afar: Linda J. Bailey, Barbara J. Dawson, M'Lissa Kesterman, Cincinnati Historical Society Library; Barbara Hall, Special Collections Department, AMPAS Library, Los Angeles; Alice Birney, Rosemary Hanes, and Wayne Shirley, Library of Congress, Washington, D.C.; Diana Lachatanere, Schomburg Center for Research in Black Culture, The New York Public Library; Ed Potten, John Rylands University Library, Deansgate, Manchester, England; Julie Shin, Whitney Museum of American Art, New York; Carla Zecher, Newberry Library, Chicago; and librarians at Fisk University, Nashville, Tennessee; E. S. Bird Library, Special Collections, Syracuse University; and Hillman Library, University of Pittsburgh.

A host of undergraduate students from the University of Pittsburgh tracked down items and reported on them to me, often with speed and clarity: Aaron Abbarno, Kacie Cope, Kevin Duffy, Leslie Gagliardo, Valerie Fabbro, Carmelo Galati, Michelle Greatti, Chivonne Harrigal, Lauren MacLaughlin, Toni Mancini, Sandra Mazzotta, Rachel Merli, Jared Tabita, Anna Talone, and Jessica Zamiska. Graduate students at the University of Pittsburgh have helped me understand parts of this project, including: Gabriella Baika, Paola Bonifazio, Daniela De Pau, Carleton Gholz, Marisa Giorgi, Chris Kaiser, Patricia Pugh Mitchell, Stefano Muneroni, Richard Purcell, Carl Schneider, and Maurizio Vito. Chris Kaiser kindly aided me in tracking down sources in the Beinecke Library at Yale University at the eleventh hour. I would be remiss not to thank the hardworking and competent staff in the Department of French and Italian at the University of Pittsburgh, Monika Losagio and Amy Nichols, who marshaled a team of assistants, including Anna Maria Branduzzi, Matt Carulli, Alyssa DiLoreto, and Danielle Marsh, to help with the details of preparing the manuscript.

I thank friends with whom at one point or another (whether they knew it or not) I discussed my work, especially Vereen Bell, Sam Fentress, Marsha Fuller, John Gunnison-Wiseman, Terry Martin, Thaddeus Mosley, William Mullen, Christina and Ellis Schmidlapp, Dennis Slavin and Julie Trubikhina, and Elsie and Rusty Smith. Pat Stack and her "cohort," Henry and Percy, shared their amazing space for writing in New York City with me. I owe much to Susan T. Vaughn, my twelfth-grade English teacher at Hillsboro High School in Nashville, Tennessee, who inspired me then to read carefully and many years later recounted her intense experience as a student at Fisk when literature was still all the rage.

I thank my mother, Betty Marion Herbert, who not only taught me to love books but also cultivated my curiosity to go beyond boundaries and over borders in the world. Speaking of which, she enrolled me in a basketball camp at Tennessee A & I in 1964 or thereabouts in the hope that I would learn something about integration firsthand; the experience of that amazing summer is somewhere in these pages. I am sad that my late stepfather, Bobby Herbert, who was intrigued with the rumors of this project, cannot read the book itself (he would have), but I am thankful nonetheless for his inspirational support. My late father, Dennis Oscar Looney, Jr., in his own way contributed to my thinking about the mixing of cultures by bringing the integrated world of jazz into our segregated life in the suburban South. We survived, and then some. Thanks to my sister, Jennifer Herbert Vick, and sister-in-law, Elizabeth Grace Herbert, who more than once supplied me with books from their respective connections. Kate and Andy Thornton and my late mother-in-law, Mary Thornton, woman of letters in an old-fashioned way, many times provided me with a quiet place to work. To my wife, Joanna Thornton, and our children, Rosamund and Virgil, great readers all three, I say thanks for the many pointers, the occasional blasts, the entertaining asides, the good dinners, and the endless patience.

WHERE POSSIBLE I have tried to use the translation of Dante's poem that the author under examination would have consulted as far as can be determined: for example, Cary for Cordelia Ray, Sinclair for Amiri Baraka, and Ciardi for Gloria Naylor. Charles Sumner cites from Thomas Brooks-bank's translation; Richard Wright (and Ralph Waldo Ellison, I assume) read Cary; Rita Dove knew the Ciardi version. It is not surprising to learn that Frances Trollope read Dante in the original, but one might not have expected the Eternal Kool Project to base their *Inferno Rap* on Cary's nineteenth-century version. When I cannot determine which translation the writer in question consulted, I have chosen from the many different translations into English according to my sense of whichever version helps me best make my argument. Singleton, Durling-Martinez, and Hollander all provide helpful commentary to which I have turned throughout this study. For citations of Dante's poem in the original, I follow the Petrocchi text as reported in the Singleton edition. Unless otherwise specified, trans-lations from other authors are my own.

The third section of the introduction on the Dante wax museum in Cincinnati appeared in a slightly different version: "'Flame-coloured Let-ters and Bugaboo Phraseology': Hiram Powers, Frances Trollope and Dante in Frontier Cincinnati," in *Hiram Powers a Firenze: Atti del Convegno di studi nel Bicentenario della nascita (1805–2005),* ed. Caterina Del Vivo (Florence: Olschki, 2007), 135–52. The section of chapter 2 on Spencer Williams appeared in an abbreviated and altered version: "Spencer Williams: An African American Filmmaker at the Gates of Hell," in *Dante, Cinema, and Television,* ed. Amilcare Iannucci (Toronto: University of Toronto Press, 2004), 129–44. A small section of the first part of chapter 3 on Amiri Baraka was published as: "The Poetics of Exile in LeRoi Jones's *The System of Dante's Hell,*" in *Exil: Transhistorische und transnationale Perspektiven,* ed. H. Koopmann (Paderborn: Mentis, 2001), 271–79. A portion of the sec-ond part of chapter 3 was originally published as "Literary Heresy: The Dantesque Metamorphosis of LeRoi Jones into Amiri Baraka," in *Meta-morphosing Dante: Appropriations, Manipulations and Rewritings in the Twenti-eth and Twenty-first Centuries,* ed. Manuele Gragnolati, Fabio Camilletti, and Fabian Lampart (Vienna and Berlin: Turia and Kant, 2010). I thank the publishers for permission to reprint.

INTRODUCTION

Dante in Malcolm X Park? That just seems weird.

The last place you'd expect to find a statue of a DWEM.

—Posted by wiredog on March 16, 2007, 8:06 A.M.,

Washington Post online

Canonicity, Hybridity, Freedom

Long before the Boston intellectual establishment sanctioned Dante Alighieri, the medieval Christian poet, as a canonical author for the prosperous readers of the gilded age, well before the New England intelligentsia began to grapple with Dante's writings and his life, and before Dante became an important rallying figure for a variety of causes in the nineteenth century in the United States and abroad, the Italian author had made it to the edges of the American frontier where he became strangely popular. How Dante's reputation flourished in Cincinnati, Ohio, in a wax museum in the late 1820s and for several decades afterward, is an interesting tale that has been neglected in the annals of Dante's reception. What makes this very early moment in Dante's popularity in the United States an appropriate starting place for this study of Dante's reception is the striking attention it gives to "a poor old negro just entering upon a state of perpetual freezing," about whom more below. *Freedom Readers: The African American Reception of Dante Alighieri and the "Divine Comedy"* argues that Dante's

1

critical fortune in the United States is tied more closely to the entangled history of the country's black and white citizens than we have ever imagined.

Freedom Readers is a literary-historical study of the surprising multitude of ways in which Dante has assumed a position of importance in African American culture, especially literary culture. It examines how African Americans have read, interpreted, and responded to Dante and his work over approximately the last two centuries, from the late 1820s on the American frontier to today, and it considers the impact of that reception on them and on their response to Dante. In many ways the African American reception of Dante follows a recognizable narrative of reception. There are texts that exemplify predictable trends in reading Dante: the Romantic rehabilitation of the author; the later nineteenth-century glorification of him as a radical writer of reform; the twentieth-century modernist rewriting; the adaptation of his epic poem into the prose of the contemporary novel; and so on. These are all moments in the African American tradition of reading Dante that fall within the ongoing reception of the medieval author in the broader culture. But surely it is unique to African American readings and rewritings of Dante to suggest that the man is a kind of abolitionist and that the *Divine Comedy* is itself a kind of slave narrative. As far as I know, only African American adaptations of Dante use the medieval author to comment upon segregation, migration, and integration.[1] This consistent response to Dante's life and poem in a political vein, this dependence on Dante to make sense of perceived injustice and to effect a change in politics to which one is opposed, underlies the play on words in the book's title, *Freedom Readers*. African American authors use Dante as if he were a "freedom rider" accompanying them on a journey through a harsh landscape of racial inequality. After all, he had been to hell and back, so why couldn't he be expected to help them deal with the segregated bus stations of Alabama and Mississippi in the early 1960s, to name only one challenge that black citizens of this country have had to overcome? If the "intent of freedom riders was to destroy state and interstate segregation policies" across the South by nonviolent activism,[2] the desire of "freedom readers" has been to confront those same policies and the political structures that enabled them—beginning with Jim Crow legislation in the nineteenth century and moving on to the civil rights struggles of the twentieth century. To be sure, some of the readers documented in this study are more confrontational than others, but they all turn to Dante for help in interpreting their paradoxical experience as citizens of the United States of America whose ancestors were likely to have arrived in this country on a slave ship. In Dante they find not only a politically engaged poet who speaks truth to power in a way that resonates with their strange experience; they also find a master craftsman of poetic language who forges a new vernacular out of the linguistic diversity around him, not unlike what authors of color have had to do in this country. Creating a poetic language, finding a voice, purifying the dialect of the tribe (as we will hear it described later in the book)—this linguistic task is the ultimate political act. And while many authors over the centuries have learned to articulate a new kind of poetry from Dante's example, for African American authors attuned to the complexities of Dante's hybrid vernacular, his poetic language becomes a model for creative expression that juxtaposes and blends classical notes and the vernacular counterpoint in striking ways.

A first step in this project is to identify the extraordinary range of imitations of Dante by artists of color in their respective historical contexts. The unusual view of Dante as a Protestant that was prominent as early as the sixteenth century makes the author more amenable to writers and artists of the thoroughly Protestant African American tradition in the nineteenth and twentieth centuries. Building on that work of identification, a goal of equal importance is to demonstrate how these imitators, some more than others, excel in their response to the original medieval model. In "Tradition and the Individual Talent," T. S. Eliot famously pointed out that a literary imitation shaped under the influence of a model may in turn cast that model in a different light, revealing unseen features of it. Joyce's *Ulysses* forces us to see Homer anew. Along those lines, the African American rewritings of Dante examined in this study should not only affect our interpretation of the *Divine Comedy* but also prompt us to assess what the methodological and theoretical implications of this history of reception might be on our understanding of African American culture. To paraphrase this interpretive work into a pair of general guiding questions, What cognitive advantage do we derive from reconsidering Dante's writing through the unique perspective provided by African American culture? And what does the reception of Dante tell us about African American culture that we might not see otherwise? An ultimate goal is to point readers in directions from which they might explore the responses to these two general questions.

I investigate this lengthy and ongoing reception through the following chronological categories in sequential chapters: (1) Colored Dante; (2) Negro Dante; (3) Black Dante; and (4) African American Dante.[3] While they are first and foremost chronological categories, each of these versions of Dante carries with it a specific semantic burden that needs to be considered and accounted for in the appropriate context. I argue in what follows that each cultural moment provides ample justification for applying these respective terms to the reception of Dante. But even so, I apply these designations with caution, aware that these terms, especially *colored* and *Negro,* when used as adjectives in the United States, even as historical markers, have often been intended to belittle the product of such a combination.[4] Is a Negro Dante, for example, some sort of lesser version of Dante, and therefore not quite as good as the original? The works I examine in this study suggest otherwise.

Translation or adaptation, broadly understood, is part of the focus of this study. How does African American culture translate Dante into formed content that has meaning and resonance to readers and viewers embedded in that tradition? And what is unique about this unheralded tradition of reception and the cultural hybridity it generates? In *The Practice of Diaspora,* Brent Edwards has proposed as a general principle of literary and cultural history that translation is the essential act defining the culture of diaspora. Translation, understood both as the literal activity of reproducing a culture's texts in a new language and more generally as the process of cultural assimilation in moving from one side to another (as the etymology of *translation* implies), links the culture that a diasporic people has emigrated out of with the culture that they have immigrated into. To understand where they are in terms of where they have come from, a people must translate their communal past—as much of it as they can remember— into their contemporary present. This process in its literal and figurative senses reveals much about the African American reception of Dante, for interpreters in this cultural tradition over the last 150 years have repeatedly called upon Dante to help them negotiate the transition from the culture of their past to that of their present. Dante, both the text and the historical figure, becomes central to the diasporic practice of readers and writers of color as they resituate themselves time and again in relation to canonical cultural paradigms. The canonical Dante is valued for having been himself an author of exile, an unusual figure of diaspora, and as such he becomes the model for a host of African American authors who see themselves in exile too and who use him to shed light on their own experience of this fate.

This is a chronology of reception that has been almost completely ignored by scholars of Dante, as well as by Americanists and African Americanists, as far as I can tell. Boswell, Friederich, Ierardo, La Piana, Levine, Milbank, and Verduin, among others, have documented Dante's critical fortune, but they have absolutely nothing to say about Dante's influence on African American culture. Among Anglo-American critics, Nick Havely, David Wallace, and Glauco Cambon are aware of this line of reception, as are the Italian critics Pietro Boitani, M. Giulia Fabi, and Walter Mauro, but no one has studied it in any depth.[5] This chronology of reception at first glance would seem at odds with Edward Said's claim that Dante's *Divine Comedy* is the foundational text in the imperial — to use his word — project of comparative literature as it developed in the twentieth century across Europe under the influence of a group of independent but like-minded Romance philologists such as Auerbach, Spitzer, and Curtius.[6] According to Said, comparative literature emerged as a discipline at the same time that a colonial Eurocentric geography was being imposed on much of the world. He argues that the conceptual framework underlying comparative literature that privileges a certain body of texts for a certain kind of comparative study is analogous to the mentality that prompted Europeans to take their administrative cultures into what seemed to them undeveloped areas and colonize them. Dante's encyclopedic summation of much of what had preceded him in medieval European culture and his idiosyncratic response to the classical tradition made his texts extremely useful in the scholarly attempt to articulate the Western literary tradition from its classical origins to the revival of classicism in the Renaissance. Thus Dante's work, especially the *Divine Comedy,* becomes a central privileged site of investigation in the modern comparatist's configuration of the literary tradition.[7]

Despite the keen attention the founding fathers of comparative literature gave to Dante,[8] there has been little notice of the African American tradition of reading and responding to the author. This tradition is often (but not always) anti-imperial, and at times uses Dante to critique the very structures of power that promote a hierarchy that keeps one group in control of another, if not colonizers versus colonized exactly, something similar enough albeit transposed to the setting of the antebellum South and the radically opposed worlds of its inhabitants: masters versus slaves. When Said observes, "And today writers and scholars from the formerly colonized world have imposed their diverse histories on, have mapped their local geographies in, the great canonical texts of the European center" (*Culture and Imperialism* 53), he is thinking of authors from the former colonial outposts of Britain, France, Belgium, and such, not specifically of writers who have responded to Dante. But what he says is strikingly apt for much of the history of Dante's reception to be considered here.[9] That is to say, that at approximately the same time as Dante is used as a foundational text in the field of comparative literature (I take Said's point), he also becomes central in a countertrend that finds its voice in writers of color across the United States from the nineteenth century to today, in a move analogous to that of Said's anticolonial authors.[10]

To be precise, in some cases the reception of Dante by writers of color in the United States over the last two centuries points toward that center that Said claims is focused on the Italian poet, but at other times Dante's reception by writers of color remains in tension with and in direct opposition to the canonical center. It is a complex and somewhat paradoxical movement, not simply the comparatist canonical Dante versus a new and radical Dante of color, but rather the comparatist canonical Dante versus a Dante of color of two different sorts (at least), one that similarly values the canonical and strives to emulate it in a variety of ways and another that seeks to critique and even upend the canonical. This seeming paradox prompts another more specific guiding question for me in this study, one with political implications: how has an imitation of Dante served as a marker that signals admittance to European culture and, paradoxically at the same time, enabled some form of rejection of it?

This dual appropriation of Dante and his work by writers of color, which holds him up as a foundational text of the Western tradition, on the one hand, and which uses him to critique the system that produces and values that sort of canonical thinking, on the other, is a feature of a response to cultural production that postcolonial theory has defined as "hybridity." Edward Said, from the same essay cited above, is helpful in parsing the notion of hybridity: "Cultural experience or indeed every cultural form is radically, quintessentially hybrid, and if it has been the practice in the West since Immanuel Kant to isolate cultural and aesthetic realms from the worldly domain, it is now time to rejoin them" (*Culture and Imperialism* 58). Said looks askance at the critical impulse of interpreting the work of art as nothing more than an aesthetic object cut off from the historical, social, and political realities that created it. The approach he correctly attributes first to Kant and the Enlightenment finds its twentieth-century followers in schools as diverse as the New Critics of the 1950s and the phenomenological criticism of Roman Ingarden and other followers of Edmund Husserl in the second half of the twentieth century.

Developing Said's idea that cultural forms are hybrid and that they need to be understood in the context of "the worldly domain," Homi Bhabha argues that hybridity is that curious formation that derives from the encounter of the colonizing power with the colonized, which the colonized then uses in turn to subvert the colonizer.[11] Hybridity comprises not only the hybrid product but also the process that creates it, a process that can then turn the product around on itself in a variety of ways. Bhabha's examples, all drawn from the annals of English colonial history in Asia and Africa, highlight the hybridity formed when metropolitan culture confronts local, indigenous cultures, with numerous cases in which the colonized culture turns the culture of the colonizer on its head. While I don't feel the need to call what I am examining in *Freedom Readers* precisely "a postcolonial Dante," I find much to suggest that Bhabha's and Said's postcolonial notion of hybridity is indeed applicable to the reception of Dante's work in African American culture, especially to the *Divine Comedy,* itself a hybrid work in more ways than one.

Dante's designation of his epic poem as a *comedy* is in part a recognition of its hybrid generic status, as he explains in the well-known letter to his patron in Verona, Can Grande della Scala. As opposed to tragedy, the genre of comedy "introduces a situation of adversity, but ends its matter in prosperity . . ." (*Epistle* 10, para. 10),[12] and in this move from high to low, the diction of comedy ranges from tragic high style to comic low style in creating a hybrid poetic mixture. For Dante the essence of comedy is the mixed nature of its linguistic fabric. His comedy has room for a description of the mystical vision of the godhead, on the one hand, and a devil farting, on the other. The art of fiction itself is figured as something of a mixed hybrid creation in the first of the two passages in the *Divine Comedy* in which the word *comedy* occurs, *Inferno* 16.128. As Geryon, the embodiment of fraud, which is presented as the counterpoint to fiction, flies up from the depths of hell to fetch the pilgrim and his guide in order to carry them down into the eighth circle, the poet feels the need to swear by the sound of the notes of his *comedìa* that what he is reporting to have seen, he really and truly saw. The monster Geryon—part dragon, snake, scorpion, with the face of a just man—is a hybrid creature *in malo,* a symbolic representation of fraud, which looks honest but will sting the second it gets a chance. Fiction, the counterpoint to fraud, works in the opposite way: it looks false but is really true. In the case of Dante's poem, it may appear that he didn't do any of the things he claims to have done, but he wants the reader to believe that he actually did. If fraud is false but appears honest at first glance, fiction by contrast is truthful though it might appear false. In other words, like the hybrid beast Geryon, the art of fiction is also hybrid. And to return to the paradox that underlies the working definition of hybridity in the postcolonial thinking of Bhabha and Said, fiction simultaneously depends on and yet rigorously undermines fraud. Dante's fiction, it turns out, is true. Or, as Charles S. Singleton put it memorably, "The fiction of the *Comedy* is that it is not fiction."[13]

We will have occasion to explore the notion of hybridity, literary and linguistic, in more detail throughout the book as we look at different interpretations and responses to Dante's hybrid poem. For now I would like to consider a recent proposal for one more hybrid category that is thoroughly in keeping with the workings of hybridity as understood in postcolonial discourse. Inverting the traditional category of "African American" in *Playing in the Dark: Whiteness and the Literary Imagination,* Toni Morrison has argued for the value of thinking about what she calls "American Africanism," a state that develops out of the creative opportunities offered by and derived from the encounter between blackness and the New World. By American Africanism she refers to a phenomenon "in which a nonwhite, Africanlike (or Africanist) presence or persona was constructed in the United States, and the imaginative uses this fabricated presence served"

(*Playing* 6). For Morrison, American Africanism describes the consistent misprision that empowers Eurocentric interpretations of black culture. She is not interested in arguing for an Afrocentric alternative, for "dominant Eurocentric scholarship [to be] *replaced* by dominant Afrocentric scholarship" (*Playing* 8); rather, she wants to explore how the encounter between black and white in the New World is shaped in the literary imagination in ways that favor white over black. In her criticism of American literature of the nineteenth and twentieth centuries, to put it simply, she examines literary blackness as it is constructed by white authors, and its curious relation to whiteness, which, it turns out, is constructed to an equal degree in those same pages. The idea of whiteness in Poe, Melville, Twain, and Hemingway is just as made up as blackness, and—Morrison's main point—the construction of whiteness depends entirely on the blackness in the literary works she examines.

In the works that I examine in this book, Dante is a source in the sense of *Quellengeschichte,* the study of literary sources which figures prominently in traditional comparative literature. But Dante is much more than merely a literary source for Morrison and other African American authors; he is a lens through which these artists approach and take the measure of European culture. And since he is critical of aspects of the dominant culture in his own day, he is invaluable to authors themselves leery of certain aspects of Western culture as a canonical author himself critical of much of what he subsumes and of much of which he is taken to represent. Perhaps Morrison's category of American Africanism provides us with a prism through which to perceive more clearly this image of Dante as a reformer whose protest against the powers that be gives him special currency among Protestant readers. That is, the consistently and sometimes overtly politicized readings of Dante's work, especially the *Inferno,* fall under the broader category of a way of reading Dante that focuses on his critique of dominant power and that then integrates that view of him and his work into the fabric of other literary projects.

The connection between Dante and African American culture has its origins in the political links between abolitionists—the outspoken adversaries of slavery in the Americas—and Italian nationalists in the Risorgimento. The politicized readings of Dante promoted by these two groups may depend in turn, at least partially, on sixteenth-century interpretations of his work by English Protestant intellectuals; their respective responses to Dante certainly have much in common with those earlier readings. We shall examine some of the connections among them in chapter 1. The historical Dante's political career and eventual exile, as well as his criticism of the papacy, his steadfast support of the Holy Roman emperor, and his belief that the two powers, spiritual and temporal, should be separated and distinct, made him into an unexpected symbol of liberty and gave him currency as a radical political thinker among English Protestants as early as the sixteenth century, as Nick Havely has explored in his work.[14] Dante's subsequent rise in popularity in the Anglo-American world depends in part on this earlier radical antiestablishmentarian "Protestant Dante." But as Antonella Braida points out in *Dante and the Romantics* (64), the political reading of the poet that comes to be associated with Foscolo and the Whigs is not embraced by all British intellectuals during the nineteenth century, reminding us to take a nuanced look at these questions of literary reception. We shouldn't expect the reception of an author as complex as Dante to be univocal.

In nineteenth-century America when the discourses of abolitionism and freedom were being declared and refined, in the decades leading up to the American Civil War in the 1860s and in the years of Reconstruction that followed, and similarly in revolutionary Europe at around the same time, the politicized view of Dante figured heavily in discussions of the poet. Many of the New England intellectual elite who promoted the study of Dante's life and works—Emerson, Lowell, Norton, and Longfellow, first among them—were also closely connected with leading abolitionists.[15] A further twist is that in these same years the various smaller political entities that filled the Italian peninsula were being shaped into a larger and more viable national state, which was formally inaugurated as Italy in 1870. Italian nationalists who argued that their compatriots were enslaved to the Austrians in the north, the Spanish Bourbons in the south, and to the Vatican throughout the peninsula, promoted Dante's unflinching criticism of the papacy in an attempt to convince their contemporaries to struggle for self-rule and determination. Giuseppe Mazzini made this case forcefully in the middle decades of the nineteenth century, and it was none other than William Lloyd Garrison, the most important American abolitionist, who edited Mazzini's writings for an Anglo-American audience in 1872. Mazzini's political Dante, inherited from Foscolo, one might say, is handed on to Garrison and through him to general readers on both sides of the Atlantic.

Dante Studies, Italy, abolitionism—each was coming into its own at approximately the same time. A major beneficiary of this confluence of intellectual activity was, unexpectedly, the slave in the American South. The slave was about to become free, at least nominally, was about to gain the opportunity to read, and was about to begin the arduous process of taking advantage of that freedom—a process that would turn him or her into a "freedom reader."[16] In keeping with the times, there is a striking tendency among these newly made African American readers to interpret Dante politically, to view Dante, the historical man (1265–1321) and the poet-pilgrim who is protagonist of the *Divine Comedy* (composed between 1307 and 1321), as a touchstone of freedom. Not surprisingly, Dante-the-pilgrim's passage from hell to heaven, like the narrative of the children of Israel fleeing Egypt in search of the Promised Land, is of heightened interest to a people with a memory of slavery.[17] In *The Man Farthest Down,* Booker T. Washington recalls first hearing the story of Exodus as a slave in Virginia and continues: "In fact, I am certain that there is hardly a day or a week goes by that I do not meet among my people some reference to this same Bible story" (240). But for counterpoint, listen to what the sociologist St. Clair Drake observes: "The urban, literate, Free Negro preachers, and even some who were slaves, elaborated a different set of key symbols from those in plantation society for whom the Exodus paradigm was paramount" (4).[18] That is, Dante is of value in the discourse against slavery because of the Exodus paradigm. But he is of value to free, literate readers of color as a symbol of liberty who grants them access to European culture. This dichotomy highlights the complexity of the intersecting traditions of reception I am tracing. In *Forgotten Readers,* Elizabeth McHenry reconstructs the literary societies of northern, urban black communities in the nineteenth century, several of which list Dante as an author worth studying,[19] and juxtaposes them to the reading and writing practices of southern blacks as represented and symbolized in the slave narrative. Dante finds a place in both those traditions. And of course the narrative of Dante-the-pilgrim's journey is of interest to religious readers for its potential relevance as an allegory on freeing one's soul from bondage to sin. Many works on the poet during the nineteenth century make reference to the theme of slavery along these lines.[20] But first things first: the canonical text of the old world must make its way to America.

Sailing with Dante to the New World

While this is a study of literary popularization, canonization, glorification, and even enshrinement, it is also a study that touches on slavery, emancipation, reconstruction, segregation, and integration. On its rather circuitous route to Cincinnati (of all places), it starts in the Gulf of Mexico at the mouth of the Mississippi River.

> I never beheld a scene so utterly desolate as this entrance of the Mississippi. Had Dante seen it, he might have drawn images of another Bolgia from its horrors. One only object rears itself above the eddying waters; this is the mast of a vessel long since wrecked in attempting to cross the bar, and it still stands, a dismal witness of the destruction that has been, and a boding prophet of that which is to come. (4)[21]

In the opening chapter of *Domestic Manners of the Americans,* Frances Trollope uses this striking allusion to Dante's *Inferno* to describe her arrival at the mouth of the Mississippi River on Christmas Day, 1827, after a seven-week voyage from London. Trollope was on her way to Nashoba, a utopian community dedicated to the education of freed slaves, established in 1825 by one of her acquaintances from England, the free-spirited abolitionist Frances Wright.[22] Nashoba was located fifteen miles inland from Memphis, Tennessee, far upriver from the Mississippi Delta. Although the greater part of Trollope's journey was over, her literary allusion suggests that she was about to enter upon the most challenging portion of the trip. Her comparison invites the reader to imagine the bleak panorama as if it were deep in Dante's hell, among the "bolgias" or "pouches" of the eighth circle, site of eternal damnation for a variety of fraudulent sinners of increasing degrees of evil in each deeper section. Trollope's description suggests that the view of the delta might have inspired Dante to conjure up another pouch farther down in hell, the worst of them all. Her use of the Italian poet in the first half of the paragraph has more literary-historical value than literary merit perhaps, but the passage assumes greater urgency and more power as it continues.

The sighting of a lone mast from a wrecked ship encourages the author to extend the Dantesque imagery in an effective way. It brings to her mind the first simile in the *Divine Comedy,* from the opening scene of the *Inferno,* which likens the protagonist of Dante's poem to a shipwrecked sailor who has barely escaped death. This opening simile is the first of an ongoing series of allusions to the myth of Ulysses. I cite it here in Henry Francis Cary's popular early nineteenth-century translation, which Trollope and her readers would have known.

> And as a man, with difficult short breath,
> Forespent with toiling, 'scaped from sea to shore,
> Turns to the perilous wide waste, and stands
> At gaze; e'en so my spirit, that yet fail'd,
> Struggling with terror, turn'd to view the straits
> That none hath passed and lived.
>
> (1:22–27)[23]

Trollope puts herself in a position analogous to that of Dante's pilgrim as she sails into the Mississippi Delta. Having survived the crossing of the Atlantic, catching sight of the shipwreck gives her pause to consider "the destruction that has been" for other less fortunate travelers. Like the sailor in Dante's simile she is safe for the time being, but like Dante the pilgrim she is about to embark on a voyage of even greater danger, for which the eerie mast can be interpreted as "a boding prophet of that which is to come." She knows Dante's poem well enough to use this allusion at the very beginning of her book to suggest to the reader that the new world she is about to enter has much in common with an inferno. Undaunted pilgrim on a mission, she sails onward, into the river channel.

After a brief stay in New Orleans, Trollope and the three children traveling with her arrived in Nashoba to their great dismay. The colony was still undeveloped: few settlers, no school, inadequate housing, poor food; and all this in a rough setting with a bad climate, at least in January. Trollope depicts Nashoba—without relying precisely on Dante—in much the same terms of desolation with which she had described the delta:

> The forest became thicker and more dreary-looking every mile we advanced but our evergrinning negro declared it was a right good road, and that we should be sure to get to Nashoba.
>
> And so we did . . . and one glance sufficed to convince me that every idea I had formed of the place was as far as possible from the truth. Desolation was the only feeling—the only word that presented itself. (27)

Trollope lasted only ten days. She quickly made plans to leave the "utopia" for a better world elsewhere on the grounds that the malarial waters surrounding the settlement endangered the health of her children. As she looked back on her brief stay at Nashoba, the only detail that tempered her miserable experience was the memory of Frances Wright's commitment to the project: "Her whole heart and soul were occupied by the hope of raising the African to the level of European intellect; and even now, that I have seen this favourite fabric of her imagination fall to pieces beneath her feet, I cannot recall the self-devotion with which she gave herself to it, without admiration" (29).[24] Wright herself was soon to abandon the project at Nashoba, but she continued to be an activist for abolitionism and women's rights until her death in 1852.

The Trollope family sailed upriver from Memphis to Cincinnati, the new boomtown in what was then called Western America, arriving on February 10, 1828. Frances Trollope liked what she saw well enough but couldn't help but be somewhat ironic: "Though I do not quite sympathise with those who consider Cincinnati as one of the wonders of the earth, I certainly think it a city of extraordinary size and importance . . ." (43). She stayed in the river town for two years; its growing population became her prime laboratory for examining the habits and ways of Americans. *Domestic Manners of the Americans,* written for her English audience back home and peppered with citations from authors like Dante, is part travel guide, part literary essay, part sociological study.[25] Above everything else, it was a book written to make money. Trollope had left England in dire financial straits, more eager to profit from investment schemes in America than to participate in idealistic causes like Nashoba. Her book proved to be the best deal with which she was involved, becoming a financial success soon after its publication in 1832, going into a fifth revised edition by 1839. Its depiction of U.S. citizens on the frontier as tobacco-spitting hayseeds amused English readers but infuriated her hosts by confirming familiar stereotypes of Americans as country cousins to the English. Controversy sold well. Although she published more than forty books before she died in Florence, Italy, in 1863, Trollope remained best known for *Domestic Manners of the Americans.*

The notorious book was not Trollope's only money-making venture in the New World. Once in Cincinnati she conceived numerous entrepreneurial schemes, presumably under the guise of research for her study of Americans. Cincinnati was the site of her Bazaar (1829–30), a shopping mall and entertainment complex modeled on Egyptian, Turkish, and fanciful gothic structures. This rambling architectural and retailing experiment reflected the nineteenth century's romanticization of Middle Eastern cultures, and with this extravaganza Orientalism had made it to the frontier.[26] The building, dubbed "Trollope's Folly" by the locals, was a monstrosity that stood for several decades; its design proved so impractical that it defied any plans to use it on a regular basis, and it continued to lose money long after Trollope left town in March 1830. As one scholar put it rather poignantly, "The Bazaar towered above her departure, a huge, grotesque monument to her hopes and failures" (Smalley li). The building was finally torn down in 1881.

The Dante Wax Museum on the Frontier, 1828

Trollope did leave behind one thriving venture, if not exactly an artistic success at least a financial one, which she first advertised as "Dante's Hell." Readers of Cincinnati's *Saturday Evening Chronicle of General Literature, Morals, and the Arts* found this advertisement on the back sheet of their four-page newspaper in the issue of August 30, 1828 (vol. 2, no. 35, p. 4, col. 2). It continued to run almost weekly into the middle of the following year after the newspaper changed its name to *The Cincinnati Chronicle and Literary Gazette.*

The proprietor of the *Western Museum* always anxious to oblige his sub-
scribers and the public and to render his Museum as attractive to them
as possible, begs to announce, that in future the entrance to the Museum
will admit to the splendid scenic exhibition of Dante's Hell, purgatory
and paradise without additional charge.

Frances Trollope knew her Dante, as we have seen, and once she had
learned enough about the citizens of this new city on the edges of Western civilization, she knew that Dante would be right for them.[27] Joining
forces with Joseph Dorfeuille, the proprietor of a local collection of natural historical oddities at the Western Museum, and a young artist who
worked for Dorfeuille, Hiram Powers, she created a chamber of horrors
called "Dante's Hell," which was an immediate success. Trollope may have
been aware of the contemporaneous revival of Dante's fortune on the
other side of the world in Florence, Italy, with the project to erect a cenotaph in the poet's honor in the church of Santa Croce, Tuscany's unofficial equivalent of Westminster Abbey, completed in 1830.[28] Decades later
Trollope and Powers would reconnect as distinguished older members of
the Anglo-American expatriate community in Florence, a group that virtually worshiped Dante. In fact, the literary entrepreneur and the artist
would both end their days in Florence, where they lie buried several feet
from one another in the Protestant Cemetery.[29] Unbeknownst to most of
their Florentine peers, their work in Cincinnati had created a unique memorial to Dante in the middle of what was, at the time, nowhere. Trollope's son Thomas recalled the creative collaboration between his mother
and Powers in Cincinnati in his memoir *What I Remember*: "And it occurred
to her to suggest to him to get up a representation of one of Dante's *bolgias* as described in the *Inferno*. The nascent sculptor, with his imaginative
brain, artistic eye, and clever fingers, caught at the idea on the instant. And
forthwith they set to work, my mother explaining the poet's conceptions,
suggesting the composition of 'tableaux,' and supplying details, while Powers designed and executed the figures and the necessary *mise en scène*" (123).
In an interview later in life, Powers himself remembered the collaboration in this way: "Soon after this, Mrs. Trollope and the French artist [her
friend Auguste Hervieu] came along . . . One of the first things I under-
took, in company with Herview [*sic*], was a representation of the infernal

regions after Dante's description. Behind a grating I made certain dark grottoes, full of stalactites and stalagmites, with shadowy ghosts and pitch forked figures, all calculated to work on the easily-excited imaginations of a Western audience, as the West then was. I found it very popular and attractive" (Bellows 404). "Dante's Hell," or as it was called more commonly, "The Infernal Regions," quickly "became the most celebrated single attraction staged by an American museum in the pre–Civil War era" (Tucker 90). And it soon became much more than a series of fixed wax tableaux. Actors playing the part of infernal greeters roamed the dark as frightened visitors gingerly made their way from one scene of the spectacle to the next. Powers eventually mechanized much of the exhibit, even adding a "metal rod as a barrier between the show and the spectators, and [he] contrived to charge it with electricity" (T. Trollope, *What I Remember* 123). There was a sign warning the spectators not to touch figures in the exhibit "written in flame-coloured letters and couched in the choicest bugaboo phraseology" (T. Trollope, "Recollections" 208). By the end of 1829, the exhibit, as described in another much longer advertisement, had grown to include "upwards of 50 wax figures (size of life) consisting of phantoms, imps, monsters, devils among which Belzebub & Lucifer are conspicuous, with a variety of human sufferers in every stage of torment" (*Cincinnati Advertiser and Ohio Phoenix,* Dec. 19, 1829).[30]

The spectacle, set up in the attic of the museum, was open to the public in the evening.[31] It recreated different sections based on Dante's hell with sinners punished by fire and brimstone as well as freezing ice. Depictions of purgatory and paradise painted on backdrops loomed behind these various animated and mechanized scenes of the underworld. A visitor from Boston, Linus Everett, described the exhibit for the Quaker *Trumpet and Universalist Magazine* in some detail, lavishing much attention on the representation of hell.[32]

On the right hand of the devil above described, and on the left of the spectator, is seen one department of this hell, which is denominated the *hell* of ice; a most heretical place, where the damned, instead of being burned in fire and brimstone, are *frozen* in eternal death! This department is filled with wax figures representing persons of all ages and conditions— and among others, I observed a beautiful child, represented as in the greatest agony, frozen fast to the foot of the infernal throne. But what added much to the *effect* was the condition of a poor old negro just entering upon a state of perpetual freezing; a sad predicament, truly, for one so constitutionally fond of a warm climate! (March 14, 1829, p. 148)

Everett's description of the "poor old negro" may be the first connection made in print between Dante's *Inferno* and African American culture. As we shall see in the chapters that follow it is a venerable association, extending from this moment on the frontiers of America to contemporary African American culture in the twenty-first century. The team of Frances Trollope and Hiram Powers sought to lend realism to the scene of the damned in their version of Dante's Hell by adding men, women, and children from all walks of life, even to the point of adding a black man. Statues of Africans occur in nineteenth-century American art, but generally not until somewhat later in the century, not until the abolitionist movement made the plight of slaves an issue in the 1840s and 1850s; in the aftermath of the Civil War images of freed slaves sometimes adorned public monuments to the soldiers and/or politicians of the North.[33] Powers's wax figure is most likely the earliest association of Dante and African American culture in art. Could this image of a black man in hell also be the earliest sculpted representation of an African American by a white artist in the United States? Alas, nothing remains of the wax figure, as far as we know, and for our knowledge of it, we must depend completely on Everett's brief description.

The language of the description suggests much about the kind of portrait Powers and Trollope intended to create. The verb *added* in the phrase "But what added much to the effect" implies that this wax figure is an additional, marginal character, in some unspecified way not quite central to the scene. And yet it is recognized as being highly effective—"But what added much to the *effect*"—Everett emphasizes this detail by italicizing *effect*. It is as if the artist had said—Everett seems to suggest—"some of my best sinners are Negroes." The patronizing phrase *poor old negro* calls to mind an Uncle Ned—the hobbling, obedient, servile, older black man of the familiar stereotype.[34] But this is an Uncle Ned who has stepped out of line, who hasn't been as obedient as he should have been, at least to God. Here is a black man who forgot who his real master was and pays the price. That he is depicted "just entering upon a state of perpetual freezing" indicates that he has just been condemned to his place in hell, where he will now freeze forever. The spectator witnesses the initial shock of the frigid setting on the dead man's soul. The condescending quip on the fate of the Negro is also revealing: "a sad predicament, truly, for one so constitutionally fond of a warm climate!"[35] This last comment raises several questions. Is the black man a free citizen of Cincinnati or is he a slave chucked into hell from some plantation way down south in Dixie? Cincinnati was an important stop on the way north to freedom; consequently many blacks passed through the city and some settled in it. It already had a sizable black presence as early as 1829, although the new immigrants were not always welcome. In fact, there was extensive antiblack rioting in the city around the time the exhibit came up.[36] In *The Origins of African American Literature,* Dickson D. Bruce comments on the racial tensions in Cincinnati in the late 1820s:

> In 1804 and 1807 Ohio had passed a series of "Black Laws" designed to discourage free people of color from entering the state, including provisions requiring proof of freedom, the posting of a substantial bond, and a guarantee, attested to by at least two white men, of good behavior. The laws were haphazardly enforced, but in 1829 city officials decided to revitalize them.
>
> Cincinnati's whites showed some division over the decision. There was actually some opposition to the enforcement policy from city newspapers; the Cincinnati Colonization Society, predictably, supported it. At least some whites used the policy as a pretext for taking matters into their own hands and decided to expel the black population forcibly, subjecting African Americans in Cincinnati to an onslaught of mob violence. (176)

It seems likely that someone like Linus Everett coming into the Powers-Trollope exhibit in these years would have been aware of these racial tensions.

Does Everett's comment about the "warm climate" refer to somewhere in the South or to the sinner's ancestral lands of Africa? Is the spectator meant to think of this sinner's punishment by freezing as the ultimate

Dantesque *contrapasso,* a punishment that in some way fits the crime, as if to say: the man enjoyed heat, now he is deprived of it forever?[37] Finally, why the exclamation point? What exactly is the joke? Perhaps there is a pun in the adverb *constitutionally,* which would have been very much in the spirit of the polished verbal wit practiced by Trollope and her associates. Of course, the "poor old negro" was not protected by the U.S. Constitution, a fact that prompted a growing number of U.S. citizens to promote the plans of the American Colonization Society, founded in 1817, and its local affiliates like the one in Cincinnati, to send free slaves back to Africa or to the Caribbean.[38] Racist humor, not always so subtle, has a long tradition in the United States, and nothing should surprise us anymore. Still, a quip like this on the wax version of Dante's *Inferno* reported in a Quaker periodical is unexpected and catches one's attention.[39]

The wax museum in Cincinnati is significant in the history of the reception of Dante for several reasons. Trollope uses her interpretation of Dante's text to respond to problems that she had earlier described in terms of the same Dantesque text. On the edges of a land where she had come seeking utopia but found instead an infernal landscape, harsh and unforgiving, she created an ersatz inferno, as if to ward off or bottle up the potential evil within the actual landscape that confronted her. She was also interested in making money. Her version of Dante may be the first commercial (nonpublishing) enterprise to capitalize so directly on the original, a model that would be imitated many times over in the coming decades and into the twentieth century with Dante's vision of hell becoming a standard source of inspiration for haunted houses on the midways of carnivals and fairs around the United States.[40] The measure of paradox that marks Trollope's use of Dante—responding to a New World inferno with the re-creation of an inferno, fighting fire with fire, as it were—characterizes other responses to Dante that we shall consider in this study.

But the most significant feature of Trollope's response to Dante for the argument of this book is the detail I have highlighted from Linus Everett's letter, that of the "poor old negro." Trollope's adaptation of hell for her Cincinnati audience, her translation of Dante, as it were, was free enough to include a diversity of racial characters including a man of African descent. In the spirit of the original text, Trollope peoples her infernal adaptation with a smattering of her own contemporaries, young and old, white and black. As I mentioned above, Trollope is most likely the first adaptor of Dante to make the collocation between the poet's work and the experience of African Americans. One wonders whether the typical visitor to the Western Museum had ever seen a work of art that dramatized the experience of a black person at all, let alone that of a black man going to hell. By all accounts the art in and of itself was marvelous in the fullest sense of the word. But the sense of wonder must have been compounded when onlookers caught sight of the black man in Trollope's exhibit, very likely their first glimpse ever of a black man framed in art. The exhibit enabled the white viewer to examine voyeuristically the fortune of the black man, moralizing all the while, as Everett does in his brief but pithy commentary on the black man's fate.

There is one final note of paradox that deserves comment. Frances Trollope had come to the United States at the behest of her friend Frances Wright to teach freed blacks at Nashoba. The utopia she came seeking was that of a new world where whites enabled liberated blacks to make progress and get on with the work of freedom. But Trollope's failure at that sort of utopian project enabled the development of another project. Dare we call it utopian too? For her establishment of Dante on the frontier, commercial though it be, with its racially integrated panorama of black and white, is but the first moment in a history of reception that will extend into the twenty-first century with ramifications for how we have come to understand the notion of freedom outlined in Dante's text. Indeed, with her version of Dante's hell, Trollope may not have turned her back on whatever it was exactly that prompted her to come to the New World in the first place. The wax museum becomes merely a different sort of teaching venue than the schoolhouse for slaves, with a different class of students.

In *A Visit to Italy,* published in 1842, Frances Trollope speaks movingly of her familiarity with Dante's poem and urges others, especially women, to make an effort to learn Italian in order to read the poet in the original. Her reason: "Methinks there is in the very machinery of Dante's poem sufficient to excite the imagination, and to send it on a voyage of discovery through regions untrodden before, and through which no hand but his can guide it" (1:335). In this same spirit of discovery, not to mention that of business, she had successfully imported Dante to the American frontier fifteen years earlier. What seemed at first a whimsical exhibit in an adjoining room of Cincinnati's Western Museum had become a thriving entertainment venue that combined theology, parlor science, and literary taste for the pleasure of the locals. At least for some of them. It is unlikely that any black citizen of Cincinnati, Natty Town as they called it, ever laid eyes on that "poor old negro." Nevertheless, I would like to see in the placement of that ephemeral wax figure at the margins of Trollope's monument to Dante a symbol that stands for the appropriation of the Italian poet by subsequent generations of African American artists. From 1828 to the twenty-first century, the "poor old negro" will undergo some radical transformations brought about by his interaction with Dante and *The Divine Comedy*. And the man of color, "evergrinning," to borrow from Trollope's lexicon, will have the last laugh.

CHAPTER 1
COLORED DANTE

For, what does a man engaged in this traffic know of humanity, justice, or the rights of a fellow man? What does he care for the sufferings of the captive, the shrieks of the agonized mother, the imploring looks and pathetic appeals of the dying slave? With the horrors of the middle passage constantly before him, does his heart relent? Looking down upon the crowded group of miserable, groaning victims of his cupidity, does a tear start in his eye? Throwing overboard the sick, for the sake of the insurance, does he reflect upon the infinite sacrifices he makes to gain a few dollars? A slave trader reflecting! What an absurdity! His conscience and heart moved! He has *no conscience,——has no heart. Look into the soul of the captain of a slave ship, and what do you see? You need not read the vision of Dante, nor visit afterwards the regions of the lost.*

—Rufus W. Clark, *The African Slave Trade* (1860)

In this chapter I examine the cultural phenomena that produce what I call Colored Dante—appropriations of the Italian poet by writers of color as well as by other nineteenth-century authors whose thinking about race and freedom is influenced by their reading of Dante. I argue that early Protestant references to the Italian author that emphasize the quality of his work and the biographical details of his life that one might associate with a reformer prepare the way for these later readings that link Dante, race, and freedom in the nineteenth century.[1] The notion of Dante as a reformer made the author more amenable to writers and artists of the African American tradition, thoroughly grounded in the Protestant religious spirit as it was (and still is).[2] I briefly consider the appropriation of Dante by William Wells Brown, the first African American novelist, who emphasizes the misfortunes of Dante's political career in his serialized novel, *Miralda; or, the Beautiful Quadroon* (1861). *Miralda* is the second redaction of what is more commonly known as *Clotelle,* published in subsequent versions in which Brown presents the more conventional image of Dante as a love poet. I then examine the image of Dante created by Cordelia Ray, a late nineteenth-century African American author whose thinking about race, civic activism, and freedom was refracted through her encounter with the medieval poet. Her fifty-two-line poem "Dante" (1885) has been ignored by students of African American literature and by critics tracking the reception of the Italian poet, as far as I can tell. And yet it is a superb example of nineteenth-century writing that foregrounds the complicated question of race in the context of a response to the *Divine Comedy,* while it also represents—one could even say it reimagines—Dante's biography. In her highly original portrait, Ray figures Dante as an abolitionist fighting for the equality of Florentine citizens, a public intellectual who resembles more a constitutional activist lawyer than the lovesick poet made popular in the second half of the nineteenth century. In 1840 Seymour Kirkup's discovery of the youthful image of Dante depicted by painters from Giotto's circle in a chapel of the Bargello[3] created an upsurge of interest in the young Dante of the *Vita Nuova,* the infatuated lover of Beatrice, which prompted an intense devotion to the poet, notably among a new wave of women readers.[4] But Ray's Dante is different. Her image of the poet is much more in line with English politicized readings, mostly eighteenth-century Whig but also earlier sixteenth-century Tudor readings, of which—I suspect—she knows nothing but with which her own interpretation is in dialogue due to her Protestant interest in Dante as a critic of the papacy.[5] Whether aware of it or not, Ray was the beneficiary of an interpretive tradition that emphasized Dante's potential for Protestant propaganda. Beginning around the mid-sixteenth century, intellectuals in England established a pattern of interpreting Dante as a radical political thinker, specifically an authority on antipapal political and doctrinal positions, in the context of Henry VIII's

struggle with the church in Rome and the ongoing cultural turmoil in Eliza-
bethan and Reformation England that followed. These interpretations,
needless to say, distort essential features of Dante's Christianity, going so
far in some cases as to liken him to Wycliffe or Luther, while at the same
time they highlight, even to the point of exaggeration, the specific line of
his thinking that was indeed critical of the papacy. This Protestant Dante
subsequently influenced Italian nationalists who promoted an idiosyncratic
understanding and use of the poet and political thinker on the eve of the
foundation of Italy. Italians needed a national hero who was critical of the
church in Rome, and if he spoke the people's language, all the better. Italian
nationalist leaders like Giuseppe Mazzini, in turn, made Anglo-American
abolitionists aware of the Italian poet as a political thinker and consequently
influenced the way in which the abolitionists understood and used Dante's
writings, especially his criticisms of the church.

Literary historians have documented how scholarly and popular interest in Dante burgeoned in the United States as the centrality of religion in
daily life began to diminish in the years after the Civil War.[6] In an unpublished lecture delivered in 1894, Charles Eliot Norton, one of the great
early scholars of Dante at Harvard, made the point unambiguously.[7] Cordelia Ray's image of Dante, however, complicates this picture, with its suggestion that a radical antiestablishmentarian "Protestant Dante" had penetrated the mentality of the abolitionists who influenced her representation
of the man and poet. Hers is a political Dante, to be sure, but with an unexpected religious genealogy. Ray's focus on the politics of freedom in her
response to the medieval poet typifies the African American interest in
Dante as a political figure, an interpretation encountered frequently in the
tradition.[8] Interestingly—and perhaps this is part of his appeal to readers
who were used to struggling and coping with defeat—Dante is recognized as a politician who ultimately lost his political battles, for which he
was punished with exile, turning him into a man without a country. At
the same time, from the beginning of this tradition in the nineteenth century to today, African American rewritings of Dante never focus on politics so much as to dismiss or disregard the religious moral overtones of
his work. In order to understand the context in which Ray developed her
thinking about Dante and the morality of freedom in the composition of
her poem, we need first to examine the curious reception of Dante as a

Protestant and then to consider how he became subsequently a touch-stone for American abolitionists and Italian nationalists before moving on to the work of Ray herself.

Dante the Protestant

Major works of Anglican theology and church history in the sixteenth century represent Dante as an authority on political and in some cases doctrinal positions that are decidedly antipapal. These works focus consistently on the same cluster of passages in the *Divine Comedy* in which the text is indeed critical of papal and church corruption, as well as on the prose treatise in Latin, *Monarchia (On Monarchy),* which examines the relations between the papacy and the Holy Roman Empire, the pope and the emperor, in detail.[9] In separate bibliographical studies Paget Toynbee, F. P. Wilson, and Jackson Campbell Boswell have performed the yeoman's job of identifying and describing the specific Anglican works that refer to Dante, setting them in the broader context of the developing struggle between Protestantism and Catholicism in England at the time. Toynbee identifies seventy-two references to Dante in printed material from the earliest in 1477 to the eve of the English Civil War in 1640; Wilson adds fourteen to that list; and Boswell finds well over another hundred unnoted references. More recently in "Dante in Reformation England," Nick Havely has begun the necessary interpretive labor (some of it also corrective) of this bibliographical foundation to understand just how Dante came to be perceived in this way in Reformation England.[10]

A key moment in the Protestant claim on Dante is the publication of *Monarchia,* which came out in 1559 in the independent city of Basel, a noted center of Protestant printing.[11] Having been placed on the *Index of Prohibited Books* in 1554 (where it remained until 1881) no doubt stirred up interest in the work.[12] Reprinted in 1566, the treatise became a central text in the debate on papal involvement in secular politics. After several centuries of relative neglect, Dante's essay would thus become a major point of contention in the growing dispute between intellectual Protestants and Catholics, precisely at that moment in English history, post–Henry VIII, when the succession of Henry's children—from Edward VI, to Bloody

Mary, to Elizabeth — rocked England's faithful as the country moved toward becoming a Protestant state. To wit, Dante's arguments on the proper relation between sacred and secular power were featured in a succession of acrimonious works that flew back and forth off the presses: Bishop Robert Horne's *An Answeare* (1566), Thomas Stapleton's *A Counterblast to Master Horne's Vayne Blaste* (1567), Bishop John Jewel's *Defence of the Apologie of the Churche of England* (1567), and John Foxe's *Acts and Monuments,* popularly known as *Foxe's Book of Martyrs* (1570). Havely has shown how the line of argument in several of these English authors is indebted to Matthias Flacius whose *Catalogus Testium Veritatis,* first published in Basel in 1556, mentions Dante in several key passages as an outspoken critic of the papacy.[13] In fact, from 1555 to 1559, John Foxe worked as a proofreader for the publisher in Basel, Oporinus or Johann Herbst, who brought to light both Flacius's *Catalogus* and Dante's *Monarchia.*[14] The convergence seems to have influenced Foxe greatly.

A few examples of how these authors cite Dante will give some sense of how he begins to play in the debate between Catholics and Protestants. To support his antipapal positions, Robert Horne introduces Dante as a critic of the papacy's move away from Christian simplicity (81r). Although he does not cite a specific passage from the Italian source, he is ready to marshal Dante in his argument against Rome. Responding to Horne in general and specifically to his attack on an author similarly embroiled in the debate, John de Feckenham, Thomas Stapleton counters by condemning the Italian poet bluntly: "Dantes a foule heretike" (334r). And in a sarcastically disparaging remark of the sort that characterizes his criticism not only of Dante but of the use of Dante as support for antipapal positions, he writes: "Nay say ye, the emperour had great lerned men on his side, experte in divinity, and in the civil and canon law. But when ye come to nomber them, ye fynd none, but the Poetes Dantes, and Petrarcha . . ." (334r). Further, on a doctrinal point, Stapleton notes that Dante's limbo contradicts the beliefs of the Protestants (334r and v). To sum up Stapleton's criticism of Dante and of those who cite him in the debate between the old and new faiths in the sixteenth century, in his own words: "Surely Dantes, for his other opinion towching the emperours subjection is counted not muche better then an heretyke" (334v). John Jewel, like Stapleton before him, brings Petrarch into the debate alongside Dante against the Roman church, mentioning Petrarch as a critic of Rome full of heresies (616). Finally, John Foxe's widely disseminated *Book of Martyrs* presents Dante as a key figure in the development of a line of argument against papal corruption that predates Luther and his followers. Foxe cites Dante's reference to the church as the Whore of Babylon in *Purgatory* 32.142–50, a key passage in the debate, which he interprets rather bluntly: "In his canticle of purgatory, he declareth the Pope to be the whore of Babilon" (1570 ed., bk. 4, p. 491).[15] He paraphrases the passage from *Paradise* 29.81 ff. on the misinterpretation of Scripture by clergy in the pulpit with its dramatic climax: "The Pope saith he, of a pastor is made a woolfe" (491). He can overargue the case for Dante's proto-Protestantism as in the claim that he "refuteth the Donation of Constantine to be a foreged and a fayned thing, as which neither dyd stand with any law or right" (491). Dante believed the Donation to be wrongheaded but nowhere does he suggest that the document was a forgery. Foxe's edition comes with shoulder notes printed in the margins, one of which couldn't be clearer: "Dantes an Italian writer against the pope" (491).[16]

As the debate between Protestants and Catholics escalated in the sixteenth century, the church would eventually call on its most effective voice to weigh in on the conflict, Cardinal Robert Bellarmine. In the 1580s and 1590s, shortly before he took up the fight against Galileo and his followers, Bellarmine established himself as an authority on Catholic doctrine by writing a massive treatise, *Disputationes . . . de Controversiis Christianae Fidei adversus huius temporis Haereticos* (On Controversies of the Christian Faith). The work was first published over twelve years between 1581 and 1593, and had a wide circulation as the authoritative statement on the church's position against Protestantism.[17] For Bellarmine, too, Dante proved an able resource. He includes an appendix at the end of the first volume which considers the more controversial passages in the *Divine Comedy*, drafted in response to a treatise by François Perrot that criticized the papacy.[18] Bellarmine's five specific points of rebuttal and explanation are as follows. (1) Dante refers to only six popes in hell, whereas Protestants had suggested that the number was much higher. The popes named are Anastasius II, Celestine V, Nicholas III, Boniface VIII, Clement V, and John XXII.[19] (2) The image of the whore on the waters at *Inferno* 19.106–8, doesn't refer to the church, but rather to pagan Rome. (3) Bellarmine reinterprets *Purgatory* 33.34–36, to conclude that Dante is not making controversial claims about the sanctity of the Eucharist. (4) Concerning *Purgatory* 33.43, Bellarmine discusses the DXV prophecy, as Werner P. Friederich observes,

> where Dante spoke of *cinquecento dieci e cinque* who, sent by God, should slay the enemy. To the Protestants this 515 seemed close enough to 1517, the beginning of Luther's reformatory activity; and their conviction that Dante thus actually had prophesied the coming of Luther was still strengthened by the fact that the Roman numbers of 515, DXV, could easily by transposed into DVX [or *dux,* the Latin for "leader"], the leader in the battle against the Church of Rome. This viewpoint seemed supported also by Inferno 1.101, where Dante spoke of the mysterious Veltro, the Greyhound that would kill the vicious she-wolf and free man—for Veltro, naturally, seemed but an anagram for Lvtero, Martin Luther. This, however, was not Bellarmine's interpretation at all; both the DUX and the Veltro, according to him, referred to Can Grande della Scala, and not to anybody else. (*Dante's Fame* 83)

(5) Bellarmine claims that at *Paradise* 29.120, Dante was critical not of indulgences in general but of priests who gave pardons to sinners for pay. Thus he tries to account for many of the significant passages in Dante's work that were being used against Catholics. Here is not the place to track the specific fortunes of Bellarmine's arguments in any more detail other than to note that this reappropriation of Dante is further evidence of the serious role his ideas played in articulating the debate for and against Protestantism during the Counter-Reformation.

Over the course of early modern English history, Protestant sympathizers would recycle Dante's criticisms against the papacy of several centuries earlier in defense of their new "true" faith. These various criticisms could be boiled down to one main point: the Roman church had corrupted itself by becoming too entangled in secular affairs. But citing certain passages from Dante's work or alluding to him in general proved useful on several other points as well. There are growing references to, among other topics, his denunciation of simony with its suggestion that priests were hawking the Holy Spirit as a kind of magical power; his promotion of the vernacular; his protonationalistic hopes for a unified state under the Holy Roman emperor; and the story of his personal tragedy that culminated in his exile.

Some readers went so far as to see him as a precursor to Luther. The association of Dante with Luther, sometimes presented in a positive light but most often raised as a criticism, figures heavily in nineteenth-century discussions of Dante as an author of reform and protest. The points that connect Dante and Luther are more or less those same topics that make the Italian poet useful first for the Protestant-Catholic debate originating in the sixteenth century, and subsequently for the interlinked causes of the nineteenth century, Anglo-American abolitionism and Italian nationalism. By way of transition to considering Dante in the context of these two political movements, I want to examine the way several nineteenth-century writers link him with Luther, thus going further to identify Dante as a Protestant.

Of the various nineteenth-century American thinkers who knew about Dante, Charles Sumner may well have had the most profound understanding of the Italian poet, grounded as it was in a more careful reading of Dante's writings than was that of any of his peers. One of the founders of the Republican Party, Sumner read Dante extensively at an early moment in his intellectual development when traveling around the Italian peninsula in the late 1830s, the first of several trips to the area.[20] Once into his political career, Sumner became known for his fiery oratory characterized by a consistent and vehement denunciation of slavery. On numerous occasions he turned to Dante in his public speaking, for example, in a memorable speech that he delivered in New York on May 9, 1855, "The Antislavery Enterprise: Its Necessity, Practicability, and Dignity with Glances at the Special Duties of the North":

> I begin with the Necessity of the Antislavery Enterprise. . . . I do not dwell, Sir, on the many tales which come from the house of bondage: on the bitter sorrows undergone; on the flesh galled by manacle, or spurting blood beneath the lash; on the human form mutilated by knife, or seared by red-hot iron; on the ferocious scent of blood-hounds in chase of human prey; on the sale of fathers and mothers, husbands and wives, brothers and sisters, little children, even infants, at the auction block; on the prac-

tical prostration of all rights, all ties, and even all hope; on the deadly injury to morals, substituting concubinage for marriage, and changing the whole land of Slavery into a by-word of shame, only fitly pictured by the language of Dante, when he called his own degraded country a House of Ill Fame . . . On these things I do not dwell. (*His Complete Works,* 11–12)

The speaker alludes to the condemnation of Italy enunciated in the poem's second canticle (*Purg.* 6.76–78), an invective that moves from comparing the whole of Italy to a prostitute in a whorehouse and culminates with a stinging rebuke of Florence as a sick woman tossing on her bed. In Sumner's enlightened allusion to this passage the dissolution of the family brought on by slavery triggers a rather familiar image of the slave as concubine, which in turn prompts the notion that the land of the slaves, the South, is a den of iniquity—a sequence of images that is probably found elsewhere. But the charged reference to Dante's *bordello* gives the passage its particular resonance and erudition.

As Sumner concludes "The Antislavery Enterprise," he makes a second reference to Dante, this time to the *Inferno,* in which he actually cites the text in translation.

> Better strive in this cause, even unsuccessfully, than never strive at all. The penalty of indifference is akin to the penalty of opposition,—as is well pictured by the great Italian poet, when, among the saddest on the banks of Acheron, rending the air with outcries of torment, shrieks of anger, and smiting of hands, he finds the troop of dreary souls who had been ciphers in the great conflicts of life: —
>
> > "Mingled with whom, of their disgrace the proof,
> > Are the vile angels, who did not rebel,
> > Nor kept their faith to God, *but stood aloof.*"[21]

Adding his own emphasis, Sumner lifts a passage from Dante, whom he refers to simply as "the great Italian poet," from *Inferno* 3.37–39, among the Neutrals in ante-hell, those sinners who would never commit to a cause. It is a fitting image for U.S. citizens unable to take their stand at that specific moment in American history.

In a long speech delivered before the Senate over two days, on May 19 and 20, 1856, "The Crime against Kansas: The Apologies for the Crime; the True Remedy," Sumner again alludes to the Neutrals, referring specifically to Celestine V who made the "great refusal" (*Inf.* 3.60). Pope Celestine's abdication in 1294 after only several months in power made it possible for Boniface VIII, a target for Dante's ire, to be elected.

> Let it [Congress] now take stand between the living and dead, and cause this plague to be stayed. All this it can do; and if the interests of Slavery were not hostile, all this it would do at once, in reverent regard for justice, law, and order, driving far away all alarms of war; nor would it dare to brave the shame and punishment of the "Great Refusal." But the Slave Power dares anything; and it can be conquered only by the united masses of the People. From Congress to the People I appeal. (*His Complete Works* 245)

Sumner was expressing his disapproval of the infamous Kansas-Nebraska Bill, which prepared the way for Kansas to be admitted to the Union as a state allowing slavery. In the speech he also roundly denounced the two men who had proposed the bill, Stephen A. Douglas and Andrew Butler. Two days later in the Senate chambers, Preston S. Brooks, a congressman from South Carolina related to Butler, used a cane to beat Sumner almost to death. Despite the outpouring of public support for him, Sumner took nearly three years off to recover from the attack away from the Senate and Washington political life.

Sumner convalesced in style during a tour through Europe, even though the people of Massachusetts had voted him back into office in the Senate in 1857. He had made it clear he couldn't attend to those duties due to his fragile health, physical and mental, but his constituents wanted his empty desk in the Senate chambers to be a visible reminder of the cruelty of Brooks and his southern supporters on the eve of the Civil War. From his travels in Italy Sumner reports to a friend in the fall of 1858: "The north of Italy left a painful impression, for everywhere were white-coated Austrians. . . . I have made many little pilgrimages; — to Brescia, because there was the original of Thorwaldsens's *Day & Night*; to Verona, because it sheltered Dante in his exile; to Vicenza, because it was home of the architect Palladio, & to Worms, because of Luther. These days have been sweet & happy" (*Letters* 1:516).[22] Of note, first, is the reference to Dante in exile. Sumner proposes to visit Verona "because it sheltered Dante," commemorating the city for its welcome of the estranged poet. The balcony of Romeo and Juliet is not on the itinerary. I don't know of other readers seeking out Verona for this specific reason this early in Dante's Anglo-American reception. But as details of Dante's biography were becoming better known and more central in the reception of the poet, tourists did visit the various places of Dante's exile, even with specifically designed maps in hand.[23] After a visit to nearby Vicenza, Sumner travels to Worms, in Germany, "because of Luther." The collocation of Dante and Luther, an odd and unexpected pairing from the point of standard intellectual history, makes sense in the context of the tradition of Dante as a Protestant.

Sumner's comments in the letter have something of a casual tone but there are many other more definitive connections between Dante and Luther made by Sumner's contemporaries. In the nineteenth century Luther is often described as "the Dante of the German language" for his successful efforts at establishing a literary koiné out of the various dialects of Germany in his lifetime, which he used not to write an epic poem like the *Divine Comedy,* but to translate the Bible, an epic undertaking of a different sort that literally took God's word to the people.[24] In an anonymous review of James Lowell's *Among My Books,* a critic writing from a Roman Catholic perspective uses the category of reformer to criticize Luther and Lutheran-inspired interpretations of Dante in line with Lowell's reading of the Italian poet: "Dante proved himself a reformer of the most aggressive kind. The difference between him and Luther was that Dante endeavored to reform men by means of the church; Luther endeavored to destroy the church rather than reform himself."[25] "The poem is a *practical* one,— it is the work of an ardent reformer," writes Oscar Kuhns in a letter to the editor of *The Dial* magazine in 1897 in reference to the *Divine Comedy*; he continues: "[Dante's] religious ideals are high, and as sound as those of today. . . . In many respects they coincide with those of Luther himself" (110). Not all commentators would go so far in their assessment of Dante's views, but many readers in the second half of the nineteenth century were impressed with the voice of protest they heard in his writing.

Volume 75 of the *Westminster Review* (1861), a British journal of review articles also published out of New York in an American edition, is revealing for its collocation of articles that focus on Dante as well as Italian nationalism and abolitionism. The volume includes essays on "The Neapolitan and Roman Questions" (59–80); "American Slavery: The Impending Crisis" (81–91); "Cavour and Garibaldi" (91–108); "Dante and His English Translators" (108–24); "The Sicilian Revolution" (178–92); and "Austria and Her Reforms" (268–81). These are presumably the kind of essays that would satisfy an intellectual reader of the 1860s in the United States. The piece on Dante is a lengthy review article that examines sixteen translations of the *Divine Comedy,* published between 1802 and 1859. One of the translations from 1859, *The Trilogy, or Dante's Three Visions,* by an Englishman, J. W. Thomas, is of special interest for its ideological approach to Dante's poem. Of it, the anonymous reviewer states:

> If the hatred of Catholicism has been a cause, (and we feel sure it has been a principal cause), why Dante has been so little read in England, we must allow that Mr. Thomas is doing good service by a bold endeavour to divert its virulence. Finding that Englishmen will not read Dante because he is so strictly and entirely a Catholic, he offers the suggestion that the notion has all along been erroneous, and that Dante, though born too soon in time, was really a Protestant, just as the old Patriarchs are said to have been really Christians. It is difficult to characterize severely enough the amount of misapprehension which this view exhibits. (123)

In the middle of the nineteenth century, J. W. Thomas, whose initials appropriately stand for John Wesley, rendered Dante in a translation with commentary that highlights and exaggerates his antipapal attitudes at every possible passage.[26] Our anonymous reviewer continues: "The warmth of Mr. Thomas' charity and the soundness of his own Protestant orthodoxy have forced him to ascribe new motives and views to Dante, which Dante himself would have been the very first to repudiate. It would be impossible, we believe, to exaggerate what would have been his hatred of the essentials of Protestantism" (123). The reviewer then provides a lengthy list of the punishments of numerous sinners—schismatics, heretics, blasphemers, and traitors—as described in Dante's *Inferno* to conclude on this note:

"We must leave it to the reader to imagine what combination and increase of these torments would have been devised as sufficient for Martin Luther" (123).

Throughout Thomas's translation and commentary, there are allusions and references to Protestantism, as, for example, when he cites Samuel Wesley, John's brother, on Brutus (1:350). In the preface, however, he states outright: "But he [Dante] is equally worthy of the high esteem and reverential study of British Protestants, as an illustrious *Precursor of the Reformation*" (x). In a separate introductory piece that precedes the translation, "On the Religious Opinions of Dante," Thomas outlines similarities between Dante's thinking and that of Luther (xli–xlvii). The specific points don't matter as much to my argument as does the simple fact that here was a Protestant promoter of Dante who peddled an identifiably Protestant translation of the poet. Thomas completed the second volume of his translation, *The Vision of Purgatory,* in 1862, and used the occasion to respond to the Westminster reviewer in an introductory essay, "On the Catholicism of Dante," in which he outlines twelve major similarities between Dante and the English theologian and religious reformer John Wycliffe, identified as "The Morning Star of the Reformation" (viii–xi). The gist of Thomas's argument is that Dante's Catholicism is evangelical and pure and therefore more like Protestantism than its Roman counterpart. In a separate essay on the doctrine of purgatory, Thomas argues that the poem's second canticle should be read as an allegory or parable, and he uses the rest of the essay to criticize current ecclesiastical practices in Rome of which he provides ample evidence of the "holy traffic in spiritual benefits to the departed" (xxi).

Thomas dedicates the second volume to "Garibaldi and the People of Italy," which prompts a laudatory response from the Italian patriot himself, printed in the preface to the third volume on *Paradise.* The third volume came out in 1866, just after the recent celebrations in honor of Dante in 1865, at a moment of burgeoning nationalism as the state of Italy was on the verge of coming into being. The political moment prompts the following comment by Thomas: "May the happy gathering in Florence, a symbol of the unity and freedom to which Italy has at length attained, prove a means of strengthening that unity, without which her freedom cannot long be maintained, and a truthful augury of that complete emancipation of all her children from the Austrian yoke and the Papal tyranny, and from the dominion of error, superstition, and vice, which we doubt not is, in the counsels of a wise and gracious Providence, intended for her" (ix). But Thomas's *Paradise,* for all its spirit of uplift, is hardly convincing as a commentary infused by Protestantism. It is simply too difficult to read that portion of Dante's poem in a theological key different from what the author had originally intended. Consequently, the response to Thomas's Dante, such as it was, was short-lived.

While a radical Protestant Dante of the sort proposed by John Wesley Thomas was not a viable cultural figure, the proposal is nonetheless indicative of the surging interest in new popular readings of the Italian poet in the nineteenth century in Italy, England, and the United States. Several decades later the Reverend George McDermot, writing on "Dante's Theory of Papal Politics" in *Catholic World* (1897), provides a striking example of the Catholic need to recuperate Dante under pressure from these sorts of Protestant interpretations. In the first section of his essay, which he calls pointedly "Dante's Words Misinterpreted," McDermot critiques "the use Protestants and Italian revolutionists have made of his views" (356), especially in *Monarchia.* From his Catholic perspective at the end of the century, Protestants and Italian revolutionaries are a formidable and lamentable tandem. In a subsequent section, "His Faith Was Sound," the apologist asserts bluntly: "Those who claim him as a pioneer of the Reformation in the same way that they claim Huss and Wycliffe, those who think he was speculatively allied to the Albigensians or the Waldenses, misunderstand the theory of Dante" (363). By this moment in the reception of Dante, there is a serious attempt to contest the multiplying Protestant interpretations of his work. This Counter-Reformation, as it were, in the interpretation of Dante will eventually be absorbed into the ongoing scholarly work of academia devoted to an accurate exegesis of the poet's work.

In response to these many attempts in the second half of the nineteenth century to claim Dante as one sort of a thinker or another, a new kind of work began to be published of which Gauntlett Chaplin's *Dante for the People* is exemplary. In the introduction to this popularizing version of the *Divine Comedy,* the editor states unashamedly that the book's "design is to disentangle the poet, in a degree, from the theologian and the politician" (5).

That is, by 1913 when *Dante for the People* came out, there was the sense that overtly politicized translations, commentaries, and appropriations had lost sight of the real Dante and his poem. A new need emerged to reclaim Dante not as Catholic or Protestant but as a poet in his own right. Indeed, some readers were ready to enjoy this more neutral interpretation of the Italian poet, whereas others, as we shall see in the following chapters, especially readers of color, continued to interpret Dante with a political edge. But before we can move into the twentieth century in the following chapters to see how certain artists accomplish that task, we need to delve more deeply into the nineteeth-century political reception of Dante so readily dismissed by Chaplin. What exactly was he responding to?

Abolitionists and Nationalists, Americans and Italians

Italian nationalists adopted the tradition of using Dante to mount arguments in protest against the Roman church during the nineteenth century as the disparate states of the Italian peninsula lurched toward the formation of the modern country of Italy. And by extension Dante's proto-Protestant attitudes emboldened others further afield in their respective struggles against overbearing authorities, including, as we shall see, many in the United States as the young country moved toward the dissolution of its union. The movements of Anglo-American abolitionism and Italian nationalism came together as mid-nineteenth-century America looked on with interest at the political developments in Europe in 1848. Across the Italian peninsula and its adjacent islands, as well as in many other places around the Continent, rebellion was brewing: in Milan, Venice, Sicily. The Piedmontese were waging a war of independence to liberate themselves from Austrian dominion, as they had tried to do unsuccessfully in 1821. In 1848 once again they failed, but the setback this time was only temporary. Events had been set in motion that would lead to the creation of a unified country by 1870, the foundation of the modern state of Italy.

In the United States, abolitionists prepared the way for an opening to Italian political culture with a steady stream of reporting on the deteriorating relations between northern Italians and Austrians in the late 1840s and

1850s. The *North Star,* the anti-slavery newspaper founded by Frederick Douglass in 1847 and published in Rochester, New York, included a regular column with news from Europe, which often reported on the tense situation in Italy. The reports are decidedly pro-Italian in tone and frequently contain the suggestion that the Italian people under the Austrians are suffering a form of slavery. The issue of July 21, 1848 (vol. 1, no. 30), includes the following report from one of the paper's correspondents:[27]

London, June 23, 1848

Dear Douglass,

Europe is no quieter. . . . In Italy, many military operations have taken place. The Italian army has all along fought gallantly. . . . The lower provinces of the Austrian Empire [Alto-Adige, Lombardy, Veneto, Friuli-Giulia] are in terrible confusion. The danger of their entire severance is hereby increasing. *The old question of race, never entirely at rest, is being again mooted.* [my emphasis]

The American abolitionists took not only a practical interest in political developments abroad at this time but also a philosophical one: in the Italian peninsula they saw a people in the process of being unified—the author refers to its army as the "Italian" army—bound to an overwhelming power—the Austrian Empire; the abolitionists saw a nation struggling to break free. And as this citation makes clear, it was easy for them to interpret what they observed in terms of race: "*The old question of race, never entirely at rest, is being again mooted.*" The political upheavals in Italy were an occasion for a debate about race with implications for the problem of race in the Americas. In 1848 Italy's struggle to free itself from a foreign power's dominion was becoming part of the discourse of freedom.

There is much evidence that Americans, including African Americans, maintained their interest in the Italian struggle over the following decades. To pick one among many examples, several of which we will consider in more detail below, on March 19, 1867, after Congress had enacted legislation to ensure the rights of freed slaves, the Reverend E. J. Adams, a leader of the black community in Charleston, South Carolina, delivered a speech to his fellow citizens that began: "These are revolutionary times. For many years a contest, terrible in its nature, has been waged between despotism and republican principles, between freedom and slavery, until finally we behold the genius of republican liberty bearing its escutcheon upon the threshold of the capitol of every nation, waving its banner in triumph over every continent, sea and ocean. The sacred fire pent up in the bosom of the Italian nation, like the fires of Vesuvius, hath recently burst forth in all its sublimity, scattering its enemies and unshackling itself from that despotism which trampled it under its feet for nearly two centuries" (461).[28] The speaker interprets the various revolutions that have taken place around the world (in the United States, Italy, Russia, and Germany) as part of a larger almost cosmic pattern. And in his catalogue of the wave of revolutionary fervor, the Italians take pride of place. Here a prominent African American preacher speaks to a public assembly of primarily African Americans and does not hesitate to cite the Italian case as a model and parallel for his own people's circumstances. The powerful metaphor of "unshackling" the chains that bound the Italians to foreign powers is a rhetorical signal that no recently liberated slave could fail to appreciate.

The mastermind behind the revolutionary events as Italy attempted to extricate itself from the Austrians, the French, and the control of the Roman Catholic Church was Giuseppe Mazzini.[29] Mazzini grew up in the turbulent early decades of the 1800s when various foreign powers vied for control of Italy, and spasmodically active groups of Italians tried unsuccessfully to oust the occupying forces. Encouraged by his parents, Mazzini early on assumed the identity of a revolutionary on a mission to unify Italy and to revive the former glory of Rome as a secular capital. His first-hand experience of the ineffectiveness of various revolutionary groups in the 1830s prompted him to found his own organization from his base in exile in France, which he called "Giovine Italia," Young Italy. As the name suggests, Mazzini placed much emphasis on the youth of the peninsula — on their education and on their potential for insurrection, even violent revolt if necessary. His model of unified Italy depended heavily on his belief in the doctrine of progress embodied in the potential of the people under God's guidance. An important authority along these lines for Mazzini was Dante's *Monarchia,* of which he wrote: "I had imbibed that doctrine [of progress] in Dante's *Della Monarchia,* a book little read and invariably misunderstood" (*Joseph Mazzini* 19). As we saw above, this crucial minor

work, which outlines the theory behind Dante's criticism of papal inter-
ference in secular government, had become a touchstone in the furious
debate between Protestants and Catholics in the 1560s and 1570s. Mazzini's use of it situates him in that ongoing cultural debate still raging in
the nineteenth century.

In 1848 Mazzini returned to Italy after seventeen years in exile to
capitalize on the uprisings reported in the *North Star*. Disturbances sprang
up around the northern and central parts of the peninsula in Leghorn,
Genoa, Venice, and Milan, among other cities. The various uprisings culminated in the destabilization of Austrian power in the north and the temporary loss of Vatican control of Rome. Mazzini and his followers, including Garibaldi, established a new Roman state, which they hoped would
be the centerpiece of a unified Italian peninsula, but their radically open,
modern, democratic republic could not withstand the pressure put on it
by foreign powers at the request of the pope. The experiment in government lasted only one hundred days, and Mazzini, the people's leader, was
forced into exile again in 1849. He spent a brief period in Switzerland in
hopes of returning to Italy, living, he says, "as if in a whirlwind, something
like Paolo without Francesca" (*Joseph Mazzini* 204). During his later years,
he began to translate the New Testament into Italian, an undertaking very
much in keeping with the radical Protestant tradition of recasting God's
word into the language of the people (Smith, *Mazzini* 77). He spent the
final years of his life on the move around Europe as a respected but ultimately not very influential onlooker of the Italian scene, dying in Pisa
in 1872.

A prolific writer, Mazzini used his time in exile to produce what
amounts to over one hundred volumes in the national edition of his works.
A constant favorite was Dante—the first book he was allowed in prison
in 1870 was a copy of the *Divine Comedy*—in fact, Dante played an important part in the evolution of Mazzini's ideas on Italian culture and nationalism (Smith, *Mazzini* 211). In a juvenile essay he wrote in 1826, which was
published against his will nine years later, Mazzini first discusses Dante's
love of country. In a longer, more mature piece on Dante's minor works
which first appeared in 1844, "Opere minori di Dante," Mazzini made a
claim for Dante's own nationalism and patriotism, the essence of which

was frequently repeated by many others in the decades that followed: "Dante was neither Catholic, nor Ghibelline, nor Guelph; he was Christian and Italian" (*Scritti letterari* 293).[30] Later in the same essay, Mazzini elaborates: "Dante was neither a Guelph nor a Ghibelline. Like every man who burns with the flame of genius, he followed his own course aiming at a higher goal to which the masses did not aspire. Beyond the politics of the Guelphs or the Ghibellines, he saw Italian Unity. . . . Italy alone was sacred to him" (*Scritti letterari* 317). Similar passages that laud the Italian poet and stress his *italianità* abound in Mazzini's corpus and are as likely to appear in a political or a religious essay as in a literary-critical piece.[31]

While Mazzini's general knowledge of Dante informs many of his essays, his philological and editorial skills are also shaped by his reading of the poet, evident in the work he did to complete the late Ugo Foscolo's edition of the *Divine Comedy*. Foscolo (1772–1834) was a patriotic exile who died in England several years before Mazzini would seek refuge there. In addition to his own exemplary efforts for the Italian cause, Foscolo was one of the first critics to popularize Dante among British readers. Of Mazzini's dedication to completing Foscolo's edition of Dante, Denis Mack Smith notes: "In an extraordinary labour of love, without payment and without even having his name on the title-page, Mazzini completed and annotated in four volumes Foscolo's unfinished commentary on Dante's *Divine Comedy*. This, he explained, was a moral duty so that Italians could be helped to understand the heroes of their own culture" (26). By "heroes" of the culture Mazzini meant men such as Dante, but he also held Foscolo in high standing, and it is easy to interpret Mazzini's editorial anonymity as a kind of heroic false modesty. The title page reads: *La Commedia di Dante Alighieri Illustrata da Ugo Foscolo,* edited by "An Italian" (London 1842). Although completed in England under the auspices of various British patrons, this edition of Dante was a project very much for Italy and the Italians, for a people in the process of being defined in a country beginning to take shape.

It should come as no surprise that an Italian nationalist like Mazzini, or Foscolo for that matter, would turn to the greatest Italian author for nourishment and inspiration at that moment in history when there was an aggressive push to forge a unified country out of the disparate states throughout the Italian peninsula. But should one expect the abolitionists based in the United States with their own troubled history to receive sustenance from the Italian poet and from the same nationalist cause promoted in his name in Italy? Mazzini, like the reporter for the *North Star* in Europe, posited similarities among different kinds of enslavement, which other readers were then free to develop in ways that made sense to them and that resonated with their own causes. Among these others, William Lloyd Garrison, arguably the most dedicated American abolitionist, stands at the forefront.

Garrison's awareness of Dante derives in large part from his familiarity with Mazzini's writings, some of which he edited for publication in 1872 in the volume *Joseph Mazzini: His Life, Writings, and Political Principles*. Much as Garrison had presented Douglass to the reading public with his preface to the first version of Douglass's autobiography, *Narrative of the Life of Frederick Douglass, an American Slave* (1845),[32] so he does in this book with Mazzini. The two men were introduced in London in 1846, and their friendship grew stronger over the following years during which time they shared "the same hostility to every form of tyranny," Garrison reports (vii). They reconnected in 1867, as Mazzini's health was seriously on the wane, due, laments Garrison, to his excessive cigar smoking. Garrison's description of Mazzini's dependence on tobacco as "self-imposed bondage" from which he needed "immediate and unconditional emancipation," may be something of a rhetorical exaggeration, but Mazzini was to die from a cancerous tumor five years later in 1872, the year Garrison's anthology was published.

In the introduction to the volume, Garrison provides an intellectual portrait of Mazzini appropriate for Anglo-American readers, stressing the man's commitment to abolitionism in general. He cites a lengthy passage from a letter Mazzini wrote to the head of the North of England Anti-Slavery Association in 1854 and comments on its "impressive language" (xv):

> Blessed be your efforts, if they start from this high ground of a common faith; if you do not forget, whilst at work for the emancipation of the black race, the millions of white slaves, suffering, struggling, expiring in Italy, in Poland, in Hungary, through all Europe; if you always remember that free men only can achieve the work of freedom, and that Europe's ap-

peal for the abolition of slavery in their lands will not weigh all-powerful before God and men, whilst Europe herself shall be desecrated by arbitrary, tyrannical power, by czars, emperors, and popes. (xvi)

In another letter to an unidentified abolitionist which Garrison cites in the introduction, Mazzini is even more direct in the comparison between struggles in Italy and the Americas: "We are fighting the same sacred battle for freedom and the emancipation of the oppressed: you, sir, against *negro*, we against *white* slavery. The cause is truly identical" (xvi).[33] Whether or not the causes were indeed identical is beside the point: both Mazzini and Garrison believed they were.[34]

Writing in the 1870s, Garrison felt compelled to rehabilitate Mazzini's democratic and populist legacy, which had suffered with the fall of the short-lived Roman Republic in 1849 and with the establishment of a constitutional monarchy in unified Italy. Garrison conceded that it eventually fell to others like Cavour and Garibaldi to take Italy from revolution to republic in the Risorgimento, but he wanted the record to state that Mazzini had done his part to start the process. And that he had done so on a moral high ground. Garrison's choices for his anthology highlight the importance of Dante in Mazzini's development as a moral political being. In an autobiographical piece Mazzini recalls the composition of his first literary article: "The subject was Dante, whom during the years 1821 to 1827 I had learned to venerate, not only as a poet, but as the father of our nation" (*Joseph Mazzini* 5). Mazzini's literary criticism of the author was a decidedly political act with nationalistic overtones. On a more personal level, Mazzini came to identify with Dante as a fellow outcast, as he would do with Foscolo and as Foscolo had done with Dante, men without a country forced to spend much of their lives in exile—Mazzini and Foscolo outside of Italy, Dante outside of Florence.[35] Mazzini often remembered the cruel treatment of exiles before and during the period of the Risorgimento (157–63, e.g.), and many onlookers saw a connection between the modern man and his medieval counterpart along these same lines. Moncure Conway, an American expatriate and a minister in the Unitarian church based in London, referred to him as "the greatest Italian since Dante" (Smith, *Mazzini* 188), a comparison that must have pleased Mazzini since he consciously modeled himself on the Italian poet, according to some historians (Barr 149). In that vein, with a touch of playful irony, Mazzini responds to a letter from Emilie Ashurst: "Yes, I am like Dante in many things. He was thin; so am I. He was exiled *in* Italy; I am exiled *out*. The differences are very slight indeed. He was a poet; I am not. He is immortal; I shall be dead to all ten years after my death. The balance is evidently in favor of the likeness" (Hinkley 159). On a more serious note, one of Mazzini's recent biographers comments in regard to his edition of Foscolo's Dante: "Some of the annotations were actually Mazzini's, so it is hard to tell whether that Dante described as 'the great citizen, the reformer, the poet of religion, the prophet of nationality, of Italy' is Foscolo's or Mazzini's; that particular Dante certainly resembles Mazzini" (Sarti 101). It was not difficult to see similarities between the two men.

An especially poignant autograph by Mazzini, dated June 22, 1851, and signed in London, corroborates this image of the man with strong emotional ties to Dante in exile.[36] In the middle of a single sheet of paper, in a tight semicursive script, Mazzini pens a line slightly adapted from the *Divine Comedy*: "E venni dal martirio a questa pace." The verse "I came from martyrdom to this peace" (he adds the initial conjunction *e* [and] at the beginning of the line; he also alters the poetic form of *martiro* to the more standard *martirio*) comes from an episode in heaven where Dante meets his great-great-grandfather, Cacciaguida, among the Christian martyrs (*Par.* 15.148). The pilgrim's relative refers movingly to the peace of the blessed in heaven only to continue with a prophecy of the bitterness of exile that Dante will experience in due course (17.37–99). The quote must have resonated within Mazzini's memory — the small errors suggest he is not transcribing it from a written text — as a gloss on his own condition: neither he nor Dante has the peace of Cacciaguida's blessed state.[37] Both must endure, by contrast, the status of exile; and it is likely that both thought at times that martyrdom would have been a better fate. A set of quotation marks frames the line from *Paradise* with the name Dante written just beneath it. An inch below, the author signs his own name, with his Christian name in English instead of Italian, as if to inscribe his harsh fate in exile more precisely: Joseph Mazzini.

We saw above that the feature of Dante's writing that consistently caught Protestant readers' attention was his criticism of the church in Rome. The bracing rhetoric of anticlericalism was authorized in Dante's poem where he condemns at least ten popes to damnation and probably meant to suggest that more popes were damned than saved.[38] While Garrison never comments specifically on Dante's antipapal positions, he does criticize forcefully the institution of the papacy. In a letter of January 10, 1871, Garrison writes to Theodore Roosevelt, the father of the twenty-sixth president, about an upcoming celebration in honor of "Italian Unity and the Emancipation of Rome" to take place in New York City (*Letters* 6:185). In the letter, Garrison doesn't mince words about his stance on the papacy and Pius IX: "The overthrow of the despotic power of the Pope, in regard to civil liberty and the rights of conscience, removes the most formidable barrier which has ever been erected against free thought, free speech, free inquiry, and popular institutions" (185). He holds the pope responsible for having enslaved Italy, as he puts it in the fervent language of a radical abolitionist: "And let the people of Italy resolve never more to wear the fetters of civil or religious bondage" (186). It is a position with which Mazzini expressed sympathy guardedly at various points in his life,[39] although he could never say it quite as openly and emphatically as his Protestant friend from Boston.

The radical antipapist position articulated by Garrison and inspired by some of Mazzini's writings, and through him by Dante's positions, was making its way into the mainstream. Popular journalism dealt with this and other issues connected with Italian culture, as did the more specialized abolitionist publications like the *North Star* and the *Colored American.* In the March 1854 number of the *Southern Literary Messenger,* the Reverend John C. McCabe published a lengthy poem at the conclusion of his grand tour of Europe, "The Homeward Bound," which contains this stanza focused on political concerns:

> Oh! Italy, whose long dark night
>> Of chains and tears, we thought was o'er;
> We caught thy shriek of wild delight,
>> That rising over Ocean's roar,
>> Was wafted from thy lovely shore,—
> Oh! Italy, for thee we weep,
> 'Twas but thy dream in slavery's sleep!

(188)

McCabe's allusion to the political problems Italy faced in the 1850s depends on the familiar image of the country's enslavement. But for McCabe, the slave master is not an unspecified foreign foe, nor is he specifically Austrian or French; rather, the master who controls Italy is none other than Pope Pius IX.

> I saw the Pope with triple crown,
>   Sit (as they said) in Peter's Chair.
>   I heard him mumble out a prayer,—
> Oh, fisherman of Galilee,
> Can this thing thy successor be?
>
> I could not think my country dear.
>   God gave *him* power to loose and bind;
> I could not dream of freedom *there,*
>   For superstition chains the mind
>   In many a dark and serpent wind;
> And lust, and violence, and pride,
> Roll over Rome with festering tide!
>
>   (188)

The poet alludes to the complicated political position of the Roman Catholic Church during the period leading up to the reunification of the peninsula in the 1860s. The church did what it could politically to block reunification at every step of the way, but Pius IX eventually was forced into exile within the confines of the vastly shrunken Vatican state. Over the course of McCabe's poem the shackles of slavery metamorphose into the chains of superstition, the church's instrument for enslaving its subjects. A typical Protestant critique of Catholicism proceeded along these lines with the pope as master of mumbo jumbo ("I heard him mumble out a prayer"), who captures and then enslaves the minds of the gullible and superstitious faithful. Rome and the rest of Italy are enslaved to—McCabe's simplicity is harsh—"this thing." A better poet, John Milton, had made an equally harsh critique of the pope two hundred years earlier in his sonnet "On the Late Massacre in Piedmont," which alludes to the murder of Waldensian Protestants in northwestern Italy in 1655:

> Their martyr'd blood and ashes sow
> O'er all th'Italian fields where still doth sway
> The Triple Tyrant . . .
>
> (10–12, p. 25)

"Triple" because the pope wears three mitered crowns, with an additional allusion to the mystery of the Trinity as well. "Tyrant" speaks for itself. But whereas Milton's choice category of evil is an ecclesiastical monarch, for the abolitionists the embodiment of evil is a slave master. Few American abolitionists go as far as Garrison and McCabe to put the pope in this category. But Frederick Douglass can be ironic about the Vatican and the very first bishop of Rome, as the epigraph to this book makes clear. "I was glad to find him black, I have no prejudice against his color," he wrote after he saw Arnolfo di Cambio's bronze statue of St. Peter in the mother church of Christendom, putting all reverence aside. No genuflections there.

Criticism of the papacy is just one connection between the cultures of the abolitionists and the Italian nationalists. A passage from a stump speech among Douglass's papers, "The Legacy of John Brown," suggests another link and sheds some light on his thoughts about the cultures of the United States and Italy. On the eve of the Civil War with states about to secede from the Union, he proposed a way to save the slaves in a speech delivered in Boston: "I believe a Garibaldi would arise who would march into those States [of the South] with a thousand men, and summon to his standard sixty thousand, if necessary, to accomplish the freedom of the slave" (3:419). There was really no need for Douglass to make the statement hypothetical given the late date of his speech, December 3, 1860: the Union needed a Garibaldi to finish the work that John Brown (who counted at least one soldier from Garibaldi's army among his own followers) had begun in Kansas in 1855–56 and at Harper's Ferry in 1859.[40] The collocation of Garibaldi and John Brown made by Douglass is picked up by other writers, most noticeably John Cournos, who dedicates an entire section of *A Modern Plutarch* to a comparison between Garibaldi and Brown.[41]

Wendell Phillips, another leading abolitionist of the day, poses a direct and unusual connection between Dante and John Brown in a speech delivered in Boston on November 7, 1860, at the news of Lincoln's election. The speech is in many ways a eulogy of John Brown whose death was being interpreted by abolitionists as a martyrdom worth fighting for. "Why, it is not impossible that Virginia herself, clothed and in her right mind, may yet beg of New York, the dust of John Brown for some mausoleum at Richmond, as repentant Florence, robed in sackcloth, begged of Ravenna the dust of that outlawed Dante, whom a century before she had ordered to be burned alive. [Great cheering.]"[42] The audience's enthusiastic response is yet another indication of the familiarity of the Italian writer to general readers on the eve of the Civil War. The fullness of references to Dante in the abolitionists' political rhetoric is impressive. Not only Dante as idiosyncratic voice of liberty, Dante as Luther, Dante in exile, but also Dante's dust deserving of a proper memorial. It's actually a quite sophisticated train of thought, juxtaposing Richmond and New York with Florence and Ravenna, colored by the hopeful suggestion of a repentant southern capital trying to make amends. But Lincoln's election, which Phillips's speech first reports, prompted the secession of South Carolina from the United States, and most southern states quickly followed suit. Phillips's wishful rhetoric went unfulfilled.

Abraham Lincoln, for his part, never refers to Dante, the man or his works—not really surprising given Lincoln's infrequent references to other authors—nor does he refer very often to Italy despite the cataclysmic events affecting the peninsula during his time spent in public life. The truth is that the American politician had enough to worry about in the years leading up to his narrow victory in the election for president in 1860, and he certainly had his hands full from 1860 till the week before his death in 1865. Onlookers, however, do pose connections between Lincoln and Dante: most notably chronological, but even physiognomic. Briefly on this latter similarity first. None less than Charles Sumner calls Lincoln to his reader's mind by comparing the president to John Flaxman's portrait of Dante, which accompanied many nineteenth-century translations of the *Divine Comedy*: "As he stood, his form was angular, with something of that straightness in its lines which is so peculiar in the figure of Dante by Flaxman" (*Memorial* 132–33).[43] This rather odd visual perhaps depends more on Lincoln and Dante as iconic emblems of solitude than on any actual similarities in their appearances. But it is striking nonetheless. As for the chronological connections posed between the two men, Lincoln's career coincides with the burgeoning of Dante's reputation in the nineteenth century in Italy and the Anglo-American world. And his life comes to its tragic end as the nationalistic promotion of Dante is in full swing in Italy. Consequently, as members of the Italian intellectual community gathered throughout Italy in 1865 to celebrate the life and work of Dante at the six-hundredth anniversary of the poet's birth, they were in a position to respond formally when they learned of Lincoln's assassination on April 14 of that year. Among the many expressions of condolence compiled by the State Department is the following from Rector Gelastoni of the University of Pavia to the U.S. ambassador to Italy, dated May 12, 1865: "Honored Sir: A number of the students of this Royal University assembled yesterday to vote an address for the ceremonies about to take place in Florence in honor of the great Italian poet (Dante); and remembering the event in the United States that put an end to the life of ABRAHAM LINCOLN they hereby express their profound sympathy for your people, who place justice and liberty above all things, and beg me to be the interpreter of these sentiments" (*Assassination of Abraham Lincoln* 459). The celebration of Dante, which was also a celebration of Italian nationhood, became an occasion to reflect on the progress of what a letter of sympathy from the University of Perugia referred to as "Young America" (460), a label that suggested a bond in much more than age between the followers of "Giovine Italia" and the United States.[44] In Rome shortly after Lincoln's death, the Anglican congregation of expatriates had the first Protestant church in the city erected, Saint Paul's within-the-Walls. From 1872 to 1876, the church rose in a very prominent site on Via Nazionale, the grand boulevard laid out in honor of the new nation, extending from Piazza Repubblica down one side of the Quirinale hill to Trajan's Forum. The English artist Edward Burne-Jones was commissioned to complete a mosaic cycle in the apse which includes, among the Christian warriors, the very noticeable image of Lincoln alongside Garibaldi and other Italian heroes (1885–94).[45] In the apse of a modern church, Protestant no less, in ancient Rome, the capital of the new republic of Italy, in the striking medium of paleo-Christian mosaics renovated by the Pre-Raphaelite Burne-Jones, Abraham Lincoln takes his place among the saints.

This memorializing of Lincoln, the saintly hero, is matched by a vehement demonizing in print of his assassin, John Wilkes Booth. An author could do no better than George Alfred Townsend, who, when he wanted to render the frightening chaos in the aftermath of Lincoln's murder, turned immediately to Dante and knew his readers would understand exactly what he meant: "Then Mrs. Lincoln screamed, Miss Harris cried for water, and the full ghastly truth broke upon all—'The President is murdered!' The scene that ensued was as tumultuous and terrible as one of Dante's pictures of hell" (10). In a very Dantesque mode himself, the author first recalls what he heard ("piercing shrieks and cries for vengeance and unmeaning shouts"), before he tries to render a visual description of what he saw. Hell breaks loose in Ford's Theater where "the dying President's head," "the insensible lips," a dress "stained with blood," all create a "real tragedy" on the world's stage. This sort of facile allusion to Dante becomes very common in the second half of the nineteenth century, and it suggests the extent to which the author had already penetrated popular American culture.

The memorializing of Lincoln in literature finds an interesting voice in the African American poet H. Cordelia Ray, who also praises William Lloyd Garrison and Charles Sumner, among others, in a sequence of sonnets called "Champions of Freedom." But Ray's most striking work is devoted to Dante himself whom she sees as a medieval analogue to these nineteenth-century figures who are devoted to the pursuit of liberty. Ray's portrait of Dante highlights the radical reformer and seeming Protestant in a way that brings together much of what we have been discussing in this chapter.

H. Cordelia Ray, William Wells Brown

Henrietta Cordelia Ray is one of Joan Sherman's "invisible poets" of the nineteenth century, that group of "over 130 black men and women [who] published some ninety volumes and pamphlets of poetry plus hundreds of poems in black periodicals [whose] achievements, impressive both in quantity and quality, remain unacknowledged" (*Invisible Poets* xv). Ray was born into a prominent African American family in New York City in 1849. Her father, Charles Bennett Ray, was an inspirational Protestant minister who led the Bethesda Congregational Church in New York for several decades in the mid-nineteenth century. From 1839 to 1842, he served as the editor and publisher of an important newspaper in circulation among free blacks in the North, the *Colored American,* which was first published in 1837 with an agenda firmly opposed to plans for the recolonization of American blacks in Africa.[46] Many articles that appeared during Ray's tenure at the paper document an outward-looking editorial policy that frequently featured news from beyond the borders of the United States, especially from Europe where revolutionary tensions were running high.[47] The editorial ethos Ray projected, according to his daughters in their biography of him, was "strong in its advocacy of the great principle underlying humanity and justice" (*Sketch* 12).

While Charles Bennett Ray does not refer to Dante in any profound way in his publications, a younger contemporary, William Wells Brown (1814–84), also active in the publishing world of freedmen, includes a striking allusion to Dante as a political figure in a serialized novel in the *Weekly Anglo-African* in 1861. Brown's work, originally published in London in 1853, rewritten in the serialized version of 1861, then republished in Boston with significant alterations in 1864 and 1867,[48] is recognized as the first novel written by an African American.[49] Over the years, the novel has continued to receive attention for it recounts the fortunes of a mulatto slave girl born into the household of Thomas Jefferson. Indeed, an alternate subtitle for the novel's first version is *The President's Daughter.* Whether or not Brown's multiple allusions to Dante had any direct influence on the writings of Cordelia Ray, his African American voice prepares the way for her own adaptation of the Italian poet. Therefore, we should consider briefly Brown's example.

From his memoir, *The American Fugitive in Europe* (1855), we learn how William Wells Brown first came to know Dante. In the wake of the passage of the Fugitive Slave Law of 1850, Brown fled the United States to endure a self-imposed exile in England where, inspired by reading Byron's "Prophecy of Dante,"[50] he sought out a painting in London's National Gallery, Sir Joseph Noel Paton's "Dante's Dream." He reports that he took comfort from the work of art for it called to mind Dante, the lover of Beatrice and poet of exile: "But the best piece in the gallery was 'Dante meditating the episode of Francesca da Rimini and Paolo Malatesta, L'Inferno, Canto V.' . . . The marriage of the object of his affections [Beatrice] to another, and her subsequent death, and the poet's exile from his beloved

Florence, together with his death among strangers, all give an interest to the poet's writings which could not be heightened by romance itself" (*American Fugitive* 133–34). Brown's description of the painting also reflects his reading of Boccaccio's life of Dante with its emphasis on the friendship between Dante and Guido da Polenta, Francesca's father. Although a man of color and only recently freed from the hell of slavery, Brown was quickly becoming a devotee of Dante like so many other Anglo-Americans at the time. This meant, among other things, immersing himself in Boccaccio's own exaltation of the master.

In Brown's first version of the novel *Clotel* (1853), there is no allusion to Dante. But revisions to the subsequent versions of the work, renamed first *Miralda* (1861), then *Clotelle* (1864 and 1867), which he completed upon his return to the United States, do reveal the influence of the Italian poet.[51] Midway through the narratives of the three later versions, Brown refers to Dante's literary love to measure how much the slave Jerome loves the novel's heroine: "Dante did not more love his Beatrice, Swift his Stella, Waller his Saccherissa, Goldsmith his Jessamy bride, or Burns his Mary, than did Jerome his Clotelle" (58, 1867 ed.). In this catalogue of lovers, Dante and Beatrice, the only non-English pair in the group, take pride of place, but there is nothing particularly unusual about the list. Many authors make precisely this sort of reference when they allude to Dante around the time when Brown was writing. As I mentioned at the beginning of this chapter, Seymour Kirkup's discovery in 1840 of an early trecento fresco of Dante in the Florentine Bargello, then believed to be by Giotto, inspired a wave of literary responses to the youthful Dante, many of which were composed by and for women. This new vision of Dante emphasized the young and handsome poet of love lyrics over the image of the dour poet in bitter exile at the end of his life. In a letter to Gabriele Rossetti, Kirkup himself outlines the dichotomy: "The poet looks about 28 — very handsome . . . it is not the mask of a corpse of 56 — a ruin — but a fine, noble image of the Hero of Campaldino, the Lover of Beatrice" (Toynbee, *Dante* 2:640). Few of Kirkup's contemporaries develop the image of Dante as a young war hero from the poet's own allusions to his time on the battlefield in 1289 (*Inf.* 21.94–96, 22.1–9). But many authors, including Brown, were inspired to follow up on the notion of Dante as Beatrice's lover, which becomes prominent even to the point of cliché.

In the second edition of the novel, retitled *Miralda* and published serially in installments in New York's *Weekly Anglo-African* between December 1860 and March 1861, William Wells Brown includes a substantial allusion that highlights the misfortunes of Dante's political career. This passage also dramatizes the very act of reading as it describes the fugitive former slave Jerome spending time in a patrician library where his bibliophilic explorations introduce him to the other, nonamorous, and for him more important side of Dante.

> During his fortnight's stay at Colonel G.'s, Jerome spent most of his time in the magnificent library. Claude did not watch with more interest every color of the skies, the trees, the grass, and the water, to learn from nature, than did this son of a despised race search books to obtain that knowledge which his early life as a slave had denied him. Everything that he read he retained. Nothing was lost. As Sterne was beaten by his valet in learning Italian, so might Jerome's master have been beaten by his slave in acquiring a knowledge of the classics, had he been in his company. He would turn from the humor of Chaucer to the dreams of Collins with as much interest as Pope manifested at getting a look at Dryden, at Burton's Coffee-House, when only eight years old. He wept over the mishaps of Goldsmith and Savage, *and with palpitating heart followed Dante, homeless and destitute, with a sentence of fire hanging over his head, as he left his beloved Florence and wandered from city to city in search of rest, with no companion save the seven cantos of his poem, which he had written previous to the decree banishing him from his native land.* He wept with Tasso as the great writer spent years in the Hospital of St. Anne, frightened by the cries and screams of the maniacs that surrounded him. Each author left a solid and lasting impression upon his mind and added to the store of knowledge with which he was daily enriching himself. (my emphasis)[52]

In his swift survey around the literary world, Brown boldly imagines his character Jerome in the position of Laurence Sterne's servant who outdid his master in learning Italian, the relationship of master and slave totally upended in the spirit of education. The ironic collocation of terms in the phrase "beaten by his slave" catches the reader's attention with its suggestion that there is something volatile and subversive about the activity of reading. Slaves don't usually beat their masters, however we might understand that verb. In fact—and here is a further irony, perhaps—the typical male slave is arguably more likely to beat his master physically, in the sense of assaulting him, rather than by surpassing him in study. Reading is liberating, to be sure, and here we are dealing with the reading of complicated texts full of exempla that take the reader to a new level of awareness. When the author comes to Dante in the survey of Jerome's potential models, he describes the Italian without any reference whatsoever to his love poetry. Instead of Beatrice, "beloved" Florence is the object of the man's affection, but she, alas, has just rejected him and sent him into exile. This is the image of Dante the political reformer, depicted as being at odds with his state, that very figure who becomes a touchstone for many nineteenth-century abolitionists and nationalists.

Brown, then, is aware of the reception of Dante both as lover and as an engaged politician, and he incorporates the two portraits into the second version of his novel in 1861. There is no direct evidence that Henrietta Cordelia Ray read William Wells Brown, but given her family's connections, her own keen literary predilection, and Brown's sudden prominence in the 1850s and 1860s, it is reasonable to assume that she would have been familiar with the story of Clotelle in some if not all of Brown's versions. If so, she would have found support and perhaps even a direct source of inspiration for her interpretation of Dante as an exiled activist. Now we need to return to her reading of the Italian writer.

Cordelia, as she preferred to be called, first came to the public's attention for an occasional poem she wrote in honor of Abraham Lincoln, delivered at the dedication of the Freedmen's Monument in Washington, D.C., in 1876. A reporter at the ceremonies noted: "Professor Langston then announced that, by request, an original poem had been contributed by a colored lady of New York, Miss Cordelia Ray, and it would be read by Mr. William E. Mathews" (*Oration* 32). Although she composed poems to memorialize Lincoln, Frederick Douglass, and many other leaders of the struggle for racial equality, including Garrison, she has been criticized for writing "sentimental lyrics on hackneyed themes, ignoring the current issues affecting her race."[53] What little criticism there is of Ray's work might lead one to believe that the agenda of her activist family had no impact on her poetry.

Her poem "Dante," published in the *African Methodist Episcopal Church Review* in 1885 and reprinted in 1910, suggests otherwise, though one might argue that Dante himself had become a hackneyed theme in nineteenth-century literary America, in "the new Ravenna of the great poet," as Scartazzini put it (La Piana 159). American readers had given Dante a safe harbor and had taken the poet to heart. Poems inspired by Dante's life and writings came out all across the country at a phenomenal rate in newspapers, popular magazines, scholarly journals, literary anthologies, and volumes of poetry.[54] Ray's contribution to this mania is the opening poem, "Dante," in a trilogy of poems, "The Seer, the Singer, the Sage." I cite from the reprinted edition of the poem of 1910, for reasons I shall explain below.

> Rare medieval Spirit! Brooding Seer!
> Grand, lonely Poet! Scaling heights divine,
> And lifting from grave mysteries the veil,
> Through the dim centuries thou speakest still
> In tones of thunder; and subdued by awe
> We listen, for thy intuitions fine,
> Thy insight keen discovered motives hid,
> And aim close wound in aim thou couldst perceive,
> Unwinding minor aims in which 'twas wrapt.
> 10 Knit with the very fibres of thy soul,
> Thy country's weal a cherished charge became;
> And Destiny stern frowning o'er the land,
> Upheaved thy feelings and inflamed thy speech.
> Indignant at the wrongs that Florence bore,
> Florence, thy well-beloved, thy hallowed home,
> With stern denunciation thou didst wage
> Against the law's lax mandates bloody war,
> And all unawed, rebuked the false decrees
> Of kings, of conquerors, popes and cardinals,
> 20 The pure "white flower" waving in thy hand.
> Thy thought self-poised, self-centered, dragged thy soul
> Into what depths of grief and deepest pain!
> But to posterity thou didst bequeathe—

Despite the scathing of the contest fierce —
Thy reveries' illuminated page.
The groans of spirits plunged in woe's abyss,
The sweet repentance of the wistful souls
Climbing in patience Purgatory's steep,
Called thee to muse on life's strange mystery.
30   Before thy vision what fair vista stretched,
Empurpled with the glow of Paradise!
Thou heardst in dreams the harmonies sublime
Of martyr glorified and rapturous saint.
And she, Beatrice the celestial one,
Who woke thy heart's best love and sweetest joy,
Alone was meet to guide thy willing steps
From planet to fixed star, and onward still,
Above the splendor of the luminous stars,
Where blessed souls their orisons uplift,
40   And isles supernal bloom with amaranth fair,
Up to the Empyrean's crystal courts,
Where Majesty Divine enthrones itself.
And soon the perfect Vision met thy gaze,
The mystic Trinity all solved by light,
Three colors, three reflections in the one,
Christ was revealed — the Human, the Divine!
God's plan for our redemption clear to thee!
And now, O lonely Spirit, brooding Seer!
So long in conflict, weary with unrest,
50   Within the beatific realms above,
Bathed in that Light Ineffable thou dwell'st,
O yearning Soul, at last, at last in peace![55]

In her Miltonic verse, Ray conveys a deep understanding of Dante's
life and poetry as well as a strong emotional and intellectual response to
the man and his work. One of the earliest critics to comment on Ray's poetry, Hallie Q. Brown, is proud to assert the genealogical primacy of Ray's
family: "Miss Ray came of the primitive Massachusetts stock, being a direct descendant of aboriginal Indian, English and of the first Negroes of

New England" (172). This lineage is as venerable a beginning as one could construct and indeed, the critic continues, it not only produced a "gentle woman," but it also afforded Ray the leisure to engage in intellectual pursuits. Her birthright, in other words, enabled her to do things like read Dante and compose a poem about her encounter with the Italian poet. Her family, it turns out, also enabled her to view Dante in a certain light, to perceive Dante as "colored," even as a "colored American," not as a man of color, to be sure, but as an engaged citizen actively trying to use the rule of law to better his people's situation. Let me explain.

Ray's "Dante" divides into two parts, the first on Dante the man (ll. 1–22), the second on the *Divine Comedy* (ll. 23–52). It opens with the stereotypical image of Dante as the brooding Christian mystic who has much in common with the typical image of the Romantic genius: "Rare medieval spirit! Brooding Seer! / Grand, lonely Poet!" Nineteenth-century interpretations of Dante frequently portrayed the poet in these terms. The sonorous blank verse elaborates the predictable image of the poet who "lifts from grave mysteries the veil" and who speaks "in tones of thunder." At line 10 the focus shifts from Dante's impact on his reader to the man's own agenda. And here is where the poem gets interesting.

> Knit with the very fibres of thy soul,
> Thy country's weal a cherished charge became;
> And Destiny stern frowning o'er the land,
> Upheaved thy feelings and inflamed thy speech.
> (10–13)

This is the sort of portrait of the politically engaged Dante that appealed to the leaders of the Risorgimento, the man dedicated to his "country's weal," the commonwealth, and the "land." As we have seen, Giuseppe Mazzini and others, Italians and Anglo-Americans, began to promote this interpretation of Dante over the more conventional images of the mystical poet and the lover (alluded to in ll. 34–35) from the 1830s on. By contrast, Anna Julia Cooper, an African American woman writing at approximately the same time as Ray, comments on how her ideal reader "can revel in the majesty of Dante" (*A Voice from the South* 69), which would seem to be a gesture to the more typical clichéd way of reading the Italian poet.

There seems to be no political edge to Cooper's reading. But even the notion of Dante as a seer, the category that Ray uses for him, can be understood in a political context. Dante's focus on the need for a unified linguistic culture for the peninsula and his attention to the potential for a
unified political culture in his day cast him in the role of prophetic seer
for many readers of the nineteenth century. This interpretation also eventually becomes somewhat conventional, but Ray's description of Dante's
mode of political engagement alters the view of him as a creature of politics in a striking way.

> Indignant at the wrongs that Florence bore,
> Florence, thy well-beloved, thy hallowed home,
> With stern denunciation thou didst wage
> Against the law's lax mandates bloody war,
> And all unawed, rebuked the false decrees
> Of kings, of conquerors, popes and cardinals . . .
> (14–19, 1910 ed.)

Ray's focus on Dante's attachment to his state (perhaps she remembers
that the noun *paese* in Italian signifies the political entities of both town
and country) modulates from his "country's weal" (11) to "land" (12) to
"Florence" (14) to "home" (15), culminating in a more intensely personal
experience of the political at line 15. In the first version of the poem,
published in the 1885 *AME Church Review,* lines 14–15 highlight the personal and omit the reference to Florence:

> Indignant at the wrong that tortured thee—
> Proud exile, banished from thy sunny home—
> With stern denunciation . . .
> (14–16, 1885 ed.)

In the earlier version, Ray emphasizes Dante's personal experience, the
wrong *he* suffered, which she subsequently emends to the many wrongs
Florence endured in the second version. While line 15 focuses solely on
Dante in the original version, the altered text shifts the focus from the
exile to the city that had been his home. Perhaps exchanging the adjective

sunny for *hallowed* is merely to swap one stereotype for another, but at least it is to opt for a more serious stereotype. Ray conjures up Florence, one of the sacred cities in the history of Western political discourse, repeating its name in chantlike recitation. The second version of the poem, published in 1910, allows for a more profound understanding of Dante's political development in that civic setting.

In the lines that follow the reference to Florence, Ray alters the conventional portrait of Dante significantly. She depicts the man not merely as an active citizen concerned about the political well-being of his country; she goes further to describe him with terms one might use of a freedom fighter who knows how to enlist the court to aid his cause—a constitutional lawyer, if you will. Legal language characterizes the description: Dante filed an official accusation, a "denunciation" (16) against the "law's lax mandates" (17) and he "rebuked . . . decrees" (18). This is the vocabulary of the courtroom of Ray's own day, if not necessarily Dante's. Indeed, it is the vocabulary of the sort of legal and judicial activism associated with Ray's father and like-minded abolitionists, the sort of leaders familiar to readers of the *Colored American,* Garrison's *Liberator,* Douglass's *North Star,* and other antislavery publications. Furthermore, Ray's Dante engages in this manner of political legal activism against both secular and ecclesiastical governments, a point made clear in another crucial revision for the 1910 publication. The rather bland "alike of potentates and factions bold" (19, 1885 ed.) is rewritten to focus much more pointedly on the potential enemies of Dante and of Cordelia Ray's contemporaries: "Of kings, of conquerors, popes and cardinals" (19, 1910 ed.). With this new line, Ray clearly sounds an antipapist, antiecclesiastical note, which would have been unambiguous to her intended audience. And much appreciated, for this is a Dante who would make sense to activist intellectuals of the late nineteenth century, a Dante for the abolitionists and those following in their footsteps, a Dante for Protestants.

At lines 21–22, the poem returns to some of the clichés associated with traditional interpretations of Dante, before it shifts to consider Dante's poem itself. There are more clichés here too. And yet, the politicized reading of Dante that takes shape at lines 10–19 redeems the rest of this predictable poem. Ray's Dante unexpectedly becomes an activist, even if in passing. If I call her portrait of the poet a "Colored Dante," I mean it in the sense that he is fashioned out of the cultural moment that created Ray herself, the second half of the nineteenth century. But I also mean that Ray's Dante is cut of the same cloth as her father, Charles Bennett Ray, and other activist leaders in the fight against the unjust laws that enabled slavery well into nineteenth-century America. As Ray's daughters wrote of their father's work in journalism, "Under his charge, as before, the *Colored American* continued to be ably conducted and strong in its advocacy" (*Sketch* 12). Of Mr. Ray, Hallie Q. Brown writes, his "natural puritanical stamina [was] neutralized by [his] deep sense of justice and sincere desire to aid, uplift and make better" (172). *Mutatis mutandis,* it could be a description of Dante himself.

In a similar vein, Ray wrote a sequence of sonnets called "Champions of Freedom," which appears in her volume of collected poems. The subjects of these poems might lead one to contest the standard criticism of Ray's poetry as not being engaged: "William Lloyd Garrison," "Wendell Phillips," "Charles Sumner," "Robert G. Shaw," "Toussaint L'Ouverture," and "To My Father." These are poems dedicated to those who fought for the liberation of her race, in which the language frequently overlaps with the sections of her poem on Dante considered above, further indication that Dante, too, was a champion of freedom equal to these heroes of the nineteenth century. In the poem on Garrison, she writes:

> No laggard laws
> Could quench thy zeal until no slave should pine
> in galling chains, caged in the free sunshine.
> (5–7)

The phrase "laggard laws" approximates "the law's lax mandates" of her poem on Dante. In "Charles Sumner," she also recycles language used in the poem on Dante: "Thy regnant soul spurned ev'ry false decree" (12), recalling the "false decrees" Dante rebukes. In a separate poem on Lincoln, not part of the sonnet sequence, she writes: "Truth was thy guide, his mandates were thy laws" (20), a verse that recalls her depiction of Dante. Ray's activist Dante is a composite figure, part Garrison, part Sumner, part Lincoln, and part her father.

There are narratives of Dante's life in the biographical tradition, beginning with Leonardo Bruni's *Life of Dante* written sometime in the first half of the fifteenth century, which emphasize his political career and social commitment. In the second half of the nineteenth century it was not unusual for essayists or lecturers to highlight Dante's interest in political matters,[56] and, as we have seen, Dante became an important rallying figure for the promoters of Italian unification. But Ray's glimpse of an activist Dante is more specific and unusual than any other I have found. She recognized that her readers, those likely to pick up the *AME Church Review* and her own *Poems,* didn't need a mystical Christian voice or a lovesick poet as much as they needed a judicial activist. Ray's unique reinterpretation of Dante's statesmanship suggests that she may not be as traditional a poet as critics claim, nor is her verse necessarily as saccharine as has been suggested. I leave it for others to reassess Ray's poetry along such lines to see whether similar revisions affect her portraits of Thoreau, Longfellow, Milton, and Beethoven, among other canonical figures she portrays in her verse. While Ray deserves credit for her innovative view of Dante as an activist lawyer who uses the courts to realize change in society, there is no evidence that her poem "Dante" had a significant impact on subsequent interpreters, African American or other. Although one reviewer does mention the poem in praising Ray: "Miss Cordelia Ray, one of the teachers of New York City, has won for herself a place in the front rank of our literary workers. A poem, entitled 'Dante,' contributed to the *Review,* received well deserved praise, and many readers hope we shall again be charmed with offerings from the same pen" (Mossell, "Colored Woman in Verse" 66). In this review essay, the youthful Ray holds her own among Phyllis Wheatley, Sarah Foster, Frances Ellen Watkins Harper, Charlotte Grimké—very high company indeed.

Ray's Colored Dante bespeaks a moment in African American cultural history when the needs of a new and growing interpretive community of readers of color began the process of transforming European cultural material into something other than what it had been. These new readers supported a vast and thriving "colored press," of which Ray's father's own *Colored American* was one of the earliest examples.[57] In the *AME Church Review* a year after Ray published her Dante poem, the journal's editor reflected in a column on the absurdity of "colored" as an adjective:

Such a phrase as the above [the colored press] would scarcely be understood in any other land than our own; understood as all Americans understand it. To speak of a "colored" press in England, or on the Continent, would be to awaken up an idea of a paper or papers printed on
colored material or some such thing. With us, however, it is entirely
different. We know precisely what is meant. American caste has created
a nomenclature peculiarly its own. . . . The Colored press in the United
States is the press owned, published and edited by colored men, and it is
to this that we wish to call the attention of all the readers of the *Review.*
(1885–86, 2:86)

Into this context, Ray, a woman of color, introduces the Italian poet and
symbol of political independence and liberal anticlericalism, making him
into a Colored Dante.

IN CONCLUSION, during the Risorgimento, Dante became a symbol not
only of political independence and unity, but also of liberal anticlericalism
opposed to the church as a temporal power. He was viewed as a radical reformer, so much so that Frederick Douglass thought of Dante and Savonarola, and other reformers, as cut of the same cloth. In a revised version of
his famous autobiography, he refers to Dante and Savonarola as "great historical personages" of Florentine culture who lend the city "a controlling
power over mind and heart."[58] But despite his interest in these two reformers, when he first visited Florence in 1887, Douglass went straight to
the Protestant Cemetery to pay his respects at the graveside of Theodore
Parker, whose epitaph is telling for its coded language:[59]

HIS NAME IS EGRAVED IN MARBLE
HIS VIRTUES IN THE HEARTS OF THOSE HE
HELPED TO FREE FROM SLAVERY
AND SUPERSTITION.

Douglass had preached from the pulpit of Parker's Unitarian church
in Boston as a young man. Parker, who died in 1860, is remembered for
his devotion to abolitionism and for his campaign against superstition, the

latter a veiled reference to the contest between Protestantism and Catholicism.[60] Douglass was also eager to see the grave of Elizabeth Barrett
Browning, for "[her] soul . . . was devoted to liberty" (*Life and Times* 588).
He probably sought out the graves of Hiram Powers and Frances Trollope, buried nearby in the same cemetery. After his contribution to Trollope's Infernal Regions in Cincinnati in 1828, Powers had become an in-
ternationally famous sculptor. He was best known for his depiction of *The
Greek Slave,* a statue completed in 1843 that toured England and America
to great acclaim throughout the 1840s, the blockbuster show of its day.[61]
A cartoonist in *Punch* accounted for the American, and especially southern, fascination with Powers's statue by drawing a very similar image of a
young woman in chains, but black instead of white, entitled *The Virginia
Slave.* It was impossible to miss the abolitionist statement Powers was making with his sculpture, which Elizabeth Barrett Browning broadcast in her
popular poem "Hiram Powers' Greek Slave." Parker, Browning, Powers,
and Trollope were all dedicated to the struggle for freedom and civil rights
which Douglass remembered almost nostalgically as he went on his version of the grand tour in the late 1880s. And a common denominator for
them all was Dante. When a member of the press visited the elderly Douglass at home in 1889 just after the final version of his autobiography had
come out, he reported the following: "Mr. Douglass invited the reporter
into his library, and there the faces of the late Chief Justice Chase, W. Lloyd
Garrison, James S. Birney, De Strauss, L. Feuerbach, Dante, Abraham Lincoln, John Brown, and Charles Sumner looked down in smiles and respect
on the great negro sage" (Washington *Press,* Jan. 11, 1889).[62] By the 1880s
and 1890s, Dante had become a fixture in the politics of the liberal world
on a par with none less than Lincoln. American abolitionists and the promoters of Italian unity used the Italian poet to rally others to fight the
good political cause. Citizens of color in the United States, for whom the
abolitionists had agitated, were beginning to name their children Dante,
as if in thankful recognition of his contribution to their new status.[63] But
by the end of the century Colored Dante was primed to transform into
something even greater.

CHAPTER 2
NEGRO DANTE

[A] Divina Commedia, *that shall be the voice of those silent centuries*
of slavery, as Dante's poem was the voice of the long-silent epoch preceding
it, . . . is the not improbable achievement of some descendant of the slaves.

—Robert T. Kerlin, *Negro Poets and Their Poems* (1923)

This chapter, covering the period from approximately 1900 to 1950, is
devoted to Negro Dante. I begin by considering briefly how W. E. B. Du
Bois dramatizes the educational value of literature in general, Dante in particular, in his debate with Booker T. Washington over appropriate models
of education for African Americans at the turn of the century. For Du Bois,
Dante is an early humanist who paves the way for Petrarch's recovery of
antiquity, a process that will culminate in Galileo's enlightened science.
Du Bois recognizes that Dante prompts Petrarch, or perhaps even enables
him, to renew classical culture in a continuum that extends from Cicero
to Du Bois himself. In the same mode as Du Bois, who unabashedly uses
Cicero to argue for the value of literary knowledge with a sharecropper in
his cabin, artists of color considered in this chapter apply Dante to their
own local situations.

The chapter turns to a unique moment in the reception of Dante: the
imitation of the *Inferno* in the film *Go Down, Death!* (1944), by the independent African American filmmaker Spencer Williams. The film's title
comes from a poem of the same name by James Weldon Johnson, collected
in his popular volume of 1927, *God's Trombones: Seven Negro Sermons in Verse.*

In the quasi-documentary film Williams makes use of Dante in an unprecedented way. To illustrate his protagonist's experience of hell, Williams uses the 1911 silent film *L'inferno,* by Adolfo Padovan and Francesco Bertolini of Milano Films, from which he literally clips frames that he splices into his movie. We suddenly see hell through the eyes of the protagonist's soul as Dante and Vergil step gingerly around the traitors frozen in the river Cocytus of the ninth circle, with Lucifer in the background champing on the body of Judas. Spencer Williams privileges Dante, by making him the only living white person in his race movie. In this version of a Negro Dante, a celluloid image of the medieval poet integrates the segregated world depicted in Williams's film. Dante thus becomes unexpectedly a vehicle for integration.

Richard Wright in *Black Boy* (1937) and Ralph Ellison in *Invisible Man* (1952) engage in analogous acts of literary integration at approximately the same time in their respective appropriations of the medieval poet. Wright carefully uses Dante as a marker of migration to signal his departure from the segregated South as he heads for what he hopes will be the promised land of Chicago. Ellison too uses Dante as a marker of migration, but in his case it is not a literal movement from south to north, or from one geographical place to another; rather for Ellison, Dante signals a move into the territory of canonical European literature. Near the beginning of *Invisible Man* Ellison calls on Dante to point toward the literary tradition he intends to penetrate—I choose this verb bearing in mind Ellison's own reflections in preparatory notes for *Invisible Man,* which I will consider at the end of the section on Ellison below. Moving from Williams's bold use of Dante as a signifier of integration to Wright's use of the poet's text to mark migration, I conclude the chapter with an analysis of how Ellison uses Dante both to migrate into and to integrate his work with the European canon. In the process of achieving his version of literary migration and integration, Ellison claims Dante as his prophetic vernacular muse. What Williams accomplishes visually and Wright thematically, Ellison accomplishes linguistically.

Educating the People: From Cicero to Du Bois

On a spring evening at the end of the academic year in 1908, W. E. B. Du Bois delivered the commencement address at Fisk University, the venerable institution in Nashville, Tennessee. He entitled it "Galileo Galilei,"[1] but the talk went beyond a traditional recounting of the well-known struggle of the early modern scientist with the church. As Du Bois explained in opening and closing notes that he added to the text when preparing it for publication, he meant for the speech to save liberal studies at Fisk, which was threatened, as he saw it, by the new vogue in industrial, vocational education favored by Booker T. Washington around the turn of the century. The debate between their respective positions was becoming acrimonious, and while Italian culture was not a feature of the larger debate, it appears in several revealing moments. Washington, for his part, went so far as to use Italy, the symbolic repository of Western liberal culture, as a whipping boy when he wanted to give an example of how best for African Americans to learn. Describing the typical graduation ceremony at his own Tuskegee Institute, he notes proudly: "Instead of having a boy or girl read a paper on some subject like 'Beyond the Alps Lies Italy,' we have them explain and demonstrate to the audience how to build a roof, or the proper way to make cheese, or how to hatch chickens with an incubator" (*My Larger Education* 141). Devotion to Italy, as depicted in this caricature, is an obstacle to what Washington considers practical knowledge based on firsthand experience.

Du Bois saw Italy, and knowledge itself, for that matter, in a very different light. He had already eloquently made a case for the right to engage with European culture in *The Souls of Black Folk,* published in 1903, where he observes pointedly, "I sit with Shakespeare and he winces not" (67).[2] In his convocation address of 1908, he drew a parallel between Galileo and the entire Fisk community gathered before him. Galileo knew that his thinking about Copernicanism and the heliocentric solar system was right, yet he denounced his position before the tribunal in Rome in 1633, thus betraying his intellectual beliefs. As Du Bois puts it bluntly, emphasized by his italics in the version of the speech he intended to publish: *"He lied"* (22). Du Bois urges Fisk to do what it knows to be right and not betray its liberal arts curriculum for the sake of the vocational education promoted by Washington and his followers. His commencement address is a rousing speech full of the rhetoric of uplift, typical of the genre, but with added point, for the speaker himself had graduated from the historically black college twenty years earlier and in the intervening decades had

become one of the leading voices among African American intellectuals. Du Bois's education had taken him from Fisk to Harvard to Germany
and here he was back at his alma mater, the place of his rather humble
beginnings, standing before the students as a witness to the truth he was
promoting.

Near the beginning of the speech, Du Bois wonders what prompted
Galileo to think like a revolutionary intellectual. He responds: "The impulse was a new vision of the world. From the time of Dante in the thirteenth up to the blossoming of Petrarch in the fifteenth century, Italy
had been seeing life anew. Galileo was child of this awakening." For Du
Bois, Galileo builds on Dante's precedent, a view of the late medieval poet
as a protohumanist who prepares the way for those who follow, first Petrarch (but in the fourteenth century, not fifteenth, to be precise), then on
through to the scientific enlightenment. This interpretation represents a
typical reckoning of Italian intellectual history. What is suggestive is the
way Du Bois uses the chronology to establish a link between his own intellectual growth and the idea of the Renaissance as a time of progress.
And by extension he implies that the Fisk community can similarly measure its potential progress against that of the Italian Renaissance.

Education had made Du Bois into a new man, and he remained hopeful of its transformative possibilities for others. Whereas he maps out a
trajectory that begins with Dante in his comments to the Fisk students,
his own metamorphosis has more in common with Petrarch's "blossoming," as becomes clear from the chapter "Of the Meaning of Progress" in
The Souls of Black Folk. During two summers while he was still a student at
Fisk, Du Bois traipsed around the backwoods of rural Tennessee offering
himself as a teacher to whoever would listen.[3] After some preliminary
training in pedagogy and with much perseverance, he eventually found a
community in the middle of nowhere fifty miles from Nashville that took
him in: "I loved my school, and the fine faith the children had in the wisdom of their teacher was truly marvellous" (*Souls of Black Folk* 40). But the
parents had their doubts about the teacher and his mission. Since they
were sharecroppers eking out a hardscrabble existence, they would frequently pull their children from the classroom to assist them in working
the fields. But Du Bois had a strategy for countering their dependence on
their children's labor: "I knew that the doubts of the old folks about book-

learning had conquered again, and so, toiling up the hill, and getting as far into the cabin as possible, I put Cicero 'pro Archia Poeta' into the simplest English with local applications, and usually convinced them—for a week or so" (*Souls of Black Folk* 40). In a nod to the tradition of Renaissance humanism, Du Bois adapted the defense of literature encapsulated in Cicero's oration in defense of the poet Archias to make a case closer to home for the value of a liberal arts education. The classical defense of literature "with local applications," in Du Bois's telling phrase, becomes a defense of the right of farmers' children to study and learn in a ramshackle schoolhouse in rural Tennessee.

Petrarch made an analogous argument in 1341 in his *Coronation Oration*, the "first manifesto of the Renaissance."[4] Petrarch's oration articulates the value of a new program of liberal learning for his age which is inspired by his rediscovery in 1333 of none other than Cicero's speech for Archias.[5] Petrarch had discovered the Latin text lying unread in a monastic library and had then incorporated its message into his speech with his own version of "local applications," in an attempt to distinguish himself from Dante and the methods of learning used by the previous generation. Education was the key to progress; in fact, in many ways Renaissance humanism is essentially about the establishment of a new pedagogical curriculum that we first see outlined in Petrarch's speech. He delivered the Coronation Oration when he was crowned poet laureate in Rome atop the Capitoline Hill, symbol of the heights of classical culture, which he was working so diligently to recuperate. In *The Souls of Black Folk,* Du Bois has a different Capitoline Hill in view, a Tennessee knob with a sharecropper's cabin at the top. But the value he puts on progressive education is exactly the same as Petrarch's, and the stakes of his act of recuperation are no less high than the Renaissance poet's. And as Petrarch had done before him, Du Bois uses Dante, at least in passing, as a starting place from which to move forward.

As we move forward from the debates between W. E. B. Du Bois and Booker T. Washington in the first decades after the turn of the century, we come to a definitive moment in the history of African American culture, the Harlem Renaissance, or, as it is also called, the New Negro Movement.

As black immigrants from the South and the West Indies moved to New York City for work, Harlem became the center of a burgeoning self-reflective black culture in the 1920s.[6] Harlem Renaissance artist Aaron Douglas recalls almost nonchalantly that a boy growing up in a middle-class black family around this time could be expected to read Dante as readily as any other author: "I was an ardent reader of serious books throughout my elementary and high school years, reading such writers as Emerson, Bacon, Montaigne, Hugo, Dumas, Shakespeare, and Dante."[7] But this sort of reading list doesn't appear to have influenced his art or that of his contemporaries in Harlem at all. Douglas's modernist painting emphatically reflects African traditions, not European. Alain Locke's programmatic essay on a new Negro art, "The Legacy of the Ancestral Arts," in the volume he edited in 1925, *The New Negro,* urges artists like Douglas to look to Africa for creative models since "the Negro is not a cultural foundling without his own inheritance" (256). But of course there could not be a wholesale rejection of European traditions. To wit, as we shall see below, Claude McKay, a Jamaican immigrant who was the first significant writer of the Harlem Renaissance, can easily use Dante to make a point. Similarly Jean Toomer, another major literary figure during Harlem's cultural explosion, alludes to Dante with ease and on some level identifies with the Italian poet.

From the top of Meridian Hill Park in Washington, D.C., in early May of 1922, Toomer wrote to a friend in letters, Waldo Frank, commenting on the monument to Dante near where he was sitting: "A statue of Dante, farther down the hill, is obscured by the hill's slope. The Dante is a cheap affair. The figure rests on a miserable wooden base that tries to look like granite. Even the boys passing by are contemptuous of it, and pelter [*sic*] it with stones. Thus is the city made impressive and beautified. . . . How our mother, this America of ours, needs us, dear brother" (38). The bronze monument, like the copy in Lincoln Park in New York City, was cast by the Sicilian sculptor Ettore Ximenes and had been erected in 1921, to commemorate Dante's death six hundred years earlier. Like the centennial celebrations of Dante's birth in 1865 and 1965, the year of his death also became an important marker in the recuperation of the man and his work. Toomer's ironic criticism of the monument—"Thus is the city . . . beautified"—suggests that he thinks Dante deserved better. He states outright that America needs people like Frank and himself, implying that they are artists in the mold of Dante whom the public undeservedly disrespects, much as Florentines treated Dante badly and much as Washingtonians disregard the new monument. The neglect of the monument becomes a metaphor for the disregard of the artist in general.

At the same time as Italo-America was promoting Dante and Italian culture in 1921, Toomer was drafting his atypical novel, *Cane,* which would be published in 1923 with a foreword by Waldo Frank. Frank and subsequent critics sometimes strain to make a case for the novel's unusual mix of poetry and prose, through which Toomer presents the coming of age, artistically and sexually, of a variety of characters, moving between the rural black South and the urban North. The final scene of "Avey," which John F. Callahan calls "perhaps the most personal tale in *Cane*" for its autobiographical tone (*In the African-American Grain* 85), is set in the same park and on the same hill as the Dante monument.[8] While there is no direct citation of Dante in the story, one could make a case that Toomer's awareness of the Italian author gives shape to the culminating section of "Avey." Documents in the archives verify that Toomer was engaging with Dante later in his life, although there is no direct evidence that he read the poet while he was composing *Cane.*[9] Nevertheless, there are several interesting parallels between this part of *Cane* and Dante's writings. The narrator, an aspiring artist, courts a beautiful young girl, Avey, in the first part of the tale. He then loses touch with her but reconnects one night five years later and takes her to his special place on the hill above the world of Washington. A policeman whose beat includes the hill chases away the characters who linger there, recalling Cato the formidable guardian on Dante's Mount Purgatory. As Dante reconnects with Beatrice in the terrestrial garden at the top of Mount Purgatory, so Toomer's autobiographical counterpoint reintroduces himself to Avey, whom he clearly sees as angelic and inspirational, in what for him is a highly charged and transformative site of spiritual renewal. In his imagination he hears the southern spiritual "Deep River" and imagines a stream before them that they need to ford. He discourses on art: "I talked, beautifully I thought, about an art that would be born, an art that would open the way for women the likes of her" (48). Whether intentionally or not, these various details—the hill with its Edenic landscape, the Cato figure, Avey (whose name recalls Eve or Eva) as a kind of Beatrice to whom the poet will dedicate his art — recall Dante's writing about his inspirational lady in both the *Divine Comedy* and *Vita Nuova*. Moreover, the very quality of the writing itself, the mixing of poetry and prose that troubled some of Toomer's early critics, is a defining feature of Dante's *Vita Nuova*. It is as if Toomer took that youthful Dantesque work as a point of departure extending it through a loose imitation up to the moment of Dante's dramatic encounter with Beatrice at the top of Mount Purgatory in *Purgatory* 30. In the end, the parallels cease, for Avey falls dead asleep in the midst of the protagonist's discourse on art. She may inspire him momentarily, but she can't lead him to a higher level of being as Beatrice will do for Dante.

Another important Harlem Renaissance work, James Weldon Johnson's *God's Trombones: Seven Negro Sermons in Verse* (1927),[10] although seemingly removed from the worlds of Europe, unexpectedly leads us to more direct imitations of the Italian source that we are tracking in this study. Alain Locke's programmatic designs about Africa as the only legitimate source for artists of color notwithstanding, the New Negro Movement ironically prepares the way for an extraordinary cinematic imitation of Dante's *Inferno*, a Negro Dante unlike anything ever seen before which is based on one of Johnson's poetic sermons.

Spencer Williams: African American Filmmaker at the Gates of Hell

Spencer Williams, by one account "the most unsung hero of [the] entire era" of early black filmmaking (Jones, *Black Cinema Treasures* 173), estranged much of the black intelligentsia for his part in the controversial television comedy *Amos 'n' Andy*, in which he played the leading role of Andy Brown.[11] Consequently, his substantial body of work is not as well known today as it might be, despite a retrospective that ran at the Whitney Museum of Art in 1988–89.[12] Of the two main films featured in the Whitney series, Greg Tate comments, "They're Christian films made with a wink and a nod to the devil. Williams means to eat his eucharist and have his slapstick, too" (61). But there is much more to this man's art than a happy-go-lucky reverential aesthetic. And yet he seems to have been forgotten. Spike Lee, in a piece entitled "Black Films" in which he praises "our pioneers," fails even to mention Williams.[13] While I intend my discussion of Spencer Williams to draw attention to the filmmaker's career and art in the hope that it may counter the general disregard and misunderstanding of this fine artist,[14] I have a larger purpose in mind that comes into focus later in the chapter when I reconsider Williams through a lens provided by Richard Wright and Ralph Waldo Ellison.

Born in Louisiana in 1893,[15] Spencer Williams worked in the film industry in the 1920s, 1930s, and 1940s, achieving notoriety as Andy Brown in the television version of the slapstick radio comedy *Amos 'n' Andy,* which was in production at CBS from 1951 to 1953.[16] While the TV show gave white America a safe glimpse into a world it mainly knew through racial stereotypes, Williams's films were another thing altogether, though it's unlikely many whites ever saw them. Folk-dramas like *The Blood of Jesus* (1941) and *Go Down, Death!* (1944),[17] deceptively simple tales of good and evil, are set against the backdrop of the religious experience of southern blacks on the eve of the great migrations that took many men and women out of the South in search of decent jobs and a better life in the urban North.[18] Williams's films have the feel of documentaries with their gritty depiction of daily life in stark black and white images: a preacher intones rhythmically from the pulpit; a big man (played by Williams himself) tears into some fried chicken at the dining room table of his boardinghouse; young couples do the jitterbug across the dance floor of a local juke joint. The films Williams made during the forties were financed by a Jewish entrepreneur, Alfred N. Sack, "a hands-off backer who enabled him to do what few other black artists . . . had been able to do—to direct a large number of his own screenplays as he saw fit" (*Black Cinema Treasures* 34). It turned out to be a good business decision, for Williams's films played very well throughout the small-town theaters of the South, *The Blood of Jesus,* for example, quickly recovering the $15,000 it had taken to make it.[19] Southern blacks in the 1940s were aware that the way of life portrayed in many of Williams's films had all but vanished. Williams as narrator says as much in a voice-over accompanying the opening frames of *The Blood of Jesus* with a farmer tilling his field behind a mule: "Almost gone are the days when Peace ruled the earth with a firm and gentle hand . . ." These films were not as popular in the North where the newly urbanized emigrant blacks were hardly nostalgic for views of what they had recently left behind.[20] Williams's films, then, document the end of an era: the rural existence of the Negro in the South.

In one of his quasi-documentary pieces, *Go Down, Death!*, Williams made use of Dante in an unprecedented way.[21] *Go Down, Death!* takes its title from a poetic funeral eulogy composed by James Weldon Johnson in *God's Trombones: Seven Negro Sermons in Verse* (1927). H. L. Mencken singles out this specific sermon for praise in a blurb on the original dust jacket as "one of the most remarkable and moving poems of its type ever written in America."[22] The film's opening credits conclude with a dedicatory frame that contains an inscription in praise of "the Pen of the Celebrated Negro Author, JAMES WELDON JOHNSON, *Now of Sainted Memory,*" who had died in 1938, six years before the film came out. The text of Johnson's sermon is the focus of the penultimate sequence of the film. The film tells the story of Jim Bottoms, played by Spencer Williams, whose juke joint has been losing money ever since a charismatic Baptist preacher arrived in town. The film score emphasizes the two worlds at odds in the story as it shifts from church hymns to jazz dance music and back again. This is a film about good and evil, symbolized by the Mount Zion Church and the Red Rooster Inn, and the men in charge of each institution, the pastor and the bar owner.[23] Jim and his cronies scheme to frame the preacher, by photographing him with three floozies who are posing as potential converts to his congregation. His henchmen snap the shot just as one of the women, brandishing a whiskey bottle and revealing a glimpse of her thigh, plants an unexpected kiss on the preacher. Jim's landlady, Carrie, an older woman who raised him after his parents died when he was a baby, sees through his dastardly plan to blackmail the preacher. With the help of divine intervention, she finds the incriminating photographs, but Jim catches her with them, and, wrestling her to the ground, he accidently knocks her head against the metal safe in which he had hidden the photographs. Sister Carrie, as her fellow congregation members call her, never recovers, dying peacefully with the pastor and her friends from church at her bedside. The last words to issue from her lips are coordinated with the text of Johnson's sermon: "I'm going home."

The narrative cuts to her funeral with the preacher delivering the eulogy, lifted from Johnson's text with slight alterations. The conceit under-

lying the sermon is that God tells Death to "go down" and relieve Carrie
of the burden of life:

> Day before yesterday morning,
> God was looking down from his great, high heaven,
> Looking down on all his children,
> And his eye fell on Sister Caroline,
> Tossing on her bed of pain.

God commands his right-hand angel to call Death.

> And Death heard the summons,
> And he leaped on his fastest horse,
> Pale as a sheet in the moonlight.
> Up the golden street Death galloped,
> And the hoofs of his horse struck fire from the gold,
> But they didn't make no sound.
> Up Death rode to the Great White Throne,
> And waited for God's command.

> And God said: Go down, Death, go down,
> Go down to Savannah, Georgia, . . .
> And find Sister Caroline.

Here we have our first glimpse of the genius of Williams as a cinematic
imitator. At those points in the sermon where the text refers to Death on
horseback, Williams borrows footage from an unidentified earlier film of
a figure cloaked in black riding on a white horse over the horizon. Necessity
is the mother of invention. Constrained by a tight budget, Williams used
what he could find in the archives to illustrate details in Johnson's sermon
rather than shoot new frames or keep the camera fixed on the preacher for
the entire eulogy. When the sermon refers to "heaven's pearly gates," the
camera cuts to another borrowed sequence: two figures, an angel welcom-
ing a soul, stand outside large metal gates cushioned comfortably among
the clouds, which then swing open, to the soul's delight. Repeated four

times, this image is recycled from Williams's earlier film, *The Blood of Jesus*, along with a recurrent image of angels moving in a slow geometric dance up a walkway, a cinematic depiction of Jacob's ladder.[24]

Sister Carrie is resting in the bosom of Jesus, but things are taking a turn for the worse for Jim, whose conscience begins to speak out about the murder. We see him chain-smoking and frantically downing shots of whiskey, while the voice of his conscience cackles away, harping on what he has done. Jim leaps up from a table at his bar, pulls out a pistol, and begins to shoot at the disembodied voice. Harassed to distraction, he leaves the building and wanders aimlessly until he enters a desertlike terrain where he eventually collapses. Before him looms an image of the Gates of Hell decked out with a skull and crossbones and crowned with an inscription in English, ABANDON ALL HOPE, YE WHO ENTER HERE, an obvious allusion to the entrance to hell at the beginning of *Inferno* 3. The line in English and the simple design suggest that it was a prop created by Williams for the shot. While the vision of these gates provides an effective structural counterpoint to the pearly gates seen earlier during the preacher's sermon, their construction is markedly inferior, even shabby by comparison with the wrought-iron gates that swing open to welcome Sister Carrie's soul to heaven. Williams is hard pressed to match the production quality of the films he incorporates into his work.

If Williams improvises a cardboard or plywood prop for his gates of hell, what follows is of another order altogether. To illustrate Jim's experience of hell, Williams turns once again to the archives, this time to the 1911 silent film, *L'inferno,* by Adolfo Padovan and Francesco Bertolini of Milano Films, from which he literally clips frames that he splices into his movie.[25] We see hell from the perspective of Jim's soul as Dante and Vergil move through the traitors frozen in the river Cocytus toward Lucifer in the background at the pit of hell. The camera cuts back to Jim lying on the ground looking at the scene before him as his conscience reprimands him for killing the woman who brought him up. There are, then, short clips from the filmed version of the *Inferno*: from cantos 5, 6, and 18; a quick cut to Jim again; then cantos 19, 21–22, and 34, once more, before the gates of hell shut. The entire sequence of frames in hell takes less than one minute. We return to the boardinghouse of Mama Carrie (Jim's name for her) where the pastor tells Betty Jean, his fiancée and Carrie's niece, that Jim has been found dead at the mouth of Buck's Canyon.[26] The film ends with Jasper, the pastor, consoling Betty Jean, which parallels another scene earlier in the film where he reports her aunt's death.

The poor production values of *Go Down, Death!* might lead one to assume that a financially strapped Williams made do with whatever pieces of the Dante original he could get his hands on. But the quality of the final product does not detract from the deliberate, intelligent reading of Dante behind Williams's allusive adaptation of the cinematic *Inferno,* from whose fifty or so scenes he chooses six that suit the allegorical purposes of the narrative of *Go Down, Death!*[27] That we first race down to the bottom of hell among the traitors suggests that this is the ultimate destination for Jim, who murdered his surrogate mother. The narrative then pulls back and focuses briefly on other circles where Jim might have gone had the sin of his undoing not been so heinous.[28] The image of windswept lovers illustrating canto 5 alludes to Jim's jealous lust for Betty Jean, about which his conscience pricks him as he begins to hallucinate at the movie's end: "You love her, don't you, Jim." There is a brief image of gluttons from canto 6, recalling how Jim, a big man, shoved food in his face as he taunted Mama Carrie about the photographs. The snipped sequence from canto 18 of the flatterers immersed in their excrement may recall several moments in the film where Jim resorts to flattery to get his way. Or it may recall Dante's reference in canto 18 to Thais, a courtesan of Babylon, who compliments her nervous customer in Dante's version of the story with stereotypical flattery. How was it, the lover asks with some trepidation, to which she exclaims, it was wonderful! The three prostitutes in *Go Down, Death!* have mastered the art of flattery along with their other skills in ways that might suggest Thais to a careful reader. The image of simonists from canto 19, of those who use church power and office inappropriately, may reflect what Jim tried to get the church members to do or it may simply allude to his disrespect for the holiness of the pastor's position. A scene from cantos 21–22 follows in which devils punish grafters. Mama Carrie acknowledges Jim's entanglement in graft and other ill-conceived uses of money when she says, "I'm going to one that you can't bribe, one that you can't pay off with money and lie to. I'm going to the Lord." And finally we return to Lucifer, whose massive face gnaws incessantly on the sinner in his mouth. When the gates to hell shut, Jim is dead.

I cannot say with certainty how Williams came upon his copy of the 1911 *L'inferno,* though examination of various copies makes it clear that he did not work from the version of the film distributed in the United States.[29] The Italian financier of the original project, Gustavo Lombardo, marketed the film cleverly and distributed it widely after it was released in 1911. In keeping with his description on the film's publicity poster as "concessionario per tutto il mondo" (distributor for the whole world), Lombardo saw to it that the film was released in England and the United States, with the title *Dante's Inferno,* in France as *L'enfer,* and in Germany as *Die Hölle.*[30] By one estimate, the film grossed $2 million in the United States alone.[31] Williams's active life in the film industry put him in a position to acquire a copy of the Italian original, which would have been less valuable to an American distributor with intertitles in Italian. It's likely that Williams got his copy from Alfred N. Sack of Sack Amusement Enterprises, who not only put up the money for the production of *Go Down, Death!* but also saw to its distribution. In addition to producing many all-Negro feature films and shorts, Sack distributed foreign art films in the South. And "in Dallas—where his various companies had their headquarters—[he opened] the Coronet Theatre, in 1948, which he claimed to be the first art- and foreign-film theatre in the Southwest" (Slide 177).

Although no one has yet found any contemporary reviews of *Go Down, Death!,* the Production Code Administration (PCA) files in the Library of the Academy of Motion Picture Arts and Sciences provide an interesting glimpse into the way in which the film was received upon distribution. The presence of a file on it in the PCA Collection indicates that the film was submitted for certification, which suggests that it may have been intended for larger venues beyond the boundaries of the southern chitlin' circuit, that network of bars and clubs run by and for African Americans, associated with the dish served there, chitterlings, or pig intestines. In fact, the PCA files include reports from regional censorship boards in Maryland, Ohio, and New York, all of which recommend specific deletions from the film. The Maryland board censors the scene where Mabel, one of the prostitutes, flirts with the preacher, revealing her leg, and requests that the line of dialogue "Gee, but I could really go to town with that guy!" be cut. Maryland censors make these recommendations twice, first in October

1944, then later in July 1946, suggesting that the film might not have been ready for release until the later date or that the later date is merely a re-release. The New York board recommends the following deletion: "In Hades episode, eliminate all views of women where naked breasts are visible." The Ohio board proposed the most radical cuts, at least for my project: "Eliminate entire sequence depicting 'hell' including scenes of 'devil' chewing man and all scenes of people in 'hell.'" Thankfully, in the version as it now stands none of these cuts was made, which would have reduced the film to a very mundane status. One would like to know more about the composition of the Ohio board and the specific reasoning behind its radical proposal. Was it an all-white board that passed judgment on this all-black film? Thomas Cripps claims that "the Negro minister who sat on Chicago's board of censors was a rarity" (*Black Film as Genre* 7). Did the board members have any inkling of what Spencer Williams was doing with his elaborate allusions to Dante through his use of the Milano Films *L'inferno*? Was there, perhaps, the sense that this black man had no right to lay claim to a white man's hell? Did the noticeably white devil of Padovan and Bertolini make them uncomfortable? We don't have any information to allow us to answer these questions, as far as I know, beyond the brief reports in the PCA files I've cited above.[32]

Dante Meets Amos 'n' Andy

Go Down, Death! is a race movie, made by a black director with an all-black cast, meant for black audiences primarily in the segregated theaters of the South. But one white presence in the film stands out: Dante. To be sure, Dante's guide through hell, Vergil, whom we see throughout the frames Williams uses, is also white, but he is a special case, a spirit from limbo, the refuge in the *Inferno* for saintly pagans. The sinners we glimpse in the frames from the cinematic hell are also white, as is Lucifer himself. In fact, Williams may have scotched and burned the frames to lighten the skin tone of the archdevil. But it is the pilgrim who stands out in his whiteness. Why does Spencer Williams privilege Dante, the ultimate "dead white European male," in this way, making him the only living white person in his film? What value does Dante have for Spencer Williams?

Dante's authoritative appeal as a source for Williams is enhanced by the gothic horror of his particular vision of hell. Claude McKay, a prominent Jamaican-born American Negro writer who was a contemporary of Williams, notes in a 1932 letter to Max Eastman, "Dante's hell has a magical power over me even though I don't believe in hell" (152). If Dante's powerful vision of human crime and divine punishment invites the suspension of disbelief in the typical modern reader—and McKay's reaction is typical—it is rendered all the more striking when cast in moving pictures. Many of the sets in the Milano Films version of the *Inferno* owe their iconographic design to Gustave Doré's illustrations, which in their own way seem to anticipate cinema.[33] The citation from the Milano Films *L'inferno* is a source you don't have to understand completely to appreciate. It has the advantage over a literary allusion of using an actual piece of the cinematic source to provide the viewer with a glimpse of hell, as seen through Jim's eyes. Imagine the experience of someone who doesn't know Italian reading a translation of the *Inferno,* who then comes upon an untranslated passage in Italian *and is able to understand it as if it were English!* That is the effect of coming upon the frames from the Milano Films *L'inferno* spliced into *Go Down, Death!* Suddenly we are there in hell with Dante as our guide to good and evil; suddenly Dante is called upon to gloss the injustices of the Negro's segregated world in the South, to pass judgment on an example of what we might call nowadays "black-on-black crime." Suddenly Dante is the Negro director's moral compass.

In the reception of the *Inferno* it is common for Dante to serve as this sort of authoritative gloss on evil, though one may wonder how many in Williams's intended audience appreciated the magnitude of the medieval authority. In fact, Dante had acquired moral currency in African American culture in the nineteenth and early twentieth centuries, as we saw in the previous chapter. He was an important symbol of freedom among the abolitionists, including Frederick Douglass (who kept an image of the Italian poet alongside those of Lincoln and John Brown in his private library at Cedar Hill outside Washington, D.C.). Douglass, William Lloyd Garrison, Charles Sumner, and others, followed with great interest the political fortunes of Italy during the Risorgimento, through which Dante was interpreted as a symbol of political and moral liberty, a voice that spoke out against hypocritical bureaucracy. If not exactly sanctioned as canonical,

Dante was a figure to be reckoned with in the increasingly complex African American tradition.

Dante, I would like to propose, was used to denote progress in the move from south to north, from rural to urban, and from folkloristic spirituality to other more Europeanized forms of worship. African American culture was becoming more bourgeois, more middle class, less rural with each passing year as more and more southern blacks moved north and became urbanized. Adrienne Seward has speculated that Williams minimizes the folk elements of the religious drama in *Go Down, Death!* in order to appeal to this new middle class. Seward also notes that the hymns in the film's soundtrack are associated more with the rather staid Methodist Church than with the rural Spiritual tradition.[34] In fact, "Ave Maria" is heard at a crucial point in the soundtrack, not exactly what comes to mind when you think of that old-time religion in a black church down South. There is no question that the film is much less of a religious folk drama than Williams's first success, *The Blood of Jesus.* A cartoonlike struggle between good and evil characterizes the first film with its predictable happy resolution of a near accidental death, whereas *Go Down, Death!* ends on a tragic note highlighted by the use of the Dante sequence. The censorship records suggest that Sack and Williams intended for the new film to circulate in areas of the country like Maryland, New York, and Ohio, where they had submitted it to those regional boards. The filmmaker and distributor may have tried to produce a film that would appeal to the different needs and tastes of audiences in these areas of the country where the series of elaborate allusions to Dante could be seen as a gesture to the rising intellectual and financial status of the Negro at this time.

Richard Wright, who had a copy of Cary's translation of the *Divine Comedy* in his library, uses Dante similarly in the autobiographical narrative of his youth, *Black Boy,* which was published in 1937 and reprinted in 1945 at approximately the same time that *Go Down, Death!* was released.[35] Two dramatic allusions to Dante frame his narrative, one near its beginning (30–31), of which Kimberly W. Benston observes, "It is noteworthy that at this point, as Richard turns away from the father, a palpable and crucial echo of European literary tradition takes his father's place. Wright recalls here the scene of Vergil the master and father lifting Dante (the child and pilgrim) over the barriers of hell, toward resurrective rebirth in a vision of the *city* of God."[36] This allusion is balanced by another at the very end of the novel in a passage where the narrator meditates on what it means to be leaving the South, as he travels from Memphis to Chicago by train: "I headed North . . . [thinking] that if men were lucky in their living on earth they might win some redeeming meaning for their having struggled and suffered here beneath the stars" (228). The allusion is to the ending of each canticle of Dante's poem, all three of which conclude with the same word and image, "stars."[37] Benston reads it as referring to the end of *Paradise,* which would suggest that the journey has reached its conclusion. I would argue, rather, that it seems more likely Wright is alluding to one of the other two sections of the poem, if not to both: the *Inferno,* with the suggestion that the South is a hell from which Richard has now escaped; and the *Purgatory,* the section of Dante's poem that deals with redemption and struggle. This second allusion, whatever its exact referent, is prompted by the narrator's trip out of the South and into the new urban world situated to the north. In Wright's autobiographical novel, as in Spencer Williams's film, Dante is used to mark the move from rural to urban, from poor to middle class, from colored to Negro.

The move northward is also a move from one age to another, from the feudalism of the sharecropper's hardscrabble livelihood to the industrial age. As Ralph Ellison puts it in the essay "Harlem Is Nowhere," which consists of his reflections on a psychiatric clinic in Harlem which read like a gloss on *Invisible Man,* "It is literally possible for them [American Negroes] to step from feudalism into the vortex of industrialism simply by moving across the Mason-Dixon line" (*Collected Essays* 321). In that essay of 1948, Ellison records the damage, psychological and social, that the great migration had on many who came north and failed. A generation earlier in 1925, Alain Locke states more hopefully in the opening essay of *The New Negro* that "the movement of the Negro becomes more and more a mass movement toward the larger and the more democratic chance—in the Negro's case a deliberate flight not only from countryside to city, but from medieval America to modern" ("The New Negro" 6). This mass act of migration contributes to the melting pot of Harlem out of which Locke and his peers inaugurate their renaissance of African American culture in the 1920s. Locke notes further that the sharecroppers of the South moved "northward and city-ward" not merely of their own accord but in response to the "shutting off of foreign migration" in 1924, which created a need for workers especially in heavy industry (6). After the U.S. Congress passed the Immigration Act of 1924 intended to check the influx of foreign immigrants, southern blacks left their tenant farms and migrated north and into the Midwest to replace foreigners in the mills and factories of the burgeoning industrial economy. Blacks filled the gap. But as Wright and Ellison dramatize in their respective works of fiction, not every immigrating New Negro up from the South plays the role of compliant, appreciative stopgap. As we shall see, Ellison describes the tension in this new social equation by turning to none less than Dante to account for one would-be New Negro's failure to comply. Ellison turns to European canonical writing to articulate what can go wrong when blacks are called "northward and city-ward" to fill the gap created by the lack of European immigrants, Italians among them.

But to return to Williams for a moment more. The Dantesque source also appeals to him for the structure it lends his film. The narrative of the *Inferno* becomes a device to catapult his character, Jim, into hell, anticipating the way that later African American writers, LeRoi Jones and Gloria Naylor, use Dante's poem to shed light on the moral inadequacies of their respective characters. These authors, like Williams, are drawn to the structural rigor of Dante's system of moral classification. LeRoi Jones, for his part, calls his imitation of Dante's *Inferno, The System of Dante's Hell,* while Naylor structures the narrative of her novel *Linden Hills* around the descending crescent circles of an infernal suburb in which her middle-class African American characters lose their souls. In each of these examples, which we shall consider in more detail in following chapters, the medieval source functions as a narrative model to which the artist refers in organizing the modern work. But Williams (and these other African American artists) could have found and borrowed a sense of structure from other sources, for a rigorous moral order is not unique to Dante. The Bible and religious rituals, for example, function as organizing principles of this sort in *The Blood of Jesus.* Why else, then, might the artist turn to Dante?

By splicing cuts from *L'inferno* into his film, Williams uses Dante-the-character to integrate his "All-Negro Production" (to borrow from the film's publicity flyer), engaging in a charged act of creative imitation that we might call "artistic integration." Ten years before the Supreme Court ruling that began the dismantling of official segregation in the United States, Williams is pushing the envelope in his art. As the filmmaker uses the white character to integrate the world of his Negro film, so he mixes or integrates his sources: the literary sources, James Weldon Johnson and Dante, on the one hand; the cinematic sources, cuts from *The Blood of Jesus* and other silent films, including *L'inferno,* on the other. It may seem contrary to propose that this "All-Negro Production" refers to the other race, the white race, which seems to be present only in its absence until Dante appears at the film's end. But the absence is a conspicuous one, for the characters in Williams's film repeatedly make comments that suggest the extent to which the other race (ostensibly nowhere near) is in fact just around the corner (or just over the other side of the tracks). Jim tells his cronies to go down to "Colored Street, and round up two or three of them little fly chicks," prostitutes to use as bait for the preacher. These are women whose sex appeal is measured by their whiteness and by their modified, affected accents that sound like caricatures of Caucasian speech: they talk white. Language demarcates social class and marks mobility. Of note in this regard is that James Weldon Johnson's sermon that forms the basis for the film is written in a language that, if not exactly white, is decidedly not dialect. Johnson notes in the introduction to *God's Trombones* that "practically no poetry is being written in dialect by the colored poets of today" (cited in North 10). Adopting Johnson's choice of language is another way in which Williams tries to make his art more middle class.

The plot emphasizes the class differences between Jim and Betty Jean. The voice of Jim's conscience criticizes him for even hoping for reciprocal love from Betty Jean with the claim: "You love her, don't you, Jim? But she's not your kind, Jim. Oh, she's colored all right, but she's not common!" As if to say, Jim could only love and be loved by a woman of color in the hierarchy of interpersonal relations in the segregated South, and in that hierarchy, Jim must find his match at the bottom. When Carrie confronts Jim in the middle of the film, she contrasts the only love Jim knows with the honest love between Betty Jean and the pastor, "not the kind of love you find down on Colored Street." And there is the odd momentary hallucination of a rope from a lynching on the tree Jim runs into just before he dies.[38] His conscience goads him: "See that tree over yonder? I'm going to tell you something about that tree. Now listen. They once hung a man on this tree for killing a woman. And let me tell you this. It was this very limb right here. Got enough to hang you too, Jim. Better go on from here, go on. This ain't no place for you. Run! Run! Run, run, run away, boy." The rope represents a potential flashback that the director doesn't have to give us, for we know how that scene from race relations would look. And if we didn't know, the reaction shot of Jim's terror amply fleshes out the picture for the viewer's imagination. There was arguably nothing more hellish for an African American audience, even as late as the 1940s, than the diabolical administration of retribution and vengeance through lynching. The way in which the horror of the specific image of the noose is suddenly thrust in the viewer's face reminds me of the way Hiram Powers's wax figure, that "poor old negro just entering upon a state of perpetual freezing," impresses the visitor in the Infernal Regions at Cincinnati's Western Museum, as discussed in the last section of the introduction. The marginal figure of the black man is suddenly front and center.

The revelation of Dante's moral cosmology, however, ultimately transcends issues of race. Jim's vision of his destination through the edited montage made of the frames from the silent film, with the incessant voice-over of his conscience directing his viewing, shows him what happens to those who traffic in evil, white or black. And we, the viewers in the audience, are given a didactic lesson in the horrors of evil, too. Alas, Jim is a sinner who learns about hell too late for it to do him any good. The timing is ironically emphasized in his glimpses of Dante-the-pilgrim, whose own preview of the underworld will enable him to confront evil more effectively once he has returned to life on earth. The mixing of sources, while it raises legitimate questions about race relations at the time the movie was made, suggests another way of construing the role of Dante in this otherwise predictable race movie. Spencer Williams's unexpected integration of his "Negro" film *Go Down, Death!* with the white protagonist from Dante's *Inferno* forces us to realize that the work of the medieval Italian poet is far more canonical than keepers of the tradition may have ever imagined.

WILLIAMS'S CAREER spanned a period of two and a half decades, from the late 1920s into the mid-1950s, taking us chronologically from the era of court-sanctioned segregation in the United States to the beginning of its end. In 1896 the Supreme Court had used its decision in the case of *Plessy v. Ferguson* to declare the doctrine of "separate but equal" constitutional and, therefore, not in violation of the civil rights of nonwhite American citizens. With this decision, racism was institutionalized easily, quickly, and openly throughout the United States in the first half of the twentieth century. In 1954 the Supreme Court ruled in another landmark case, *Brown v. the Board of Education* of Topeka, Kansas, to reverse the earlier decision of "separate but equal." Chief Justice Earl Warren wrote unambiguously for the majority that "separate educational facilities are inherently unequal" (Christian 388), thus beginning the slow process of dismantling the structures of disadvantage that had hindered the progress of nonwhites. As we noticed earlier, the progression from *The Blood of Jesus* to *Go Down, Death!* moves us topographically from a rural setting to an urban one, a move that parallels the contemporary migrations of African Americans from the farms of the southlands to the cities of the North or to urban areas in the South in the first half of the century. With a new generation of African Americans growing up outside the South and heightened awareness in the South itself of the right to justice under the law, things were in place for the civil rights movement to blossom in the 1950s and 1960s.

The next noteworthy moment in Spencer Williams's career after *Go Down, Death!* came with the television series *Amos 'n' Andy,* in production at CBS from 1951 to 1954. The TV show was a sitcom based on an earlier radio version in which two white actors had played the main characters in black voice. Whenever the radio actors, Charles Correll and Freeman Gosden, were photographed for publicity shots, they appeared in blackface and tattered clothes. It was for all practical purposes a minstrel show. And did it have a following! "The enormity of the program's popularity as a radio show is attested in the fact that in its early days many of the nation's hotel dining rooms began to follow the custom of three Pittsburgh hotels and suspended service between 7:00 and 7:15 P. M. and turned up their radios while the program was being aired" (Clayton 66–67). Although Williams and the other black actors hired to play the leads in the TV version struggled to elevate the level of the show's discourse by dressing better and refraining from dialect,[39] it was still undeniably a show marked by malignant racial stereotypes to which the NAACP and others took exception. Sponsors withdrew their support for fear of retribution from the African American community, which prompted CBS eventually to take the show out of production. Reruns played regularly, but the cast didn't earn a penny from those screenings, creating what Clayton calls the "tragedy of Amos 'n' Andy" (66). When Clayton interviewed Williams in 1961, the actor was barely surviving on Social Security and GI benefits. Typecast as a minstrel fool, his earlier career all but forgotten, the actor had not had a single job since the TV series ended. CBS had even blocked an attempt by the cast to organize a touring vaudeville-type production of the show. Williams died in 1969 in obscurity.

Ralph Waldo Ellison's Prophetic Vernacular Muse

Where does Dante fit into this picture as Williams's career bottoms out in the 1950s? Just as *Amos 'n' Andy* is showing up on the cathode-ray tube, Ralph Ellison finishes an intense seven-year period of writing his magisterial novel *Invisible Man,* published in 1952 to great acclaim. There is a radical discomfiture between *Invisible Man* and *Amos 'n' Andy,* although they are products of the same moment and milieu, the same segregated Negro world. Whereas the reality represented in Williams's television show exists in a time warp, Ellison's depicted world is under constant pressure to the point that it finally erupts into the violence of the Harlem riots of 1935, refracted through the author's direct experience of the 1943 riots. The riots and the political and economic exploitation that causes them force the protagonist underground from where he narrates the novel, saying in the book's memorable last sentence: "Who knows but that, on the lower frequencies, I speak for you?"

Several critics have pointed out thematic and structural parallels between Ellison's work and Dante's *Inferno,*[40] but no one seems to have noted the striking similarity in the design of their narratives. Meili Steele's observations on Ellison's narrative design are as applicable to the *Divine Comedy* as to *Invisible Man*: "It is a first-person retrospective narrative about how the protagonist comes to be able to tell the story. . . . Ellison's first-person retrospective narrative uses the distance between the narrating self of the present and experiencing selves of the past to create a hermeneutic tension"

(188–89). The design of the *Divine Comedy* allows for a similar play between different moments in the protagonist's experience. I mentioned in the introduction that a standard critical starting place distinguishes Dante-the-pilgrim who experienced the miraculous journey through the afterlife in 1300 from Dante-the-poet who struggles in the present (from 1307 to 1321) to write that journey down in poetic form having returned from hell, purgatory, and heaven. The hermeneutic tension between those two periods in Dante's life creates the poem's dynamic as it moves between past and present, posing such questions as: How can I write down what I saw? Now that I am a new man, how did what I see affect my abilities to write down anything at all? One could describe this structural device as a kind of narrative "double consciousness," to use the concept W. E. B. Du Bois promotes in *The Souls of Black Folk*; that is, "this sense of always looking at one's self through the eyes of others" (2). The divided Negro, Du Bois explains, longs "to merge his double self into a better and truer self . . . to be both a Negro and an American" (2–3). To create a new identity that combines the experiences and memories of two cultures, Africa and America—the ongoing challenge that confronts people of color in the United States—is analogous to the creation of the new man that arises from overcoming the sort of split narrative that Ellison and Dante deploy. Much as the reader's challenge is to grapple with the implications of Dante's pilgrim who then becomes the poet whose work we read, so must the reader think through the ethical implications of Invisible Man's voice narrating from an infernal coal cellar beneath the streets as he reconstructs his life to account for how he ended up there in the first place. The critical retrospection shared by Dante's poet and Ellison's narrator generates the meaning of their respective works.

There is another more obvious connection between the two works that bears scrutiny. Ellison foregrounds his awareness of Dante's poetic project with a direct allusion to the medieval writer in *Invisible Man* when the protagonist describes the way he listens to jazz in the novel's prologue: "I not only entered the music, but descended, like Dante, into its depths" (8). My reconstruction of how Ellison came to compose this specific sentence at the opening of the novel tells us something not only about his allegiance to Dante but also about his compositional technique. The Ralph Waldo Ellison Papers, Manuscript Division, Library of Congress, contain no fewer than six different typed versions of the Prologue to *Invisible Man* in addition to several undated handwritten notes, all of which shed light on the opening allusion to Dante. To my knowledge no one has analyzed these drafts of *Invisible Man* from the perspective of textual bibliography to understand the novel as a material product of written culture in the way that Bradley and Callahan have edited the massive quantity of typescripts and computer printouts that compose the material substratum of Ellison's second novel, of which *Juneteenth* is a substantial portion.[41] I offer my investigation of the material production of this passage as a model for what someone else might do with the other drafts preliminary to the printing of *Invisible Man.* Small though this single sentence may be, it is crucial to my understanding of Ellison's relation to Dante and by extension to my reading of the modern author's work as a whole.

Assembling the sequence of typed drafts of the prologue to *Invisible Man* in the likely order of their composition (which for the sake of simplicity I will designate as versions A though F), one comes upon the following note, handwritten in pen and pencil on a 3 × 5 inch piece of paper with the long side pointing up, which seems to precede the drafts: "Impressionistic opening section when he is within depths of music and hears water in mains, this water must itself seem to talk to him. These are the Muses making prophsey" [*sic*].[42] Ellison had written the first two words in pencil and then continued — starting over on top of those initial words — with a fountain pen. The script is a big and clumsy cursive, seemingly scribbled in a rush, with two to four words per line on the card. The passage fills about three-fourths of the card. Much as the water in the plumbing running down the walls of his basement hovel communicates prophetically to Invisible Man, so the idea for the passage appears to have been something of an inspiration to Ellison himself. At least his handwriting suggests that he worked fast to get it down. Is the crucial word *prophsey* with two syllables a hurried misspelling or is it the black vernacular speaking in this moment of rushed inspiration? And, if the latter, is it an unintended slip of the pen or is it an intentional channeling of dialect? There is no way to be sure.[43]

The earliest full draft of the prologue is a typescript (version A) over which Ellison returned to make emendations in pen and pencil, adding, striking, and correcting.[44] The allusion to Dante is not typed out in A,

but at a later moment Ellison has gone back over the typescript and inserted this draft of the sentence in pencil: "I not only entered the music
but descended, like Dante, into its depths." The added sentence is placed
precisely at a literal juncture between two separate pieces of typing paper
that the author has cut and stapled together to form a single 8 × 11 inch
sheet. Ellison took a page of typescript and cut it horizontally so that only
one and a half lines of typed text remain at the top in this configuration:

> waited for the other voices to speak. I found myself hearing not only
> in time, but in space as well.

He cut the page about one inch down from the top edge on the left margin,
proceeding horizontally for about four inches, cutting up the page one-half
inch to trim around the last word in the second line, *well,* then proceeding
horizontally across the page's next four inches, to finish about one-half inch
down on the right. It is impossible to say how much of the original typescript he removed with this cut, but I hypothesize that he must have cut off
at least an early version of the sentence that interests me, which I believe
read originally, as it does in version B: "I not only ? the muse but descended,
like ? into the depths." Having clipped it away, he then combined the page
with another page whose top margins had been clipped to dovetail with
the cropped page as described above so as to create a new sheet. Precisely at
the point where the two sheets are stapled together the author penciled
in the sentence on Dante. The text in version C leads me to conclude that
he added this line to A only after having completed C—that is, he emended
A in light of what he eventually composed in C.

Versions B and C are identical, in fact C is a literal carbon copy of B,
with the major exception that the author subsequently used C as his working copy upon which to introduce a new wave of changes by hand in pen
and pencil. In B, Ellison produced a clean typescript incorporating the
handwritten changes added to the typescript of A. He then put it away
and worked instead on the copy of it, version C. In version B the allusion
to Dante hasn't yet crystallized; we find instead: "I not only ? the muse but
descended, , like ? into the depths." Two question marks hold the place for
what will come in subsequent versions. And one notes the typographical
error of a superfluous second comma after "descended."

and amazingly scientific. His body was one single flow of rhythmic action.

He hit the yokel a hundred times while the yokel held up his arms in surprised. But

suddenly the yokel struck one blow and knocked science, speed and footwork

as cold as a well-digger's posterior. under the spell of reefer I discovered new analytical way of lis-

tening to music. The unheard sounds came through, and each melodic line

stood out clearly from the rest, said its piece, and waited for the other

voices to speak. That night I found myself hearing not only in time, but

in space as well. I not only entered the music but descended, like Dante

into depths. Beneath the swiftness of the hot tempo there was a slower

and I entered it and looked around and heard an old woman singing a

spiritual as full of mute (welstomene) pain as a flamenco, and beneath that

was a still lower level on which I saw a beautiful girl the color of ivory

pleading in a voice like my sister's as she stood naked before a group of

slaveowners who bidded for her to be their sleve, and below that I found a

lower level and a more rapid tempo and I heard someone shout:

"Brothers and sisters, my text this morning is the 'Blackness of

In version C, which is larded with all sorts of corrections, overwrites, and insertions, we catch a glimpse of the author at his desk working over the revised typescript, thinking through the revisions. In C's draft of the sentence on Dante, Ellison has written over the two question marks that remain barely visible under the bold black stroke of his fountain pen. Over the first question mark he writes *heard,* which he then cancels, writing *entered* above it. Despite the fact that we are dealing with Louis Armstrong's music the issue here is not simply how one hears it but rather how one viscerally participates in it. Ellison then emends *muse* to *music* by writing -*ic* on top of the -*e* in *muse.* He doesn't correct the additional comma in the middle of the sentence; something more important lies just ahead. Over the second question mark, he writes DANTE in capital letters. Finally, in the last clause he changes *the* to *its.* The essential transformations have occurred in the line, and in fact in version D, which is completely retyped, we have the sentence as it now stands in the printed editions: "I not only entered the music but descended, like Dante, into its depths." Though he continues to make changes here and there to the text of the prologue in versions E and F, which he prepares as he readies the final typescript for submission to the press, he leaves the sentence with the reference to Dante alone from this point on. Dante replaces the question mark. Dante fills the gap. And once Dante entered Ellison's text, he stayed there. But what does this reference to the Italian medieval poet mean?

The allusion to Dante signals an allegiance to the canonical literature of the Western tradition with which Ellison wants to align his work. The array of allusions in this allegorical novel is complex, and Dante is an important part of the mix. The actual placement of the inserted sentence is telling coming as it does on the heels of several other references and immediately before the text's first extended surreal passage. In the prologue's second sentence, after the dramatic opening line, the author situates himself in relation to the venerable tradition of American writing of the nineteenth century: "I am an invisible man. No, I am not a spook like those who haunted Edgar Allan Poe . . ." (3). It is well documented that Ellison fancied himself in some ways inheritor to the legacy of Melville (the novel's first epigraph is from *Benito Cereno*), Hawthorne, Thoreau, not to mention Emerson, for whom he had been named, all New Englanders responsible for the Golden Day in American letters in the nineteenth century.[45]

Perhaps the southerner Poe's somewhat more marginal canonical status marks a good starting place for Ellison, who was in his own way an upstart on the twentieth-century literary scene. Further on in the prologue the protagonist mentions a different "but great American tradition of tinkers. That makes me kin to Ford, Edison and Franklin" (7). From the early republic's high literary tradition to that of the homespun American entrepreneurial inventor: Ellison values both.

The tinker in the story uses his technological savvy to rig up a radio-phonograph to listen to the music of Louis Armstrong, who represents yet a third indigenous American tradition that informs Ellison's work, that of vernacular art especially associated with black (Ellison would most often say Negro) culture. And it is the presence of Armstrong's bluesy jazz that prompts the allusion to Dante in the first place. To describe the protagonist's sensation of listening to Armstrong's "What Did I Do to Be So Black and Blue?" after smoking marijuana, Ellison turns to Dante: "I not only entered the music but descended, like Dante, into its depths" (8). The reference to Dante is the first to a European cultural figure setting him up in opposition to the American figures that have preceded him in the text. I count T. S. Eliot, from whose play *The Family Reunion* Ellison took the novel's second epigraph, as a hybrid Anglo-American despite his having immigrated to England in 1914 and taken on British citizenship in 1927. As I will discuss below, it is precisely the duality of national cultures in Eliot that Ellison values.

This juxtaposition of American traditions and the European tradition which Dante represents is actually hinted at in the author's emendations, to return to the archives for a moment. The original idea on the 3×5 inch sheet in Ellison's hurried hand which will eventually morph into the sentence with the allusion to Dante mentions both "music" and "Muses": "Impressionistic opening section when he is within depths of music and hears water in mains, this water must itself seem to talk to him. These are the Muses making prophsey." The sequence of emendations suggests that the author is grappling with that contrast, trying to determine the best way to describe what has hold of his character, music or the muses. The line removed from version A (in my hypothetical reconstruction of Ellison's editing practice) has "muse": "I not only ? the muse but descended, like ? into the depths." The same line is reproduced in B and C, the copy

of B, with the author writing over the line in C, changing *muse* to *music.* In
the traditional archaic way of describing inspiration, in the openings to
Homer's *Iliad* and *Odyssey,* for example, the muse enters the poet, not vice
versa. Similarly in Dante's *Inferno,* in a passage at the beginning of the
poem, *Inferno* 2.7–9, and one near the end of the first canticle at *Inferno*
32.1–12, the muses are invoked to take action. Dante does not call on
them to enter him as does Homer but he invites them to help him with
his poetry. They act on him, not vice versa. It made more sense to Ellison
as he edited this line to emphasize the protagonist's active relationship to
music rather than to the muse or muses.

Furthermore, to separate "music" from "muse" emphatically distinguishes the realm of Louis Armstrong and his black vernacular from the literary world of Homer, Dante, and other epic poets who call on the muses
for inspiration. That is, the juxtaposition of music and muse represents a
tension between, once again, not merely American and European cultures
but, more to the point, American vernacular culture and European classicism in the form of the epic muse.[46] We have seen how Richard Wright,
Ellison's most important literary mentor, uses Dante to mark the dramatic
move of the American black from the feudalism of the South to the industrial North in *Black Boy.* Ellison extends Wright's use of Dante to highlight
a new kind of mobility, not literal, not social, but the literary mobility of
a new kind of American writer who signals his arrival among the canonical writers of old Europe with an energized allusion to Dante. Ellison mi-
grates to Europe but not literally as did Wright in 1946 much to the cha-
grin of his young protégé; rather, Ellison enters the territory of European
culture via the literary tradition Dante represents.

In another undated but presumably early note found in the archives,
Ellison suggests that the act of migration itself is infernal in a Dantesque
sense by associating it with other words that recall the topography of Dante's
hell.[47] The words that make up the note are on an 8½ × 11 inch sheet of
paper and are divided into two columns. The column on the left consists
of a list of fourteen nouns; it is written in ink and dashed off hurriedly, as
is Ellison's wont. Most of the words are spelled out in capital letters giving
them a proclamatory quality, as if they were being declared. To the right
and at the center of the page is an abbreviated list, a sort of heading, which
seems to announce what the column to the left is really about: "CRIME"

and "EXPIATION." Beneath this pair is the only phrase in the note, a tag in slang: "Going to END of LINE." I reproduce the note schematically here.

ICE	CRIME
FIRE	EXPIATION
ROT	
labyrinth	
MAZE	Going to END of LINE
HEll	
Abyss	
MOUNTAINS	
VALLEYS	
EXILE	
MIGRATION	
LOSTNESS	
SubMERGENCE	
SILENCE	

The longer list contains the features of an infernal topography of the sort that Dante imagines in the *Inferno*. In fact, every single word could be said to have a correspondent in Dante's vision of hell with the exception, perhaps, of *migration*, which, as we have noted above, has a special significance to black Americans of Ellison's generation. The unexpected occurrence of the term emphasizes all the more the extent to which migration is being recast as infernal too. For Richard Wright, the first impression of migration is that it is an escape out of hell, but the sharecropper immigrating to the North realizes all too soon that the perceived paradise is a place of exile, a labyrinth, an abyss, a fill-in-the-blank with any of the nouns from the list above, in short, a new and different setting that is nothing less than hell. Migration north becomes almost a form of punishment or expiation for the simple crime of being black in the segregated South. Wright's autobiographical *Black Boy* (1937), with its Dantesque transitions from South to North, is followed by his first novel, *Native Son* (1940), in which Bigger Thomas, the protagonist, is living in a hellish Chicago slum where four people share a rat-infested room. No surprise, Wright protests, if someone emerges from such a setting to become a social misfit—a rapist and a murderer—the fate of Bigger. Migration leads ultimately to "Death on the City Pavements" in Wright's harsh phrase (*12 Million Black Voices* 91). In *Invisible Man,* Ellison also comes to share a similar perception of the injustice of social relations, even in the North; thus one may account for his addition of *migration* to the list of infernal sites and actions.

Ellison's list represents a Dantesque way of thinking about crime and punishment. While it's not the sort of detailed system that LeRoi Jones/Amiri Baraka will embrace in the next generation of African American rewritings of Dante's *Inferno,* it is an attempt to imagine a sequence of geographical settings through which the artist could effectively depict evil. In addition to the nouns of place that sound hellish, Ellison includes several words that reflect an existential malaise often articulated by writers confronting evil in the middle of the twentieth century: *exile, migration, lostness, submergence, silence.* Culminating in silence, the writer's ultimate hell, the list addresses what one might say was the fate of blacks moving north in the hope of becoming New Negroes. Migration is a form of exile in which the immigrant is frequently lost, often submerged, and eventually silenced as in the cases of Bigger Thomas and Invisible Man. The unusual form *lostness* signals the writer's desperate attempt to make sense of the gravity of the situation as he meditates on the condition of the lost. The solecism speaks volumes.

Ellison's love of language prompts him to complement the list with a vernacular tag taken from railroad jargon that riffs playfully on the more formal topographical designations: "going to end of line." To go to the end of the line is to arrive at the last stop beyond which there is nothing. It is an apt euphemism for going to hell. The image of the train it evokes calls to mind once again the fate of immigrants heading northward from the feudal South to the industrial North. If Wright depicts the excited agony of the train trips north that inevitably lead to disappointment, depression, poverty, or even death on the pavements (*12 Million Black Voices* 98–100), Ellison is able to balance his immersion in hell with a love of language. He concludes the essay "The Little Man at Chehaw Station" with this claim: "Where there's a melting pot there's smoke, and where there's smoke it is not simply optimistic to expect fire, it's imperative to watch for the phoenix's vernacular, but transcendent, rising" (*Collected Essays* 523).[48] We need to understand just how Ellison comes to this hopeful statement about a transcendent vernacular, solecisms and all.

Migration, both from Europe to North America and from the South of the United States northward, contributes to the melting pot out of which will rise the transcendent vernacular. The mixing of European and American and African American voices gives the American vernacular its distinctiveness. But there is another more fundamental fusion that underlies the American vernacular Ellison is seeking to perfect. In his provocative essay of 1970, "What America Would Be Like without Blacks," Ellison makes the claim that cultural fusion has been successful since "most American whites are culturally part Negro American without even realizing it" (*Collected Essays* 584). In fact, the first example of the seemingly radical cultural fusion to which Ellison alludes is linguistic: "For one thing, the American nation is in a sense the product of the American language, a colloquial speech that began emerging long before the British colonials and the Africans were transformed into Americans" (*Collected Essays* 585). The modern language available to Americans is derived from a vernacular mix based on British and African ingredients (along with other European languages too), a hybrid mix that even preceded the political maneuverings that created the new nation at the end of the eighteenth century. Enslaved Africans brought more than the banjo and okra along with them across the Atlantic: they brought a multitude of languages, and through the filter of that great linguistic variety they began to adopt and adapt the colonial languages they encountered, especially British English. The nation's Constitution may have legally excluded Africans from participation in its political life, but Africans could not be kept out of the process that would create a new national language. Ellison tellingly refers to the formation of the national hybrid language as an act of "vernacular revolt" (*Collected Essays* 585). And more directly in "Roscoe Dunjee and the American Language": "I suspect that in the effort to adapt the American language, to make it tell the truth about processes and relationships between people in this country, there somehow lay the beginnings of the American Revolution" (*Collected Essays* 457).[49] The formation of the new hybrid American language was a fundamentally political act according to Ellison.

In an interview from 1965 with Robert Penn Warren, Ellison makes a hopeful claim about the impact of black on white in this formative linguistic process. Imagining what might be the positive effects of desegregation in the years to follow, he proposes that "the dictionary will become more accurate, the language a bit purified, and the singing in the schools will sound better" (*Who Speaks for the Negro?* 334). The potential for linguistic change catches Ellison's attention. With desegregation, the vernacular will do nothing less than rise and transcend the limits of racial discrimination. And in a utopian mode he proposes that as the country moves toward a more perfect union, the country's language will reflect that perfection in a newfound purity and wholeness.

Some of the thinking behind Ellison's notion of a new American language derives from the example of T. S. Eliot, whose "The Waste Land" was a crucial text in Ellison's intellectual development at Tuskegee Institute. The poem introduced him to the symbolist modernism of the best American writing at the time.[50] In particular its emphasis on colloquial speech—the poem's working title before Ezra Pound edited it was "He Do the Police in Different Voices"—resonated with Ellison's own sense of how his artistic language should sound.[51] And as Michael North has shown in *The Dialect of Modernism,* the colloquialisms of Eliot, Pound, Stein, and other modernist authors were often inspired by the vernacular speech of black America. The dialect of modernism, to borrow from North, owes much to the dialect of Joel Chandler Harris's Uncle Remus stories. Modernist American authors found their own collective voice in English by turning to the dialect of African American culture, from which they benefited immensely even as they belittled it. Ellison, for his part, wanted to forge a new vehicle of expression that would adequately represent the experiences of Americans of color without sacrificing their communal voice. To do so he would model his writing on Eliot's incorporation of direct speech in his complex symbolist poetry. Positioned among multiple traditions, American (including African American), British, and European, Eliot taught Ellison that the literary artist can straddle different worlds at the same time.[52]

The main lesson here was that the literary artist can do this linguistically. Ellison took to heart Eliot's claim that the writer should purify the people's language.[53] In "Little Gidding," the final section of *Four Quartets,*

Eliot declares that one of the charges of the writer is "to purify the dialect of the tribe" (l. 127). The phrase is uttered by his ghostly mentor as they patrol a desolate urban landscape, perhaps wartime London after a German bombing raid, in the hours before dawn. Composed in a modified form of *terza rima,* the scene in Eliot's poem is inspired by Dante's encounter with the soul of his master Brunetto Latini in *Inferno* 15. The narrator of "Little Gidding" dramatizes the modern poet's act of literary imitation when he says, "So I assumed a double part, and cried / And heard another's voice cry: 'What! Are *you* here?'" This allusion to the initial moment when the pilgrim catches sight of Brunetto rewrites or, perhaps it is more accurate to say, translates Dante's expression of surprise upon seeing his teacher in hell among the sodomites: "Siete voi qui, ser Brunetto?" (*Inf.* 15.30). Eliot's italicized *you* emphasizes the pronoun, perhaps in an attempt to recreate how the rhythm of Dante's line, as well as the pronoun's redundancy in the original, calls attention to the *voi* in the Italian.

Ellison knew the Dantesque passage from "Little Gidding" well. Included in the archives among his papers is a typed two-page copy of this specific section of the poem without the first six lines but containing the rest of the passage from lines 84 to 149.[54] The first six lines use dense symbolism to describe a bombing raid during an "interminable night" (79), "after the dark dove with the flickering tongue" (81)—that is, Nazi bombers—had done their damage and flown back to Germany. Ellison's disregard of the opening suggests that he wants to remove the passage from its historical context and focus on other aspects of its content. It is a rough copy replete with typographical errors, one inadvertently omitted line (115), and no attempt to indicate the integrity of Eliot's tercets. That Ellison read it over is clear for he has emended the finished typed copy with pen as neatly as possible, correcting line 127, for example, where he had typed *trive* to read *tribe.* At the head of the page he adds this statement: "From Little Giddings [*sic*], discovered by me July 51 [*sic*] 1948 after I had written my scene in which IVM encounters blind man." Ellison dramatizes the moment of his own discovery of the passage and in the excitement mistakenly types *51* for *15* for the date of the fateful day. But at the same time he wants to be clear about the precedence of his own creativity over Eliot's. Before he read this passage in "Little Gidding" he wrote something that he considers similar—the encounter of his narrator, whom he calls IVM or Invisible Man, with the blind preacher Barbee—and he wants posterity to know that it would have been impossible for him to imitate Eliot given the chronology of his reading and writing. While I accept his claim, his anxiety about Eliot's possible influence is palpable.[55]

There are no annotations on these pages, thus there is no direct evidence that Ellison was even aware of the full genealogy extending from Dante to Eliot to himself. But there is a crucial indirect connection that links the three authors. The central claim in Eliot's poem about purifying the dialect of the tribe is inspired in part by Dante's own sense of the responsibility of the poet articulated in his incomplete theoretical treatise *De vulgari eloquentia* (On the Eloquence of the Vernacular). Dante discusses the ideal model for the Italian vernacular and concludes that none of the fourteen dialects he examines in his essay is appropriate in and of itself, but taken together they all share some unstated quality that is constitutive of the illustrious vernacular he is in search of. In his Italian poetry Dante tries to exemplify that idealized form of the vernacular, although in truth he does depend heavily on his own Florentine dialect of which he is critical. In short, as a vernacular poet he tries to purify the dialect of his people.

Ellison too sees his task as a writer in precisely these terms. The challenge is to seek out and perfect the best, most appropriate, suitable form of expression in which to write. As he puts it: "It is he [the Negro] who insists that we purify the American language by demanding that there be a closer correlation between the meaning of words and reality, between ideal and conduct, between our assertions and our actions" (*Collected Essays* 587). We saw above that the formation of the American language is political for Ellison, and here we note that the purification of that language once formed is equally a political act. It may be that the act of purification is precisely the formation itself of the language. The Negro, the Negro American, the black American—he uses all three labels just before he writes the sentence cited above in this paragraph—has the awesome responsibility of putting "pressure upon the nation to live up to its ideals" (*Collected Essays* 587). This act of speaking truth to power or of telling it like it is (to put it in the vernacular) is how the people's language gets purified. Purifying the dialect for Ellison means not only bringing together British and African linguistic roots in a cohesive American vernacular cultural fusion; it means doing so in a way that eliminates injustice, that struggles for democracy, that strives for a more perfect union. The political act of forming the new American hybrid language is the ultimate act of purification for Ellison.[56]

The linguistic product of this purification is based on "an integrative, vernacular note" (*Collected Essays* 511). In the "integrative vernacular," Ellison goes on to say, styles clash and out of that cultural confusion there often arises comedy, whether intentional or not. The crucial point for Ellison is that the vernacular thus understood is essentially American and democratic, deriving from "an American compulsion to improvise upon the given" (511). Improvising upon the given, playing off the standard, compromising the classic—these are all ways to describe the process of creating something new by blending, melding, fusing vernacular and classical into a new hybrid cultural product. Actually, Ellison thinks of the vernacular itself as the process by which this new hybrid is created: "I see the vernacular as a dynamic *process* in which the most refined styles from the past are continually merged with the play-it-by-eye-and-by-ear improvisation which we invent in our efforts to control our environment and entertain ourselves" (my emphasis, *Collected Essays* 612). In fragmentary notes that underlie the essay from which this quote is taken, "Going to the Territory," Ellison elaborates on forms of linguistic improvisation:

> Language was our most easily available toy so we played with it endlessly. Not only in the form of pig latin and bubalub [*sic*], but in ways which we improvised ourselves. There were recess periods during which a group of us mystified our schoolmates by pretending to communicate with Italian phrases which we'd learned in studying the dynamics of musical interpretation, and like many Americans we delighted in nonsense and double-talk. . . . Americans are not as versatile with foreign languages as Europeans, but our flexibility in dealing with the variety of American English idioms [is great]. In the counterpoint between Standard English and the vernacular we give expression to what Henry James refered [*sic*] to as the American joke.[57]

The creation of the vernacular is a process that overcomes the differences, whether of class, race, religion, or other categories, within American society. Language brings unity to diversity, and it does so in the United States with a sense of humor. Here it is helpful to recall that Dante designates his poem a comedy in part to recognize its hybrid generic status. The genre of comedy "introduces a situation of adversity, but ends its matter in prosperity . . ." (*Epistle* 10, para. 10),[58] and in this move from high to low, the diction of comedy ranges from tragic high style to comic low style in creating a hybrid poetic mixture. For Dante the essence of comedy is the mixed nature of its linguistic fabric. Ellison would agree.

Another early note found among Ellison's papers in the archives deserves comment as an additional example of cultural fusion.[59] The 8½ × 11 inch sheet contains three faces in profile, moving from left to right the first clearly an African American man, the second a younger Caucasian male whose hairstyle and ear mimic the curve of both a bass and treble clef, the third a curious mix of the previous two with stylized hair, flamboyantly bearded cheeks, and Negroid lips. The hair and especially the sideburns recall portraits of Pushkin in whom Ellison may have been interested for the story of his mixed race. Pushkin's great-grandfather was from Africa, either Ethiopia or Cameroon.[60] Above the head of the African American in profile is a bar of an unidentified piece of music, ten or so notes, perhaps a riff of jazz. Among all the faces is a cluster of multiple versions of the letter *S* capitalized, written with a fountain pen, as if Ellison were testing the nib with one version of the letter nearly on top of the next. To the lower right he has actually drawn an ink pen's nib suggesting that it is the source from which all the images on the page emerge. In the upper left corner of the page there is a single word, the only one on the entire sheet, isolated somewhat, but if one reads from left to right it is the first thing one notices, in fact it appears to have been written twice it is so bold: *Aristotle*.

I submit this not only as another example of the stuff bubbling up from within Ellison's creative well, his mind's reservoir and workshop, but also as a visual image of the kind of vernacular mixture he refers to repeatedly in his prose as the essence of American culture. Two modern men, one black, one white, are in the presence of Aristotle, a representative of classical Greek culture, alongside what may be a riff of jazz, the vernacular American culture par excellence. Ellison refers to the founder of Invisible Man's college as "this black Aristotle" (118), perhaps indicating a train of thought similar to the one represented here in images. And it may be that Pushkin looks on in approval of the vernacular mixture coming out of the writer's pen. A strange brew perhaps, but to borrow Ellison's words from near the end of "The Little Man at Chehaw Station," "Seen in the clear, pluralistic, melting-pot light of American cultural possibility, there was no contradiction" (*Collected Essays* 523).

I need now to return to the very first item I mentioned at the beginning of this excursion into the archives of Ellison's papers. There is an additional sentence on the 3 × 5 inch sheet where I began, which I would be remiss not to point out. Beneath the passage that forms the underlying images of music and muses—"Impressionistic opening section when he is within depths of music and hears water in mains, this water must itself seem to talk to him. These are the Muses making prophsey"—which the author will understand eventually in the context of Dante, Ellison jots down another incomplete sentence in pencil: "penetrates hymen with a fountain pen." The fragment refers to someone's loss of virginity. But whose? I take Ellison's reflection on the pen as penis as an attempt to articulate how the act of writing leads him out of a protected youthful world associated with a simplistic notion of language and literature into a new literary world of more complex symbolism expressed in an innovative language that is striving to become more pure. This literary and linguistic mix is created by the fusion of American and European models with Dante at the gates to the European literary world. To be sure, there are many other figures in that world that interest Ellison—Kafka, Dostoyevsky, Eliot stand out, perhaps Pushkin is there too—but Dante, at least here in the prologue, takes pride of place. The allusion to Dante announces that the author is no longer a virginal ingenue trying to write the great American novel in a vacuum. It marks Ellison's realization that to write about "the beautiful absurdity of their American identity and mine" (*Invisible Man* 550), paradoxically he must embrace European canonical writing too. Dante leads the way into those depths.

ELLISON'S NARRATIVE, set in the 1930s but narrated from the perspective of the author's contemporary moment, represents Negro life as it was and predicts how it is about to change in 1952 and beyond. The underground existence of Invisible Man is prophetic of various modes of action and reaction embraced by blacks in the following decades of revolution.

A Negro of the 1930s, by the end of the novel Ellison's protagonist has metamorphosed into a new kind of character but is not quite ready to emerge from his underground world. Ellison didn't have the exact term to define his character just yet, thus one of the reasons for the image of invisibility repeated throughout the book. Invisible Man, who was in search of American democratic values and identity, was in the process of becoming black. However, between segregation and integration would first come revolution. And Dante was there.

CHAPTER 3
BLACK DANTE

It is simply, again, that someone is trying to tell you write is white.

—LeRoi Jones/Amiri Baraka,

"Black Writing," *Home: Social Essays* (1966)

In this chapter on Black Dante I focus on the period from the late 1950s to the mid-1970s. During the Black Revolution, Dante retains his potential as a powerful model of activism and emancipation, as seen in the early work of LeRoi Jones, who uses the medieval poet to express a new kind of militant black identity. With reference to the autobiography of Frederick Douglass, Barbara Johnson restates the suggestion by Lévi-Strauss that the act of writing enslaves, claiming that it is actually the control of access to writing that enslaves a man like Douglass (48). In contrast to these positions, however, the function of writing about Dante and the control over access to the part of the tradition that Dante inhabits can liberate the black writer. At least it liberates LeRoi Jones, turning him into a new man with a new name, Amiri Baraka, whose experimental literary project culminates in *The System of Dante's Hell* in 1965. Dante's poem (specifically in the Sinclair translation) provides a grid for the narrative of Baraka's autobiographical novel, and at the same time the Italian poet's description of hell functions for Baraka like a gloss on many of his own experiences. Whereas for Ralph Ellison and Richard Wright, Dante marks a way into the world of European culture, Baraka uses Dante first to measure the growing distance between himself and European literature, then, paradoxically, to separate himself totally from it. His Dante is a marker of separation rather than integration.

The Dante encountered in this chapter is highly politicized but not like that of Cordelia Ray and the abolitionists who based their understanding of the poet on contested interpretations of Protestants and Catholics, as we explored in chapter 1. Baraka is oblivious to that earlier history of reading—so much so that one could say he thoroughly dehistoricizes Dante from previous African American ways of appropriating the Italian writer; moreover, in contrast to Ellison one might even say that he de-Europeanizes Dante. Baraka's radical response to the poet at once confirms and belies Edward Said's claim that Dante's *Divine Comedy* is essentially an imperial text that is foundational to the imperial discipline of comparative literature: that Baraka can found his struggle against imperialist culture, as he sees it, on none other than this specific poem suggests the extent to which it is a richer and more complex text than even Said imagined. To see exactly how Baraka does this, we must read through *The System of Dante's Hell* to take stock of the fullness of its allusiveness to the Italian model. For all the critical attention to Baraka, surprisingly no one has undertaken the necessary work of sorting out his allusions to Dante in any systematic way. In the first section of this chapter we need to see exactly what he has done in relation to his principal source before proceeding in the second to examine his use of sources in general. This will enable us, then, in the third section to examine how Baraka's radical adaptation of Dante affects his thinking in unexpected ways. It becomes difficult, if not impossible, for Baraka to leave Dante behind, much as he might try.

LeRoi Jones, *The System of Dante's Hell*

Under the name of LeRoi Jones, Amiri Baraka published an autobiographical novel in 1965, *The System of Dante's Hell,* which together with other early works earned him the unofficial title "poet laureate of . . . the Black Revolution" (Schneck 19).[1] In what many readers would consider a tone of ironic understatement, an early reviewer of the novel noted, "Mr. Jones rejects the formal logic of exposition; he invites verbal and emotional accidents, willingly or willfully connecting ideas and impressions that have no common focus outside his own mind" (Capouya 4). The fragmentary syntax and the episodic narrative are only half the challenge for the reader. The novel—Baraka's first and principal example of lengthy prose fiction—takes a hard look at the author's world between the late 1930s and the early 1960s, recasting it from the autobiographical perspective of the narrator, Roi, and juxtaposing it with Dante's hell. It is an unexpected and odd comparison, as our reviewer suggests: "To Dante's fierce certainties the 20th century opposes its despair of any certainty. . . . The static and fragmentary lyricism of much of the novel, then, is an expression of the intellectual and moral lost motion of the age" (4).

Baraka's early reviewer claims that the fragmentary form of *The System of Dante's Hell* renders the author's vision difficult to understand. It may be that this incomprehensibility prompts Baraka to turn to Dante for a system to lend his autobiographical story some semblance of a rational structure. In fact, Dante provides a grid for his narrative and more, for at the same time in the Italian poet's elaborate and memorable description of hell, Baraka finds a gloss on many of his own experiences. He borrows a narrative structural device from Dante's *Inferno* that brings with it content, including nothing less than an implied ethical system. Moreover, through the imitated narrative he also comes to perceive more clearly another system, one that is not merely literary and ethical but also decidedly political. Dante's hell enables Baraka to understand better the system underlying his own experience of hell on earth, or, as we shall hear him say later in his own words, the system of "America . . . a hell run by devils."

Baraka first read Dante at Howard University in the early 1950s with Nathan Scott, a professor of English and religious studies, an experience that transformed him: "Nathan Scott's preaching about Dante conveyed an *intellectual* love for literature that I hadn't seen. . . . And it was due directly to this that I later went back to Dante to read what I was able" (*Autobiography* 75). We saw in chapter 1 that literary historians document how the reception of Dante waxed as religious faith waned in the United States at the end of the nineteenth century, and that for many, including a former student of Charles Eliot Norton, the great Dantista from Harvard, "reading Dante . . . 'was almost an act of worship.' "[2] Amiri Baraka's initial encounter with Dante through the lectures of the charismatic Scott in a sense continues this New England tradition, transplanted to Howard in the twentieth century. In an interview in 1981, Baraka explained that Scott's course was a yearlong survey of Western literature. He continued: "We got all the biggies, everybody we were supposed to get in that one-year survey course; and when he came to Dante, he [Nathan Scott] was so in love with it. And now I understand why. Because he was religious. I didn't know that. He was a Reverend . . . something like that. He was a Doctor of Divinity, as well as a PhD" (*Conversations* 214–15).[3] Scott represents the rarified world of Dante Studies, rooted in the abolitionist and Protestant culture of the Bostonian gentry. The figured world in Dante's poem and the world of privilege that first fostered its study in the United States must have seemed equally strange to Baraka. The ivory tower, too, was an uncomfortable fit that came with limitations. Indeed, Baraka, as a sign of his rejection of that upward social mobility, would soon turn away from the world Scott represented by flunking out of Howard in 1954, only to return to Dante's poem several years later to read it on his own. He would use that rereading of Dante to position his critique of the social mobility of blacks in the United States. And he would also eventually develop a critical attitude toward the use of authors like Dante himself.

After his time at Howard (1952–54), Baraka joined the U.S. Air Force, serving until 1957, an experience to which he alludes in certain sections of *The System of Dante's Hell.* In 1991 William J. Harris divided Baraka's literary career into four basic periods, which begin with his dishonorable discharge from the service: the Beat period (1957–62); the Transitional period (1963–65); the Black Nationalist period (1966–74); the Third World Marxist period (1974–91).[4] Baraka wrote portions of *The System of Dante's Hell* in the first period as he came into his own among the Beat writers in New York and during the transitional years leading up to the book's publication in 1965. Like Cordelia Ray, perceived as an "invisible poet," Baraka has been called a "skipped Beat," an overlooked writer "most readers have never heard of, in many cases because those other Beats were people of color or women" (Johnson and Damon 4). Although eclipsed by the fame of Ginsberg, O'Hara, and Olson, and others whom he emulated, Baraka held his own among the Beat writers and was enough a part of the group during his tumultuous years in Manhattan that he felt it necessary later to declare his independence from them, literally and literarily. He struggled to find his identity as an ethnic outsider among white bohemians who saw themselves as social outsiders (Watts 87–88). It was a delicate balance to maintain, and the tension deriving from the ongoing social negotiations may account for the affected tone in *The System of Dante's Hell.* He did make a name for himself both as a poet and publisher working to establish alternative publishing venues for other poets. He co-edited the journal *Yugen* with his first wife, Hettie Cohen, and he set up the mimeographed semimonthly newsletter of poetry and prose, *The Floating Bear,* co-edited with Diane di Prima, among other projects.[5]

While it is impossible to determine how much Baraka's encounter with the Beats directly influenced his interest in Dante, it is likely that they encouraged and stimulated his curiosity in the Italian author to some extent. Some of them knew the medieval poet fairly well. Di Prima recounts in her memoir, *Recollections of My Life as a Woman,* that her Italian grandfather read her Dante when she was a child (7). Ferlinghetti's long poem, *Coney Island of the Mind,* is full of references to Dante. Ginsberg compared the enigmatic and brooding William Burroughs, the sage of the Beats, to a bust of Dante.[6] This is not the place to register and interpret the many references to Dante in Beat writings; suffice it to say that as Baraka began to imagine and then write his autobiographical novel, he was surrounded by other writers who were equally interested in Dante.

The System of Dante's Hell grew organically out of several experimental pieces published over the first decade of Baraka's writing career. The 1959 issue of *The Trembling Lamb,* a literary magazine printed by Harry Gantt and distributed by the Phoenix Book Shop in New York City, contained the first appearance in print of a portion, initially called *The System of Dante's Inferno,* the last word of the title changed in the 1965 printing to *Hell.*[7] It is approximately the first third of the narrative as it eventually would be published, and it remains virtually unchanged in the subsequent versions. Two experimental short works, "Hypocrites," and "Thieves," which fit into the larger narrative where the piece in *The Trembling Lamb* leaves off, came out in an anthology Baraka edited in 1963, *The Moderns.* A third section, "THE EIGHTH DITCH (IS DRAMA," was first published in *The Floating Bear* 9 in 1961. The publication of this excerpt led to the arrest of Baraka and Diane di Prima on obscenity charges in October 1961. Baraka then prepublished three other sections that he incorporated into the final narrative, "The Christians," "The Rape," and "The Heretics," in two collections that came out in 1963 and 1964, before he assembled all the pieces into the final version with an epilogue, "Sound and Image," which came out with Grove Press in 1965.[8] Only one short section, "Personators (alchemists) Falsifiers," hadn't been published in some form earlier. The year 1965, like 1865 one hundred years before, was an important moment for Dante Studies in general, inspired by the seven-hundredth-year celebration of the Italian poet's birth. Although I can find no direct evidence that Grove Press timed the publication to come out then, the massive quantity of publications on Dante—not to mention the 5-cent U.S. postage stamp in celebration of the Italian poet—makes it highly unlikely that the press and Baraka himself would not have been aware of the celebrations and scholarly work taking place in Italy, around Europe, and in the United States. Anthony L. Pellegrini comments in his bibliography of work on Dante for that year, "As expected, the centennial year of 1965 greatly surpassed in number of Dante publications not only the recent annual norm, but also the previous centennial year of 1921. While this reflects a noteworthy growth of interest in Dante in America, on the qualitative side it is even more gratifying to note that scholars and critics have achieved new depths of understanding and appreciation of Dante's work" (73). And amidst all the scholarly work, Pellegrini's bibliography includes an entry for Baraka's novel, which reads: "Autobiographical novel about the author's early years, lyrically narrated in a series of spiritual states represented under the sign of various Dantean categories, such as incontinence, violence, fraud, etc."

The System of Dante's Hell was published the same year Baraka divorced his white wife, Hettie Cohen, and left the beatnik scene of Greenwich Village, getting "out of this downtown white hell" (*Autobiography* 198), moving to Harlem to run the Black Arts Repertory Theatre/School.[9] In-your-face political theater became his medium of choice as he settled into Harlem. Baraka left after a brief sojourn in 1965 and returned to his home in Newark, New Jersey, which would soon be convulsed in the riots of 1967 and 1968. Shortly thereafter he became a proponent of Kawaida spirituality and assumed the name Imamu (or Spiritual Leader) Ameer Baraka. Kawaida spiritual practice, based on the "moral discipline of orthodox Islam and African concepts" such as Umoja or unity, became a moral code governing the lives of Baraka and some of his fellow Black Nationalists.[10] At some point later he altered his name again, dropping "Imamu" and changing the Islamic-sounding "Ameer" to a more pan-African and secular "Amiri."

What did Baraka as a reader find in Dante that he could transform into something of his own? The title of his novel, *The System of Dante's Hell*, suggests that what he took from the Dantesque model first was a *system* or a *structure* or a *form*, as we will hear him say below. Baraka borrowed the title of his novel from the heading to a schematic table in John Sinclair's popular translation of the *Inferno* (19, 1961 ed.).[11] He reproduces the table with one significant alteration, moving the heretics from the sixth circle down to the bottom of his hell. He adds an explanatory note on where and why he repositions the heretics, and he places the entire table prominently at the start of his own narrative in the 1965 edition (*Hell* 6–7).[12] The narrative is made up of twenty episodes that focus on the main character's youth and young adulthood, with titles inspired by the *Inferno* such as "Gluttony," "Wrathful," "Seducers," "The Diviners," and "Thieves"; and they follow more or less their order in hell according to the medieval tradition codified and restructured by Dante. There is no question that Baraka alludes to a systematic infernal topography with its moral overtones as the organizing principle for his novel. But why?

Baraka is hardly the first (or last) artist to find in Dante's hell a gloss on a version of hell on earth. In 1961 he reviewed Federico Fellini's film *La Dolce Vita* as he was giving shape to his novel, and he saw a parallel between the film and Dante's vision, and by extension, I think, his own writing: "*La Dolce Vita* is Fellini saying, 'I am going to talk about all of our lives; everyone of us. I am going to get it all in. Everyone will be dealt with . . .' And, in this idea, Fellini's attempt is much in intent like the *Commedia*. He shows you each circle of our 20th century Western hell" ("La Dolce Vita" 85). Baraka makes two points in this comparison. There is, on the one hand, the sense of fullness in the respective worlds presented by Dante and Fellini, with each artist's comprehensive treatment of sinners and sin. There is in each work an epic panorama of sinners from all walks of life. Baraka doesn't note that *La Dolce Vita* includes scenes of black U.S. sailors dancing with Italian women, as well as shots of black singers and musicians, although these details must have caught his attention. Fellini's depiction of sinfulness was integrated. On the other hand, there is the encounter with the underside of life at its worst in each work. Baraka appreciates Fellini's use of Dante to critique the materialist culture of Italy as it grew during the years of a booming economy in the late 1950s and early 1960s. It is precisely this aspect of Fellini's critical adaptation that he will apply to his own rewriting of Dante. That is, Baraka will similarly use Dante to critique aspects of his own society that appear infernal to him. He seems incapable of doing so with a sense of humor, and in this he differs from Fellini, who pulls off his critique with a tone of serious comedy much as Dante himself does in key passages of the *Divine Comedy.*

Baraka is writing about the hell of growing up black in the segregated America of the 1930s and 1940s and the frustrations of coping with that racist system in the 1950s and early 1960s. He focuses progressively on what it means to develop as a writer in that sort of world, and he seems troubled especially by what he takes to be a paradoxical question: how one cultivates an authoritative voice as a black man if one's sources come predominately from white authors. Just before *System* is published but after most of the novel had already been written, Baraka writes an extensive review article, "A Dark Bag," on several books by African poets or African American poets in the March 1964 issue of *Poetry.* The article is highly critical of the writing by Americans of color that Baraka perceived to be in vogue at that time, including much of the material anthologized in *American Negro Poetry,* edited by Arna Bontemps. He is critical of many black African writers in English, but he singles out several francophone authors for praise. He directs his complaints specifically against writers of color who aspired to rise to the middle class and who "thought of literature as a way of proving they were not 'inferior'" (395). An example of the kind of writing to avoid is Ellison's: "Ralph Ellison's extra-literary commercial is usually about European Literature, the fact that he has done some reading in it" (395). Ellison's advertised allegiance to Europe is precisely the problem. The reference to his work as a "commercial," extraliterary no less, is a clever way of implying that he has sold out, but it may also be an envious commentary on Baraka's assumption of Ellison's financial success.[13] In contrast, the best writing of color should not imitate the literary models of white writers regardless of the potential for profit. The black artist should consider his own race a legitimate and necessary subject and find appropriate sources accordingly. He goes so far as to imply

that the review in the establishment journal *Poetry* might be his last literary contribution as he shifts his energies to a more direct form of activism for his people (394). In a telling chronological detail, Baraka writes
another piece, "State/meant," the year after the publication of *System* in
1965, in which he goes much further in his demands of the artist whom
he now refers to as black: "The Black Artist's role in America is to aid in the
destruction of America as he knows it" (*Home* 251). The latent militancy
of 1964 has exploded by 1966: LeRoi Jones has become Amiri Baraka,
the Negro bohemian has transformed into the black artist. We need to
examine *The System of Dante's Hell* to see what brought about this radical
transformation.

The following table, which contrasts Sinclair's schematic table with
the order of episodes in Baraka's narrative, shows that Baraka consistently
uses Sinclair to map out the sections of his novel.

Beyond this Dantesque grid just how much does Dante's poem really
influence the composition of Baraka's novel? Most readers have concluded
not much. Here's the beginning of the narrative: "But Dante's hell is heaven.
Look at things in another light. Not always the smarting blue glare press-
ing through the glass. Another light, or darkness. Wherever we'd go to rest.
By the simple rivers of our time. Dark cold water slapping long wooden
logs jammed 10 yards down in the weird slime, 6 or 12 of them hold up a
pier. Water, wherever we'd rest." Baraka begins his novel with an adversa-
tive conjunction thus setting the tone of his version of Dante, which will
be in contrast to the medieval model, played off against it, rather than a
continuation of it. Perhaps he is inspired to use this mode of opening from
his reading of Ezra Pound. According to Diane di Prima, Baraka wanted
to be known as the black Pound, a claim we'll consider below when we
look in more detail at the narrative models that inform Baraka's work.[14]
Pound opens his epic *Cantos* with a conjunction: "And then went down to
the ship." Perhaps Pound's initial "and" alludes to the first word of Homer's
Odyssey in the original Greek, "man": "Andra moi ennepe, Mousa" (About
the man, Muse, sing into me).[15] The suggestion in Pound's case (the same
is true of James Joyce's *Ulysses*) is that his work is meant to be read as
a continuation of Homer's. Baraka, for his part, opens with a double sally
against the Dantesque model and against an important American epic
intermediary for him of that model. The gist of the opening line is that

Sequence of episodes in Baraka's *The System of Dante's Hell*:	Sequence in Sinclair's schematic map of The System of Dante's Hell
Neutrals: The Vestibule	Neutrals
Heathen: No. 1	Circle 1. Virtuous Heathen
Heathen: No. 2	
THE INCONTINENT: Lasciviousness	Circle 2. Lascivious
Gluttony	Circle 3. Gluttons
INCONTINENT: The Prodigal	Circle 4. Avaricious and Prodigal
Wrathful	Circle 5. Wrathful
	Circle 6. Heretics
Seven (The Destruction of America	Circle 7. Violent
Seducers	Circle 8. (1) Panders and Seducers
The Flatterers	(2) Flatterers
Simonists	(3) Simonists
The Diviners	(4) Diviners
Circle 8 (Ditch 5) Grafters (Barrators)	(5) Barrators
Hypocrite(s)	(6) Hypocrites
Thieves	(7) Thieves
The Eighth Ditch (Is Drama	(8) Fraudulent counsellors
The Ninth Ditch: Makers of Discord	(9) Makers of discord
Personators (alchemists) Falsifiers	(10) Falsifiers
Circle 9: Bolgia 1—Treachery To Kindred	Circle 9. (1) to kindred
	(2) to country and cause
6. The Heretics	(3) to guests
	(4) to lords and benefactors
Sound and Image	

Baraka's story will be different from other versions of Dante, including Pound's, and that Baraka's version will be a tale far worse than the original in comparison to which it will seem like heaven, so much will he outdo his model.

The second line of Baraka's proemium enjoins the reader to be prepared for the unexpected, to see things differently, to see things in a new light. The narrator continues: "Another light, or darkness." The challenge to the reader, then, is to see things in the dark and to see things that are dark, literally and figuratively, a challenge that eventually becomes one of the novel's themes. If *Invisible Man* turns not being seen at all into a theme, *System* focuses on how to perceive things in darkness, on how to perceive and appreciate even the darkness itself. Indeed, darkness and color become apt metaphors in Baraka's writing for the social gradations of the classes on a scale that runs from white to black, with yellow, brown, and other shades in between. Rewriting Dante's *Inferno* is a process that enables Baraka to reflect on the social setting of his youth in Newark and adulthood beyond that and to see those various colors in a new light.

The first section of the novel, "Neutrals: The Vestibule," emphasizes community, with the communal perspective encapsulated in the first person plural pronouns, "we" and "our," recalling the insistence on community at the beginning of Dante's poem: "In the middle of *our* life's journey" (*Inf.* 1.1). The narrative begins with a reference to a river, Baraka's version of Acheron, where he would go as a boy and alongside which others presumably would gather, as the sinners do in Dante's *Inferno* 3, before they are ferried over into hell proper. For Baraka, however, the river is a place of rest and refuge.

At *Inferno* 2, Dante invokes the muses and through them his memory in order to recollect what he had experienced as pilgrim on his journey through hell. Baraka, too, calls his memory to action. First, he refers to the recollecting powers of his mind in the third person: "The mind fastens past landscapes" (10). Then he issues a command to his memory as it begins to produce a multitude of images from his past: "Each face will come to me now" (12), and later "I remember each face . . ." (21). Dante reassures the reader over and over again that he is recreating the experience of the past exactly as it happened. The truthfulness of memory is not an issue for Baraka's narrator, who is more interested in presenting a poeticized view of the sites he remembers from his past, in phrases like "Fire escapes of imagination" (10). This sort of poetic image, in turn, can prompt a memory such as the night when the young Roi sneaked out his window to the rooftop: "Then shinnied down to the ground. I hid out all night with some italians" (12). On this transitional note the first chapter of the novel ends as the protagonist moves surreptitiously out of his house and into the world of white culture, represented by the Italian Americans of Newark. Dante clearly belongs to that Italian American world, even more so, one might think, than he does to Baraka and the Negro world from which he and his protagonist are emerging. When Baraka states, "Neutrals: The breakup of my sensibility" (9), he suggests that the application of the Dantesque category to his situation challenges his own understanding of himself and his surroundings. Moving out of his world and into another by way of Dante and Italian culture paradoxically marks the beginning of the transition from LeRoi Jones to Amiri Baraka.

As the narrative progresses Baraka amplifies Dante's category of "virtuous heathen" into two parts, "Heathen: No. 1" and "Heathen: No. 2." Dante's introduction of a separate place on the edge of hell where pagans are not punished was strikingly original. In *Inferno* 4 the poet elaborated upon the traditional Christian notion of limbo where the Hebrew patriarchs were placed until Christ's harrowing of hell liberated them and lifted them into the Christian heaven. Limbo was also thought to be the final resting place for the souls of babies who died before they could be brought fully into the body of Christ through the sacrament of baptism. To these two groups Dante added many of the historical and legendary heroes of Greece and Rome, including warriors and philosophers, as well as three prominent Muslims of the Middle Ages. Baraka is oblivious to all these subtleties. For him, heathen suggests the impulse to explore one's sexuality. In the two sections of "Heathen," he alludes repeatedly to sexual encounters, primarily homosexual ones. The partners in these various trysts are the beasts who impede Roi's progress as a pilgrim. "Another beast in another wood," comments the narrator as he tallies an additional conquest (20). Oddly, Baraka does not include a section later in his version of the seventh circle that corresponds to Dante's place deeper in hell for homosexuals, where they are punished for being violent against nature and are described in some detail in *Inferno* 15–16. Dante's episode is memorable, among other reasons, for its depiction of the pilgrim's unexpected encounter with his teacher, Brunetto Latini among the sodomites—the passage to which T. S. Eliot alludes in some detail in *The Waste Land* and which Ellison reverentially types up. One wonders whether Baraka really read this scene in the *Inferno*. Or does the absence of a direct imitation of Dante's section on homosexuality reflect ambivalence within Baraka about addressing the subject in its proper Dantesque category as a form of unnatural violence?

Uncontrolled sexual desire makes one out to be a heathen in Baraka's rewriting of Dante, and Roi's homosexuality in particular induces extreme self-loathing at times: "You've done everything you said you wdn't. Everything you said you despised" (13). This self-loathing then modulates into the recreation of a Dantesque narrative device, the direct address to the reader. "I am myself. Insert the word disgust. A verb. Get rid of the 'am.' Break out. Kill it. Rip the thing to shreds. This thing, if you read it, will jam your face in my shit. Now say something intelligent!" (15) The narrator often vents his spleen in this kind of confrontational rhetoric, but here the passage is noteworthy for the way it shifts from Roi's disgust with himself to aggressive anger with the reader. *The System of Dante's Hell* is a *Bildungsroman,* a "novel of education" that shows the development of its protagonist, but it may be that the most marked development takes place in the reader, especially for the reader unfamiliar with the sort of infernal world Baraka describes in his novel.

The narrative moves into a section that is an imitation of Dante's treatment of circles 2 through 5 in which incontinent sins are punished: lust, gluttony, greed and prodigality, anger and sullenness. In the section on the lascivious, Roi's uncontrolled exploration of his sexuality continues. No mention of Francesca, Cleopatra, Achilles, or others who might have caught Baraka's attention from even a perfunctory reading of *Inferno* 5. We begin to realize that his rewriting is a very free imitation. And yet he makes an effort to keep the reader focused on possible Dantesque echoes, as when the narrator observes, "Passd the neutrals into the first circle" and "But to the next level" (23). Such asides are characteristic of Dante's original, enabling the reader to follow along as the pilgrim descends. For example, canto 5 in Sinclair's translation opens: "Thus I descended from the first circle down into the second" (5.1–2). Another passage in this short section calls attention to itself for its allusion to Dante's text. The fear of desire out of control prompts this comment: "Anger is nothing. To me fear is much more. As if trees bled" (25). Trees bleed dramatically in *Inferno* 13, where Dante describes the punishment in the wood of the suicides. The allusion suggests that the fear of desire and its momentary satisfaction in homosexuality has caused the narrator to entertain thoughts of suicide.

We progress deeper into Baraka's hell, past gluttony and among the prodigal. He omits the avaricious, although he includes them in his version of Sinclair's map. This section contains several pointed references to literary sources, an indication that the project of rewriting Dante's *Inferno* forces the author to rethink a series of relationships with other literary predecessors and contemporaries. Rewriting Dante casts Baraka inevitably into an epic mode, a position in which he is not always comfortable. "Incontinent: The Prodigal" opens with a recollection of Baraka's early adolescence: "On a porch that summer, in night, in my body's skin, drunk, sitting stiff-legged in a rocking chair. Vita Nuova" (29). The young teenager is about to come of age, hence his reference to the youthful work of Dante, *Vita Nuova,* or *New Life.* Dante's *New Life* describes his passion for Beatrice and ends with a pledge that he will say about her in a subsequent work that which has never been said about any other woman. The literary project to imitate Dante the poet has shaded over into an imitation of the man's life too. Other possible models are available for Roi to follow, the Beats in particular. But even his first reference to them is riddled with ambiguity: "Olson broke, Allen losing his hair. The faces seep together" (31). Charles Olson and Allen Ginsberg aren't allowed the authority of models worthy of extended imitation in this passage. Contrast that with the reference to the older generation of modernist poets: "Eliot, Pound, Cummings, Apollinaire were living across from Kresges. I was erudite and talked to light-skinned women" (31). Baraka associates the high modernist tradition with an intellectual power that enables him to attract previously unattainable women, a power that he will reject later on. Lust is now being conflated with literary affiliations.

When Dante the pilgrim passes among the wrathful sinners, he assumes the essential characteristic of their sin, becoming angry at a soul he recognizes from the world above. Baraka is not such a careful reader of

Dante to recreate this sort of detail. But the short chapter on "Wrathful" does begin with a butcher telling off the young Roi for some unstated mischievous deed: "Fuck you, he repeated in his chin." The wash of memory then becomes mellow, hardly angry at all, and the chapter ends on a very different and unexpected note: "Forgive me."

The order of Dante's *Inferno* moves from circles 2 through 5, from various sins of incontinence, to circle 6, the peculiar Christian sin of heresy, and on to circle 7 of the violent. Baraka, however, moves from his section on wrathful sinners, the last sin of incontinence, to the violent, skipping the heretics. Baraka locates heresy at the end of his narrative, at the bottom of hell, aware that this contradicts Dante's order, which places them in the sixth of nine circles. He explains the move in a note appended to the entry for the heretics on the schematic map at the beginning of the novel: "I put The Heretics in the deepest part of hell, though Dante had them spared on higher ground. [New paragraph] It is heresy, against one's own sources, running in terror, from one's deepest responses and insights . . . the denial of feeling . . . that I see as basest evil" (7). We will consider Baraka's reasons for rearranging Dante's structural design in more detail below when we come to the final section of his narrative, "The Heretics." In an odd way Baraka's rearrangement reflects tensions in Dante's original narrative regarding the structural design of the whole and the position of the heretics in relation to it. For Dante's classification of heresy also calls attention to itself. John Freccero (cited in Singleton's commentary) observes, "Here is the only instance in Dante's moral system where an error of the speculative intellect is punished in hell, a fact which no pagan, neither Cicero, nor Aristotle, nor Virgil would have been able to understand" (*Inferno: Commentary* 143). In a curious (and most likely unintended) way, Baraka's reclassification of the heretics reflects Dante's own reconsideration of this specific category in the classical ethical scheme that underlies his Christian plan.

Baraka's rewriting of the entire seventh circle of the violent (*Inf.* 12–17) is a mere page and a half. Entitled "SEVEN (The Destruction of America," the author's characteristic open parenthesis leads to a poetic meditation on the fate of native Americans at the hands of "White man." Dante has little to say about imperial colonizing violence, although he does include among the violent against others Alexander the Great and Dionysus of

Sicily, two ancient imperialist conquerors (*Inf.* 12.105–8). A closer reading would have revealed them to Baraka. This section of *The System of
Dante's Hell* ends with a direct allusion to Dante's plan of hell as articulated in *Inferno* 11, at a moment in the narrative between circles 6 and 7
when Vergil and his charge pause for the pilgrim to acclimate to the sights,
smells, and sounds of deeper hell. At the pilgrim's request they pass the
time wisely with a brief lesson on infernal topography and structure.
Vergil explains to Dante that the seventh circle is divided into three rings,
the third divided further into a tripartite structure. The rings correspond to
the violent against others, self, and God, nature, and art (*Inf.* 11.16–66),
that is, murderers, suicides, blasphemers, sodomites, and usurers. But
Baraka doesn't examine the theology and ethical philosophy that account
for these divisions. Rather, he has lifted from Sinclair's edition the following general description, which I reproduce respecting Baraka's line-breaks
and typographical arrangement (36):

Violence
        against others,
                    against one's self,
                                against
God, Nature and Art.

Baraka is not interested in matching moments from his experience with
the precise section in Dante's *Inferno* where the Italian poet deals with the
given illicit activity. He is not concerned with reconciling sections like
"The Flatterers" in which he mentions a grisly murder (41) with the appropriate section in his chapter on the violent, "Seven." But then Dante,
too, as noted earlier in regard to Dido, often must make artistic decisions
about where to locate a given sinner who has committed at least two different sins.

    In his version of the eighth circle, Baraka imitates Dante's structural
design more fully. Dante divided the circle of the sinners guilty of simple
fraud into ten subcategories. Deeper down one encounters the ninth circle
of treacherous fraud, which Dante divided into four sections. Beyond and
below is Satan himself. Baraka respects the original plan of an eighth circle

made up of ten sections for a narrative sequence that constitutes over a third of the novel. Sinclair translates Dante's term for the subsections of the eighth circle, *bolgia,* as *ditch* (the more accurate translation is *pouch*), which Baraka borrows to describe the eighth and ninth sections of his sequence. Baraka reduces the four subsections of Dante's ninth circle to one. Then he appends his long story of the heretics in its iconoclastic reordered position. Finally, he adds a short epilogue to the entire work called "Sound and Image."

The prose in the various sections dedicated to Baraka's eighth circle is full of memories of his adolescence. The narrator often mentions people by name, recalling things that they did in their youth, good and bad. As in Baraka's rewriting of Dante's seventh circle, here there is no consistency in his attempt to match a given action or sin to a certain part of the circle. No seduction among the "Seducers," oddly enough. No flattery among "The Flatterers." No church corruption in "Simonists." But in several sections deeper in the eighth circle, Baraka does find more exact correspondences, especially in "The Ninth Ditch: Makers of Discord," which we shall consider in its proper order.

Although the imitation of Dante's text remains loose, at times Baraka wants to mark his awareness of it. In "Simonists," for example, he opens the section in this way: "Again, back. Dancing, again. The portions of the mountain under light and shade at noonday. Cf. *Purg.* iv. 'When it is 3 P.M. in Italy, it is 6 P.M. at Jerusalem and 6 A.M. in Purgatory'" (47). This looks like an actual quotation from Dante's text or at least from a commentary on *Purgatory,* but it is not. This reference, the only one in the novel to Dante's *Purgatory,* is botched or bogus—one can't be sure which. There is no passage in Dante's poem that reads as Baraka has it; nor does the sequence of time zones in Baraka's quote jibe with the general sense of *Purgatory* 4. In the canto, the pilgrim and Vergil do discuss the spatial and temporal reorientation necessary to make sense of things in the southern hemisphere where they have emerged from hell. But at the beginning of the canto (4.15), the sun has already climbed fifty degrees in the sky making it about 9:20 A.M. (according to Sinclair 64n3). And by the end of the canto, Vergil remarks that it is noon in Purgatory and dusk in Morocco (4.136–39). So Baraka's version is out of sync with time in the Dantesque model. What function might this passage have for Baraka other than to signal a dependency (and an inaccurate one at that) on Dante's poem? There is some humorous appeal in a seemingly erudite allusion to the canonical model, which might catch the unwary critic off guard. Baraka might have chuckled had he read an analysis like this one: "For an explanation of the co-extensiveness of times, Baraka cites the *Purgatorio* directly . . ."[16] Baraka's allusion to Dante's *Purgatory,* at least here in this passage, is a great send-up of the poetry of literary allusion and a tease, if not outright parody, of those critics who delight in it.

Perhaps there are other reasons for the imprecise allusion to *Purgatory.* In Dante's *Inferno,* Vergil occasionally intuits the time with an ability to read the unseen skies and he uses the information to urge the pilgrim onward toward his destination. Baraka may allude to this sort of communication further below: "In hell the sky is black" (54). But in the *Purgatory* the skies are visible, and the narrator or Vergil himself will occasionally refer to the astronomical clock that marks the time of the pilgrim's sojourn in the other world. Baraka's narrative has a static, timeless quality to it that defies a definitive chronology. The passage alluded to from Dante emphasizes, paradoxically, that time doesn't matter in Baraka's novel.

In "Simonists" there is another deliberate reference to Dante's text, specifically *Inferno* 19. Dante found in the canonical story of Simon Magus a magician who tried to put a price on the power of the Holy Spirit and buy it, as related in Acts of the Apostles 8:9–24. In the apocryphal Acts of Peter, which Dante seems to have some vague knowledge of, Simon uses his magic to challenge the religious authority of Peter. Simon flies above the Roman forum to the wonder of the crowd until Peter prays to God that he crash to the ground. God answers Peter's prayer. The punishment that fits the sin in Dante's vision of hell for the simonists, among them several popes, is to be buried head downward with an eternal flame licking the soles of their feet that stick out above the ground. Baraka doesn't elaborate on the fullness of this image, but he refers to someone being thrown out of a window, the culmination of some sort of domestic tragedy: "Simonist, thrown down from second story" (47). On the same page there is an enigmatic reference to Dis, the deeper hell of graver, malicious sins, where we find ourselves at this point in the narrative. And then another reference to Dante's sinners: "Magicians, falling from the heavens" (47).

The section ends by mentioning the third bolgia of the eighth circle and suggesting that there is a question about how to label these sinners: "Simoniacs, Simonists, Bolgia academic brown leaves" (48).

In the next section, "The Diviners," Baraka continues with a reference to *Inferno* 20, to the punishment of the diviners in Dante's canto: "Heads twisted backwards, out to the yards, stalks" (49). On the same page, the narrator remembers another friend of his youth in an allusion that conflates *Inferno* 19 and 20, the cantos of the simonists and the diviners: "John Wieners is Michael Scott, made blind by God. Tears for everything. The fruit of his days in the past. Is past, as from a tower, he fell. Simon, dead also. Under various thumbs, our suns will pass." At *Inferno* 20.116–17, Dante refers to Michael Scot, a scholar who was a member of Frederick II's court in Palermo in the first half of the thirteenth century. Presumably Baraka is reporting that Wieners has suffered a fate analogous to Scot's, something like that of Simon Magus. This is one of those passages where one senses an attempt on the part of Baraka to turn his prose into something like Poundian verse. Pound's poetic line, however, is often distinguished by its metrical play, something often lacking in Baraka's writing. If Pound is the inspiration for this passage, Baraka's text is not up to the model.

Among the diviners, the young Roi wanders in and out of pool halls on the streets of Newark, a member of a gang called the Cavaliers. He refers to the setting as part of a hellish landscape, which one of his friends has been able to flee: "Escape Bolgia in a buick" (53). Different strands of the population attend different churches appropriate to their respective social status. The narrator has his church; "the negroes from the projects" have theirs (53); "The poor went to Jemmy's church" (54). And he concludes: "Jehovah *me fecit*" (54). It is a surprising conclusion to the section on the diviners for the narrator to express the sentiment "God made me" in the sacred language of Latin, and with the Hebrew name of the Creator from the Old Testament no less. But God's creation of Roi has to be reconciled with Roi's destructive behavior toward himself and others. In another allusion to Dante's *Inferno* in "The Diviners," the narrator states: "This is high tragedy. I will be deformed in hell" (52). In the original, Vergil points out one of the diviners to the pilgrim: "Eurypylus was his name, and thus my high tragedy sings of him" (20.113). So here, Baraka likens his novel to Dante's memory of Vergil's epic poem, *The Aeneid,* written in a high tragic style.

Baraka describes his coming of age as a homosexual and his willing in-doctrination into Western culture in the next section, "Circle 8 (Ditch 5) Grafters (Barrators)." The analogous section in Dante's original deals with political corruption in counterpoint to the ecclesiastical corruption of the simonists; it has nothing to do with homosexuality. But Baraka uses the notion of corruption in general as a point of departure to explore his own personal shortcomings as a "faggot," to use a term that recurs throughout the novel and in his nonfiction too. Moreover, Western culture represented in this section by references to Joyce, Proust, Eliot, Yeats, and Rachmani-noff, comes into the narrator's life as a wonderful but potentially corrupt-ing and eventually effeminate influence. Here Baraka attempts to liberate himself from his sexual history. After one encounter with an older man in Chicago who reminds him of his father, he writes in a diary, "Am I like that? Those trysts with R?" (58). But he can also claim, "One more guy and it was over" (58). And he concludes the section, "I am myself after all. The dead are what move me. The various dead" (59). Negotiating his re-lationship with Western culture is more complicated than negotiating his various sexual relationships. The dead poets of the past beckon him, one in particular, Dante, whose "dead poetry" (*Purg.* 1.7) has him enthralled. It will prove much more difficult to be rid of the various poetic sources Baraka will soon feel the need to leave behind than to rid himself of these scattered male lovers.

As we move deeper into Baraka's hell, his writing becomes more original. He begins to experiment with more confidence in the pieces he writes between 1959 and 1963. "Hypocrite(s)" first saw the light along with the section that follows it, "Thieves," in an anthology Baraka edited in 1963, *The Moderns*. The section focuses momentarily on hypocritical Chris-tians but shifts to give us a list of acquaintances from Baraka's youth, pre-sented as if they were characters in a play. The section ends with a cryptic closing phrase and signature: "Yrs t., Caiaphas" (68). The sinners being punished for hypocrisy in Dante's *Inferno* 23 march slowly in heavy leaden cloaks with a gilded edge over the body of Caiaphas, the archhypocrite who urged the Jews to look for a scapegoat for their sins, which they found in Jesus. Baraka keeps his eye on Dante's text as if he owes some sort of al-legiance to it. In "Thieves," he makes occasional references to snakes in recognition of the episodes of metamorphosis in the Dantesque original

(72, 76), and there is a deliberate allusion to the equivalent scene in the *Inferno* with the mentioning of the sinner who is punished there, Vanni Fucci (73).

"The Eighth Ditch (Is Drama" announces its generic status as a theatrical piece. Like Dante, Baraka experiments with different genres. This is the work that was first published in *The Floating Bear* 9 in 1961, which led to the arrest of Baraka and Diane di Prima for obscenity on October 18, 1961. The newsletter and its editors were cleared of all charges in April 1962. What was obscene about it? In *The Floating Bear* 15, Joseph LeSueur reviewed a production of *The Eighth Ditch* at the New York Poets Theatre: "Finally we come to Jones' [Baraka's] 'Dante,' which, taken literally (it shouldn't be, of course), is about a gang-bang in an army barracks, with one soldier on the receiving end.[17] It can be truly said that no holds were barred in its staging; in fact, it was so graphic, so specific, that the imagination had no place to go. Since the language, along with Beckett's in *Happy Days,* is the most supple and evocative so far this theatrical season, it's too bad the audience couldn't concentrate more on it. The acting of Alan Marlowe and Ron Faber, by the way, was professional in the best sense" (168). Di Prima observes that this was the first time Baraka had his own work staged, and she recalls how much he seemed to enjoy it (*The Floating Bear* xv).

The "Eighth Ditch" is another section of the novel that associates homosexuality and cultural awareness.[18] In "Circle 8" the context for the conflation of sex and knowledge is the sin of political corruption: here the context is false counsel. Baraka seemed to have resolved the questions raised by the issue of homosexuality earlier in the novel but here the issue poses some of those questions again. In the play two men converse in a tent: one "64" or Herman (read "her" + "man"), the other "46." The man designated 64 represents the wild uncontrolled culture of the black experience, a culture ignored at times by the younger Baraka/Jones, while 46 represents Baraka as a young man trying to negotiate the world of white Western culture and all that such a negotiation implies. The wilder 64 prompts 46 to have flashbacks of his youth and gives him visions of what the future holds. He says at one point that the year is 1947, when Baraka would have been thirteen years old. He moves across the tent to 46, taking off his shirt as he goes, while 46, uninterested, continues to read from a book. Then 64 sits beside him and touches him and declares, "I have, at least, all the black arts" (83). The playwright is using the medium of drama to explore further the relationship between different cultures, black and white, and different classes. We learn later that 64 is "an underprivileged negro youth now in the boyscouts" whereas 46 is "what's known as a middle-class Negro youth, also in the boyscouts" (85). The lower-class 64 teases 46 about his white, middle-class tastes in jazz. And yet 64 predicts that the intervening years between 1947 and the time of the play, approximately 1960, will be full of complications. He predicts it because he knows it. The narrator addresses the audience and declares the theatrical piece "a foetus drama" (84). The play is about the coming of age of a young man, sexually and intellectually. He then states: "Or if we are to remain academic . . . he is a man dying" (84). The play is about one man's choice in cultural ways of being, in habits of thinking. The question is not as simple as, will Baraka decide to be black or white? Rather, it is a question of how class and color intersect: will he accept the virtues of the underclass and forgo the pleasures of the middle class? By the time he had incorporated this piece into the narrative of his novel, the author was on the verge of deciding to follow the impulsive advice of 64, to leave the world of 46's aspirations behind.

As the drama unfolds, 64 climbs on top of 46 and initiates him into the world of homosexual sex, all the while reciting the sort of blues folk knowledge that he possesses. He then asks 46, "What's that make you think?" To which 46 replies, "I donno what it makes me think. Only thing is I guess I'll get pregnant" (87). The homosexual act inseminates 46 with a new kind of knowledge that he doesn't yet understand. Transmission of culture is reduced to and symbolized by sexual intercourse and its physiological transmission. The narrator intervenes again and tells the audience that one's past can be revisited: "The past / is passd. But you come back & see for yourself" (88). Then the drama shifts to a comical, almost Aristophanic, ending, replete with a "crooked ass peter" (88), as three guys line up to have a turn with a nonplussed 46 who only wants to hear about other kinds of blues from 64.

What does this play within the novel have to do with Dante? Vergil as guide transmits knowledge of the ancient world to Dante; moreover, he represents rational thought. Beatrice later in the *Divine Comedy* presents

Dante with access to revelation, a different kind of knowledge that complements Vergilian, classical rationalism; she transmits the pilgrim literally to a place from which he can experience revelatory knowledge on his own. Baraka knows that the epic tradition of which the *Divine Comedy* is a part turns the handing down of knowledge from one generation to the next into an important theme. His unusual take on the theme of *traditio,* with one man literally inseminating another, should not distract us from his dependence on the theme itself. In fact, the uniqueness of Baraka's version is itself indicative of the epic tradition of one poet in a later and subsequent generation trying to outdo another who preceded him. Dante, needless to say, doesn't have anything like the scene of 64 and 46, the inverse of each other, becoming whole through copulation. (Again one thinks of Aristophanes, now of the myth Plato has him relate in the *Symposium.*) In his encounter with Brunetto Latini among the sodomites, Dante suggests that homosexuality is literally a dead end (*Inf.* 15–16). Dante does portray, however, redeemed homosexual poets in *Purgatory* 26–27, although Baraka didn't progress far enough in his reading of the Italian authority to have learned of that episode. Baraka uses a drama in which one character convinces another (who is his alter ego) of the value of black culture, which he as author had rejected in favor of white culture like that of Dante's poem upon which he models the very work in which the radical drama finds its niche. It sounds more subversive than it really is. In fact, it's very similar to what Dante constructs in *Inferno* 26, in his depiction of the fraudulent counselors, the equivalent passage to Baraka's "Eighth Ditch." Dante the poet portrays the pilgrim interacting with the Homeric hero, Ulysses, through Vergil, who presumably translates Ulysses' Homeric Greek into Latin for Dante. That is, a chain of communication is set up from Homer to Vergil to Dante, which symbolizes the lines of the epic tradition from its beginning down to the medieval poet. That all of this is introduced under the rubric of false or fraudulent discourse suggests that Dante questions the veracity and direction of poetic discourse within the epic tradition. And indeed he takes liberties with that tradition in his unique version of the Ulysses story. Baraka's specific image may be a new way to figure the handing down of literary tradition, but it is not as revolutionary as it seems. Poets have been doing this to each other, as it were, for eons.

The next section, "The Ninth Ditch: Makers of Discord," was first published in an anthology that came out in 1963, *Soon, One Morning,* which may
account for its composition seeming more carefully crafted than other parts
of the novel that were written earlier without the benefit of additional editorial scrutiny. It is the most subtly constructed imitation of Dante's narrative in *The System of Dante's Hell.* In this passage the author situates the
world of the Newark gangs of his youth in terms of Dante's *Inferno* 28.
First among Dante's makers of discord in the eighth circle, ninth bolgia,
are the founders of Islam, portrayed as radical schismatics, Muhammad the
prophet and his son-in-law, Ali. Dante accepted the medieval belief that
Islam began when heretical wayward Christians created a schism within
the church. Their punishment in hell, consequently, is to be mangled and
cleft into pieces by a devil, whose violent actions force them to embody the
sort of suffering they brought about within the political entities of which
they were a part. The schismatic's body is cleft in retribution for the way
the schismatic cleaved the body politic. In his version of this section of
hell Baraka continues to focus on his teenage years. He is about sixteen or
seventeen, attending parties around Newark in a wintry landscape in the
late 1940s, early 1950s. He takes buses across town to some unidentified
house and then descends into the basement for intense dancing with people
he doesn't know. Our hero is already showing his literary aspirations, alluding to conversations with a girl about Dylan Thomas and Baudelaire
(94). Roi recalls that members of his gang, the Cavaliers, were in a struggle with boys from another tougher gang, the Dukes: "They had taken up
the practice of wearing berets. Along with the army jackets (& bellbot-
tom pants which was natural for people in that strange twist of ourselves,
that civil strife our bodies screamed for . . . Now, too, you readers!)" (98).
In a Dantesque mode Baraka commands the reader to pay attention to
the passage in order to highlight the connection he makes to his medieval
source. Dante's makers of discord—Baraka borrows Sinclair's phrase to
describe the sinners—are guilty of creating civil strife. The very names
of the Newark gangs are medievalizing: Cavaliers and Dukes. Earlier in the
passage when the narrator first mentions them, he makes a passing reference to "Mahomet" (97), in Sinclair's spelling. It may be that the rival gang,
the Dukes, plays the part of "Mahomet" in a local Jersey version of a reli-

gious dispute. But like many other details in Baraka's narrative, it is difficult to identify the exact purpose of the allusion.

Baraka has his text of Sinclair's translation of Dante open to *Inferno* 28.
The final example of a schismatic in *Inferno* 28 is the troubadour poet, Bertran de Born, who succeeded in dividing Henry II from his son in the complicated political landscape of twelfth-century France. Bertran appears at
the end of Dante's canto memorably with his detached head in hand like a
man holding a lantern, articulating the principle of the punishment fitting
the crime: "Thus is observed in me the retribution" (*Inf.* 28.142). Bertran
sheds light on how the two Newark gangs act when they come together in
the crowded basement at the house party: "Tonight someone said something about the records. Whose property or the music wasn't right or some
idea came up to spread themselves. Like Jefferson wanting Louisiana, or
Bertran deBorn given dignity in Hell. There was a scuffle & the Dukes won"
(98). The Dukes are territorial, as gangs are, and as Jefferson was when
he negotiated the Louisiana Purchase with the French, and as Bertran de
Born was when he tried to rally one faction of the French nobility against
another. Baraka focuses on Bertran over several other sinners in Dante's
canto, probably in part because he was a poet. The striking observation of
Bertran (whose last name Baraka misspells) "given dignity in Hell" is lifted
straight from Sinclair's notes, where the scholar writes, "The quality of
the sinners seems to rise from figure to figure, from the brutal squalor of
Mahomet to the strange dignity of Bertran" (357). Bertran does have an
unexpected dignity in Dante's hell, which Baraka appreciated. It is possible,
though, that he simply lifted the insight along with the phrase from Sinclair's commentary. Roi, for his part, is trying to lay low, hiding behind his
persona as a poet in love: "I sat down talking to a girl I knew was too ugly
to attract attention" (99).

The references to Dante's text culminate when an angry member of
the Dukes leaves the party only to return armed and ready for a fight: "He
came back with six guys and a meat cleaver. Rushed down the stairs and
made the whole place no man's land. . . . 'Where's that muthafucka.' Lovely
Dante at night under his flame taking heaven. A place, a system, where all
is dealt with . . . as is proper. 'I'm gonna kill that muthafucka.' Waived
the cleaver and I crept backwards while his mob shuffled faces. 'I'm gonna

kill *somebody.*'" (99). The narrator describes the chaos that ensued, including how his own face was grazed by the cleaver, now an "axe," until "they finally disappeared up the stairs, all the fighters. [New paragraph] When we came out & went slow upstairs the fat guy was spread out in the snow & Nicks was slapping him in his face with the side of the cleaver. He bled under the light on the grey snow & his men had left him there to die" (100). The Duke with the cleaver has become Dante's devil dispensing punishment to the gang members. But the devil gets his due for it is the Duke gang member who has been cut up and left to bleed to death out on the sidewalk. This suggests further that the reference to "Mahomet" earlier may be an attempt to link the Dukes to the role of Muhammad in *Inferno* 28. Roi himself has metamorphosed into a new person; from talking of Dylan Thomas and Baudelaire, to cultivating his literary interests that the others envied (97), to hiding strategically behind a conversation with an unattractive girl, he has turned into none less than the poet: "Lovely Dante at night under his flame taking heaven." This is Dante who has emerged from hell to see the stars of heaven once again, a sentimental poet whom the others don't understand, not even his friends. This is a utopian Dante who will dream up "a place, a system where all is dealt with as is proper." This is the pilgrim as adolescent in Newark who survives to become our poet in New York.

Despite the fact that Baraka emphasizes Bertran de Born over Muhammad in his imitation of the schismatics, his reference to "Mahomet" implies a growing attraction to the world of Islam and respect for it. It is intriguing to reflect on the development of the ideological positions in the future Black Nationalist and sometime practitioner of Islam. The extent to which Dante's portrayal of Islam may have had, paradoxically, an impact on the radical transformation of LeRoi Jones into Amiri Baraka deserves further consideration.[19]

"Personators (alchemists) Falsifiers" is the last section of Baraka's eighth circle, corresponding appropriately to the tenth bolgia of the eighth circle in Dante's original, *Inferno* 29–31. This is the only section of the entire novel that was not prepublished in some other venue. The section is a meditation on the protagonist's relationship with organized Christianity and his desire for other kinds of spiritual life. It opens with a verse sequence in which the narrator wonders whether or not he is a good and God-fearing man. The world of God, especially reinterpreted through Baraka's experience of reading Dante, is a world of systems. He writes: "Those 12 years of God, all strength followed (and the walks into halls, and their dusty windows. They would quote something, or remember who was who. Who was placed, made to enter the pure world of system. As our lives slip through the fingers of giants. . . . He will not pray again" (102). The narrator decides to reject the world of the Christian God to whom he had prayed at times earlier in his life. He is unimpressed with the ability of others to quote from Scripture. He is also troubled by the reaction to place others in "the pure world of system." Christianity's hierarchical impulse to classify, especially Dante's medieval Christian urge to arrange reality in a system, troubles Baraka. Life can pass before one knows it, he seems to suggest in the line "As our lives slip through the fingers of giants." That line also keys the passage to its source from *Inferno* 31.130–45, where Dante describes how a giant at the bottom of the eighth circle, Antaeus, picked Vergil and him up and carried them down to the lowest pit of hell, the ninth circle. It is a transition passage in Dante, and it functions that way in Baraka too. This section of Baraka's narrative leads us up to the next section with its final passage like a kind of catchword at the bottom of the page pointing to the new word at the top of the next page: "THE RAPE" (105).

Dante's ninth circle of the treacherous is divided into four subsections of increasing heinousness: treachery to kindred, to country, to guests, and to lords and benefactors. Baraka recreates only the first of these four in a story about how he and his friends abuse a drunken prostitute, "Circle 9: Bolgia 1—Treachery to Kindred. The Rape" (107–17). Roi is back from college and reconnecting with old friends from high school over the summer. At a party full of light-skinned women, he and his buddies meet an older woman who is "skinny, dark and drunk" (109) and offer to drive her home from East Orange to Newark, through Montclair, a drive that takes them from middle-class black neighborhoods through upper-middle-class white areas, through places where "some car full of Negroes up there wd be spotted by the police" (115). Once they learn that she carries a venereal disease, they throw her out of the car. Baraka's description of her lying on the ground like a cadaver in a morgue suggests that he thinks they killed her. Before he can jump out of the car to help her, as he implies he is about to do, his friends restrain him, all the while celebrating his leading role in pushing the whore from the car. Again, as in several earlier sections of *System,* we are far removed from Dante's text. The main connection appears to be that Roi's treatment of the black prostitute is a form of cultural betrayal. His ridicule and rejection of her is a rejection of all blacks and of blackness in general, including his own. The passage ends with Roi questioning everyone's allegiance to him (117) and the "new life" (115) he embraces through such cruel escapades.

The book's final episode, "The Heretics," stands out as the longest single piece in the narrative. It is the episode of *System* that has received the most critical attention from Baraka's readers, due in part to its length and to its prose, which exhibits a more recognizable beginning, middle, and end, than does the prose of the rest of the narrative. Moreover, its thematic treatment of Roi's sexual explorations has caught the attention of many of Baraka's readers, especially more recent ones.[20] As I noted above, Baraka locates the heretics at the end of the novel, at the very bottom of his reconstruction of hell, aware that this contradicts Dante's order, which places them, instead, in the sixth of nine circles. Marc Cogan clarifies that for Dante heresy (like violence) is a sin tied to the irascible appetite; it is not a sin of maliciousness like the sins deeper down in the eighth and ninth circles of Dante's hell (60–68). Baraka's shifting of heresy further down in his narrative depends on his own redefined literary understanding of the sin. He explains in a note that accompanies his schematic map, "I put The Heretics in the deepest part of hell, though Dante had them spared on higher ground. [New paragraph] It is heresy, against one's own sources, running in terror, from one's deepest responses and insights . . . the denial of feeling . . . that I see as basest evil" (7). This is of course a moment of autocriticism, for Baraka saw himself as a cultural and literary heretic in his attempt to blend in with white culture early in his life, especially in the time he spent in Greenwich Village in the years leading up to the novel's publication in 1965. In the story, Roi describes himself as an imitation white boy whose "quick new jersey speech, full of italian idiom, and the invention of the jews" (128) perplexes and charms the rural southern blacks he meets near the Air Force base where he is stationed in Louisiana. These encounters force Roi to confront directly the social dichotomy of being split down the center, of having a double consciousness, half black, half white.

The heresy, therefore, is of a black man trying to act white and, worse, refusing to learn from the rude and uneducated (but untainted) blacks of the South.[21] By extension it is heretical for the black writer to ignore his race and write as if he were white. For Baraka this comes down to appealing to the wrong sources, middle class over lower class, as he often puts it, and European over African.

Baraka's exact title for the chapter is "6. The Heretics," the number recalling the circle for the heretics in Dante's order. For Baraka, however, we are in the pit of hell where we should expect to see, therefore, Satan, as we do at the end of Dante's narrative. He opens the chapter with an epigraph in italics and quotation marks taken from Sinclair's notes to *Inferno* 9, page 128:

> *"The whole of lower Hell is surrounded by a great wall, which is defended by rebel angels and immediately within which are punished the arch-heretics and their followers."*
>
> *And then, the city of Dis, "the stronghold of Satan, named after him, . . . the deeper Hell of willful sin."* (119)

Baraka generalizes correctly from Sinclair's scholarly note that once inside the gates of lower hell, once past the point of *Inferno* 9 in the original narrative, we are within Satan's domain proper. Given this calculation, Baraka's repositioning of the episode of the heretics is not quite as unorthodox or heretical as it may seem. The action of the story reaches its climax in a neighborhood on the other side of the tracks in Shreveport, Louisiana, called "the Bottom," where servicemen would often go for a night out.[22] The neighborhood's name is one way to emphasize that we are in deepest hell; the Dantesque landscape furthers the impression. The setting is full of "Damned and burning souls" (126). A bar Roi enters "was filled with shades. Ghosts" (128). At another moment, perhaps in a flashback, the narrator reflects, "All frauds, the cold mosques glitter winters" and "Infidels fat niggers at the gates" (136), recalling the mosques of *Inferno* 8.70–73 and the drama at the gates in *Inferno* 9. Finally, throughout "The Heretics," the author alludes to the cruel and savage forest in which his character wanders, the Dantesque image par excellence. "The old wood. Eyes of the damned uncomprehending" (134), becomes an image for nothing less than white Western civilization, especially its literary culture, which entraps Roi and by extension Baraka.[23]

Roi meets a whore with a heart of gold named Peaches, who will provide him with the opportunity to learn how to be black. It is as if the whore he threw out of the car in "Treachery to Kindred" had been reincarnated at this later moment in Roi's life. He has a chance to make amends. Where the narrative analogy would lead the reader to expect some version of Satan, instead Roi meets quite unexpectedly his saving grace. He hasn't had a guide—no Vergil or Beatrice—during his journey throughout the novel. When Roi first lays eyes on his would-be lady, he is compared to Dante: "He pointed like Odysseus wd. Like Virgil, the weary shade, at some circle. For Dante, me, the yng wild virgin of the universe to look" (126). There is nothing sexually virginal about Roi. But it remains for him to be initiated into the mysteries of the culture of his birthright, black culture. Later as Roi and Peaches dance, he recognizes that "my history . . . ended, here, the light white talking jig, died in the arms of some sentry of Africa. . . . No one the white world wanted or would look at" (129–30). Roi says to himself as Peaches undresses him, "Please, you don't know me. Not what's in my head. I'm beautiful. Stephen Dedalus. . . . My soul is white, pure white, soars" (140). His unvoiced plea is that she respect him for his apprenticeship in Western culture, for his similarity to Joyce's protagonist in *Portrait of the Artist as a Young Man*. At the very opening of the story he declares his allegiance to "Thomas, Joyce, Eliot, Pound" (119), but by suggesting that these authors are part of his heretical education, he is prepared to leave them behind as soon as he finds a new guide for the future. Once he succumbs to Peaches, he performs and leaves, only to return to accept her invitation to move in for a while. He thinks to himself as she serves him watermelon in bed the next day, "And I felt myself smiling and it seemed that things had come to an order" (147). A good system, in other words, to counter all the bad in the narrator's life. He continues, "And felt the world grow together as I hadn't known it. All lies before, I thought. All fraud and sickness. This was the world. . . . A real world, of flesh, of smells, of soft black harmonies and color" (148).

But the bottom of hell isn't the place for a kind spirit like Peaches, whether or not she is meant to recall Beatrice, nor can the narrative end on such a blissful note if it is to remain true to its primary model. Roi, assuming the role of husband, jokes about going out to shop for his new bride and buys her among other things some peaches. On his way back to her house, he has a change of heart about being with her, which a citation of the opening line from *Inferno* 9 glosses: "That color which cowardice brought out in me" (149). Dante uses the line to depict the pilgrim's face when he turns pale upon realizing that his fearless guide Vergil is suddenly afraid. Vergil has realized that he is no longer in control of the situation and that the pilgrim's life is at risk, for he is in danger of being turned into stone at the walls of the City of Dis. The color of cowardice is white. To turn from Peaches and what she represents for Roi is to turn back toward whiteness and the fear that accompanies it. It is to risk a kind of petrifaction. Moreover, it is to turn toward a form of heresy, as Baraka's subsequent allusion makes clear. Here is the quoted verse in its narrative context in *System*: "It was a cloud I think came up. Something touched me. 'That color which cowardice brought out in me.' Fire burns around the tombs. Closed from the earth. A despair came down. Alien grace" (149). In Dante's *Inferno,* God punishes the heretics by having them burned in open tombs. This is what Roi now risks as he leaves Peaches behind in the hopes that he might "find sweet grace alone" (150). In an earlier lyric piece, "A Poem for Neutrals," Baraka alludes to this same passage in *Inferno* 9, just before Dante encounters the heretics beyond the gates of the City of Dis. There, however, his journey is interrupted:

> It is not Dante,
> nor Yeats. But the loud and drunken
> pilgrim, I knew so well
> in my youth. And grew to stone
> waiting for the change
> (*Dead Lecturer* 13)

Baraka identifies with the pilgrim (though he is not "loud and drunken" in Dante's original), distinguishing him from Dante the poet. In this lyric version of the descent into hell, Baraka's pilgrim is petrified before he can make it out and grow into the poet. The epic version of the descent in *System* offers different possibilities.

As Roi walks away from the house of Peaches, a rain begins to fall. Its timing suggests a rite of purification: "And a light rain came down. I walked away from the house. Up the road, to go out of Bottom" (150). This could be, it should be, the moment when the pilgrim exits hell and sees the stars once again. Instead, three "tall strong black boys" beat him nearly to death for being a "Mr. Half-white muthafucka" (151). As the novel ends the protagonist does indeed see stars but not the salvific kind offered by the Dantesque model: "Crazy out of my head. Stars were out" (152). He is picked up by authorities and taken away to an institution. The last line of the story has Roi revived in a different kind of infernal setting: "I woke up 2 days later, with white men, screaming for God to help me" (152). But it is a form of hell no less.

In an epilogue to the novel, "Sound and Image," the narrative voice forcefully describes a vision of hell on earth:

> Hell in the head.
> The torture of being the unseen object, and, the constantly observed subject.
> The flame of social dichotomy. Split open down the center, which is the early legacy of the black man unfocused on blackness. (153)

Baraka's definition of hell ultimately does not derive from anything specific in Dante's text. Rather, hell is the state of mind of the black man who must cope with the effects of being invisible in the white world. The "unseen object" of this social critique is Ralph Ellison's invisible man. Baraka's reference to "the flame of social dichotomy" and being "split open down the center" describes the impact of being, paradoxically, an invisible man under constant observation, of being an exile lost in one's own country. The divisive tension between being totally ignored by one's society to being hounded to death leads the author's autobiographical self to do things that bring about his eventual ruin. The tension leads him to a white institutional hell, perhaps the psychiatric ward of a hospital, which also stands for the sanitized danger of the canonical hell represented by Western literary models like Joyce, Eliot, Pound, and of course Dante. Roi, the narrator, Baraka—whatever his identity—needs to break loose.

A New Narrative Model

The System of Dante's Hell takes the *Inferno's* structural and moral topography as an organizing principle, but critics have questioned the extent to which its experimental prose actually parallels Dante's poem.[24] While there is clearly some merit to the question of how Dantesque the work actually is, we have seen above, for example, in the analysis of "The Ninth Ditch: Makers of Discord," just how carefully Baraka can imitate and follow Dante's text when it suits his artistic design. He has it in him to make his narrative resemble Dante's as closely as he wants it to. So why doesn't he do so consistently? And if not Dante, then which other narrative models does he consider and reject and which does he eventually settle upon as he rewrites the narrative of the *Inferno*?

The reader's experience of the work's episodic narrative is akin to the experience of reading a composition by Burroughs, Ginsberg, Olson, or one of the other Beat artists whom Baraka had admired early on in his career. As we have seen, the novel is characterized by free association, disjunctive connections, unexpected juxtapositions, and other features that challenge the reader's ability to follow the plot of the autobiographical narrative. Its mix of genres, along with its mix of discourse, sometimes poetic, sometimes prosaic, further complicates any progressive reading from the novel's beginning to its end. One may legitimately question whether, or the extent to which, the work actually should even be considered a novel. Just beneath the title, the cover of the first edition proclaims that it is "a novel by LeRoi Jones," as if there might be some question about its genre. This same phrase is repeated on the inside front flap of the original dust jacket, and the work is identified as a novel again on the copyright page. The paratextual apparatus of the book functions to counter any confusion engendered in the reader's mind about the work's generic status. Whatever it may be, the press wants to assure the reader that it actually is indeed a novel.

In the official press release for the publication of the book, Baraka describes the design of his narrative in musical terms: "Pieces from *The System of Dante's Hell* are all part of a musical-literary scheme, and have literally come together as narrative after the accretion of single images, silences, and what I call 'association complexes.' These are the individual sounded notes and phrases that build to form motifs that are jammed together to make straighter narrative" (1).[25] Here he refers to the novel with the sort of language he uses in his musical criticism: "notes" combine to make "phrases" (this particular word functions readily for music and literature) that create "motifs" (another term that suits musical and literary criticism) to make a narrative. By "association complexes," he means the fabric of memories that compose his stream of consciousness narrative. Baraka then continues by claiming provocatively that the first half of the novel resembles Sonny Rollins's *Oleo* and that the work's overall rhythm, "the total rhythm form I collect my words around," derives its inspiration from Cecil Taylor's *Of What*.[26] But as intriguing as these parallels to avant-jazz musical compositions are, I am hard-pressed to identify the specific internal structures of Baraka's narrative which justify such a claim.[27] In fact, stream of consciousness may be the most apt description of its design.

In *The System of Dante's Hell* the author points to his sources in many passages, as we have seen, mentioning them by name or alluding to them in other obvious ways. In other places, for example in the press release, Baraka comments openly about the literary influences on his writing: "My influences have been Joyce, Dante, Burroughs, Ginsberg, Olson . . ." (2). Joyce, who perfects the technique of stream of consciousness narrative, stands in for modernist authors in general. Baraka mentions Dante, of course, followed by the Beats. Allegiance to these sources represents a form of heresy for him, and he will break his ties with them through the writing of the novel—although he can't explain how the break happens until after it has occurred. That is, it is not a premeditated break.[28] The phenomenon of using one's literary predecessors while simultaneously distancing oneself from them is a common device among writers in the epic tradition. In fact, an agonistic relationship with one's literary predecessors is arguably a constituent element of epic discourse. Vergil uses Homer to be different from Homer; Dante uses Vergil to distinguish himself from Vergilian epic; Ezra Pound uses Homer, Vergil, and Dante in ways that allow him as a modernist epic poet to separate himself from the group. For his part, Baraka uses Dante as his guide into the world of Western literary culture in the process of differentiating himself from the canonical European model and these other practitioners—the modernists and the

Beats—of what he will come to label, as in the epigraph to this chapter, "white writing." One could say that he takes the conventional epic agon between generations of poets and turns it into an act of rebellion.

In *System* Baraka refers to Joyce, Eliot, and Pound as sources of inspiration on several occasions, and in fact it proves complicated to break completely away from the modernists who taught him how to write in a new vein. While Baraka uses Joyce's stream of consciousness narrative technique, his protagonist Roi fancies himself a Stephen Dedalus at two moments in the narrative (58, 140), and he refers to Joyce at the beginning of the episode of the heretics (119). The narrator mentions Eliot in two passages (58, 134), but Baraka himself seemed to take only a passing interest in Eliot's specific literary projects. In fact, in an earlier note Baraka dismisses him as a mere "rhetorician."[29] As we've seen above, a model Baraka did have in mind as he drafted his prose and as he reconfigured previously published pieces into a whole narrative is the poetry of Ezra Pound, especially his *Cantos*. Baraka's eccentric style of abbreviation and his seemingly random manipulation of typography may be inspired by Pound; in any case, Pound's example lends these practices a kind of authority. Roi refers directly to Pound twice in *System* (31, 119), in one passage associating his reading of the American poet with his own erudition and by extension with his fascination with white culture: "Eliot, Pound, Cummings, Apollinaire . . . I was erudite and talked to light-skinned women" (31). To imitate Pound, then, is to give in to a kind of literature and cultural life that leads the would-be black poet astray. Later he refers to Pound at the opening of the episode on the heretics, suggesting that reading such an author is a heretical act of self-indulgence, which does no more than focus Baraka on "how beautiful I was" (119). Pound's complex narrative, marked by literary and historical references to many different traditions, is a difficult model to imitate and surpass.

Baraka as a black Pound is a puzzling, even oxymoronic image given Pound's known attitude on race. James Laughlin, Pound's publisher at New Directions Press, reports that the iconoclastic poet "practiced what I believe the rhetoricians call tapinosis, the application of colorful slang to serious topics, and we were given Villon and the troubadours, or even Dante, in his vernacular" (*Pound as Wuz* 168). It was a vernacular that often featured a black accent (*Pound as Wuz* 5). Pound doing a minstrel Dante in blackface must share the stage here with Baraka sending up a black Dante. In the process of creating this version of the medieval poet wearing a mask—his version of a modernist work of liberation that looks to Dante for some of its inspiration—Baraka was overlooking other traditions to which he later turned as he forged new literary alliances. He openly admits this in *6 Persons,* an incomplete prose piece written in the mid-1970s that continues the autobiographical explorations of *The System of Dante's Hell*: "You left the village & went to Harlem. You thought less about Ezra Pound & more about black people" (*6 Persons* 97).[30] By this point in Baraka's career, Pound's modernist verse stands for everything that is a negative alternative to black culture. Pound has come to stand for Europe and white writing.

Baraka's growing alienation from white culture in general was accompanied by an increasing discomfort with its literature. In the process of negotiating these various possible models it may come as a surprise that the Negro writers who had come into their own in the previous decades—especially Wright, Ellison, Baldwin—are not sources of inspiration for Baraka. As far as I can tell, Baraka does not allude to Wright in *System,* although he maintained a respectful appreciation of Wright as writer and Marxist intellectual, especially for his early works.[31] From what we have learned earlier about Baraka's troubled relationship with Ellison, the surprise would be if he did turn to Ellison's novel as a source. He never mentions the possibility that *Invisible Man* might function as a narrative source or model for *System,* even though Roi and Ellison's protagonist have much in common. In *Invisible Man,* as in the *Divine Comedy* and *Portrait of the Artist as a Young Man,* the hero goes on a journey in search of knowledge. It is a typical epic quest that occurs on two levels: the hero must descend into another world to confront the dead, and, as the protagonist makes this descent, the poet for his part must come to grips with the literary dead. Baraka, whose narrator states, "The dead are what move me" (59), gives us his version of such a twofold epic journey in *The System of Dante's Hell.* Similarly Roi and Rufus, the protagonist of Baldwin's *Another Country,* seem to share enough that one could imagine Baldwin's novel as a model of sorts for Baraka, but the influence of Baldwin, too, goes unremarked by Baraka.[32]

I have been pointing out everything that Baraka's *System of Dante's Hell* is not. It does not seem to be as consistently conscious a rewriting of Dante's poem as one might assume from the book's title, its opening table lifted from Sinclair's translation, and the various allusions to Dante. It is not as much a work like that of the Beats as one might expect. Nor is it really the musical-literary innovation that Baraka's comments in the press release imply. It is neither openly modernist nor a renewed version of the established Negro writing preceding Baraka's arrival on the literary scene. Then what is it? How can we best describe its narrative models?

Baraka's move away from the literary scene of the Village and up to Harlem is paralleled by a shift to radically different models in his writing. In an interview with Debra L. Edwards, he explains the role his novel played in furthering his artistic development. In response to Edwards's question "So you had arrived by the time of *Dante's Hell* at a purely black aesthetic?" he states:

> No, what *Dante* actually did was move me away from the earlier derivative works. When I came to *Dante,* I then consciously determined that I was going to stop writing like other folks, like the Creeleys and the Olsons and all those other people. So what I did was write that book without thought to any kind of artifice but just straight ahead, whatever came to me to write. I used the Dante form because it was a form that I could quickly impose upon it. Yet the content would be as free as I could make it, but I thought I would impose this form so the book wouldn't just float away. I would at least try to construct some kind of systematic portrait of my own mind and life. That was probably the breakaway book, in terms of the breakaway from older, more derivative forms and getting more clearly into my own voice. (*Conversations* 156)[33]

For a modern writer to claim, "I used the Dante form" to break away from "more derivative forms," sounds contradictory.[34] Another piece by Baraka from approximately the same time as his interview with Edwards may help resolve the contradiction. In "The Revolutionary Tradition in Afro-American Literature," Baraka writes condescendingly of the Europeanized Negro authors like Phillis Wheatley and Jupiter Hammon, who were not willing to challenge the system and therefore are of little consequence to the contemporary black writer. Given the traditional interpretation of Cordelia Ray and the oratorical sonority of her Colored Dante, Baraka most likely would classify her in the same negative category as Wheatley and

Hammon, however deserving she is, in my opinion, of a different and more positive interpretation. Baraka juxtaposes these poets with another less educated, less accommodating, less authoritative writer, the slave, and sees his own authentic creative origins there: "In the slave narratives . . . are found the beginnings of a genuine Afro-American written literature" (*LJ/AB Reader* 314). He includes William Wells Brown, whom we discussed as a precursor to Cordelia Ray, among the radical creators of this revolutionary literary tradition (314–15). Baraka's "breakaway from older, more derivative forms," his break with the Beat poets and other models, is a move toward an innovative form of narrative that has the slave autobiography as its generic source. If, as Baraka claims in the passage that serves as a gloss on the schematic map at the beginning of *System,* "it is heresy" to be "against one's own sources" (*System* 7), here we observe the black author going back via Dante to the most original source in his own tradition, the writings of the slave.

In *The Autobiography of LeRoi Jones,* Amiri Baraka—that is, Jones, once he has been emancipated and is no longer a literary heretic—puts it in these terms:

> At the same time I had begun a long prose work. It was as if I wanted *to shake off the stylistic shackles of the gang* I'd hung with and styled myself after. I consciously wrote as deeply into my psyche as I could go. I didn't even want the words to "make sense." I had the theme in my mind. My early life, in Newark, at Howard, in the Air Force, but the theme was just something against which I wanted to play endless variations. Each section had its own dynamic and pain. Going so deep into myself was like descending into Hell. I called it *The System of Dante's Hell.* (*Autobiography* 166, my emphasis)

The image of the emancipated slave is an apt one for the author's stylistic liberation from the Beats and the Greenwich Village crowd and his literary modernist models.[35] In 2003 he offers a variation on this theme by referring to his stylistic breakthrough as "A breakout!" as if from prison ("Amiri Baraka Analyzes How He Writes" 7). By extension we can understand the liberation to be from Western writers in general. If we take *The System of Dante's Hell* as a latter-day slave narrative of sorts—as at least one critic has done—the gesture of shaking off "the stylistic shackles of the gang I'd hung with" comes full circle.[36] Baraka goes back beyond the Beats and other Western authors, through Dante, to take his inspiration from the genre of the slave narrative *so as not to write like a slave!* In keeping with the genre of autobiography, this is as much a constructed attitude as it is the description of something Baraka actually did. The author is rewriting his own history for posterity. For how can he really abandon the Western tradition without also forfeiting its language first and foremost? Rather, with this claim Baraka announces that he will take his stand and appropriate the literary models of the West as he sees fit. It is a declaration not so much about casting off one tradition for another, but about devising strategies for re-engaging the tradition of the master in a new way. The challenge is to make Dante speak a new language, to translate him into a new American vernacular, somehow to take him thoroughly out of Europe.

Unlike Ellison, whose laudatory appreciation of the American melting pot we considered in the previous chapter, Baraka grows to condemn the hybrid mix of America as he sees it. How then can he incorporate or integrate a translated Dante into his black world? In an essay on the "The Myth of a 'Negro Literature'" of 1962, Baraka claims that there is no good Negro literature because all the proponents trotted forth are thoroughly middle class. The challenge to a writer like himself is precisely "to survive the constant and willful dilutions of the black middle class" (*Home* 106). Dilution is dangerous. Moreover, as the black writer must reposition himself in regard to white, middle-class culture, so the American writer must be wary of the diluting effects of European culture. Baraka makes this point rather humorously: "For an American, black or white, to say that some hideous imitation of Alexander Pope means more to him, emotionally, than the blues of Ray Charles or Lightnin' Hopkins, it would be required for him to have completely disappeared into the American Academy's vision of a Europeanized and colonial American culture, or to be lying" (113). For the American writer of color, then, there is the risk of double dilution, from both European and American white culture. Under these circumstances, it would seem that Dante would simply have to be abandoned rather than adapted into some new form. But Baraka is not yet finished with the Italian poet despite the constraints of these various positions.

Amiri Baraka: From Dante's System to the System

The schematic table that lays out the divisions of hell near the beginning of the Sinclair translation of the *Inferno* suggests to Baraka the image of the system; indeed he takes his title *The System of Dante's Hell* from that table. The sort of apparatus accompanying Sinclair's translation has a venerable lineage that goes back to some of the earliest printed editions of Dante's poem. The organization of hell elaborated by the poet lends itself to the creation of such schematic maps, although Dante himself never actually added one to his text as far as we know. In *Inferno* 11, Vergil does provide the ready and willing pilgrim with a verbal outline of hell, while the pilgrim pauses in order to acclimate himself to the terrible stench rising from farther down below. The table in Sinclair derives from Vergil's remarks in canto 11, which description in turn owes much to popular notions of the seven deadly sins and to the medieval Dominican theology of Thomas Aquinas, and through him, Aristotle's *Nicomachean Ethics* and Cicero's *De Officiis*. Aristotle's general categories of immoral actions that fall broadly under the rubrics of incontinence, violence, and fraud, are supplemented with specific medieval Christian sins like heresy, sodomy, and usury. Medieval theologians classified the latter two sins as manifestations of violence, while they considered the former a unique *sui generis* sin that fell between the evils of incontinence and violence. Dante's originality in conflating Christian and classical categories of sin with elements of high and low medieval culture continues to surprise his readers. It is easy to see why some readers from the very beginning have attributed to Dante's poem a radical heterodoxy.[37]

The reader who first comes to Baraka's rewriting of Dante—with its own hybrid contamination of popular and canonical, low and high, epic narrative, theatrical, and lyric fragments, works and traditions associated with the worlds of black and white—has reason to be as amazed as Dante's readers are by the *Divine Comedy*. The system Baraka took from Dante works well in organizing the narrative as a series of autobiographical episodes that take us deeper and deeper into Roi's private hell. The journey described in the novel prepares Roi the pilgrim and would-be poet to become Baraka the activist. His personal maturation, in fact, may be encapsulated in the term *system,* which suggests a range of both aesthetic and political categories that are more fully visible by the end of the narrative.

The literary activism that will distinguish Baraka's career from this point on in his life is brought about by the merging of the separate categories contained in the notion of "system."

This transformation of the notion of "system" itself in Baraka's thinking is striking. We saw above how the author conjured up a utopian Dante who dreams of "a place, a system where all is dealt with as is proper" in the episode of gangs and civil discord in *System* (99). But sometime shortly after he published *The System of Dante's Hell,* Baraka began to subject the notion of "system" to the same transmogrifying force that he himself was undergoing, in moving from the aestheticized LeRoi Jones to the politicized Amiri Baraka. Consequently, the structural category of "system" acquired a new meaning in Baraka's lexicon as "the system," that is, the established and entrenched culture against which Baraka was urging his contemporaries to struggle. This comes across clearly in an unpublished piece by Baraka housed at the Schomburg Center. The text is stored in a folder marked 1971, but there is no date on the piece itself and it could be from an earlier moment in Baraka's career. In fact, in some ways it recalls his "State/meant" of 1966.[38] On a single sheet, Baraka types in double-spaced format the following:

America is a hell, run by devils. These devils walk among us, tempt us, either to become, be, what they are, or die! And they will kill us: whether on anonymous subways, in the "fashionable" slick groovy communism of the lower east side, in vite-nam, the congo, or at the Audubon Ballroom. They will kill us, if we let them. Or turn us into the sleek killer whore that America is.

Clay is a captive, and a victim. He is the spectre of our failure (if we do fail) and the grim example of our fathers, who, no matter how they protest against "the system" still <u>enjoy</u> their inch of subway space, ~~It was also their blindness, and this blindness is another spectre~~ as masters of blindness. A blindness that is helping to kill their sons (suns), as example, as stance, as would sit in invisible Naacp's, holding session at bowling allies, while Malcolm, or Patrice, or Walter Bowe, are left to be massacred by the beasts.

No More Clays!

No More Murder Must Be Tolerated!!

DEVIL

~~WHITE~~ America Must Die!!!

(Either we will be extremists, and free men, masters of the earth,
or we will remain sick blind ~~funny~~ slaves, chained to the freezing
winds that blow up out of the vacuum caused by the white man's
missing soul.
Your move . . .)[39]

The cultural, political, and economic apparatus of white America, of,
as he calls it, Devil America, operates the system that Baraka struggles with
at this moment in the middle of his Black Nationalist period (1965–74).
In the single sentence that constitutes the fifth paragraph of the passage,
Baraka has scribbled out "White" and written in pen above it "DEVIL," recalling the militant language of Malcolm X (who was assassinated in the
Audubon Ballroom, hence the reference to it) in his early phase: "DEVIL
America Must Die!!!" His criticism here is of the failure of "our fathers"
who have protested against the political economic system but have done
little to change it. It is essentially a twofold protest against the system of
white America, which is at once paternalistic and patronizing, and against
those black Americans who are too accommodating to it. The guiding image
for Baraka's redefinition of the term *system* is taken from his play, *Dutch-
man,* in which the black character, Clay, is eventually murdered for not
giving in to the seductive appeal of a white woman on the subway. He is a
failure for not fighting back against the system before it's too late, which
leads Baraka to proclaim: "No More Clays!" The term, then, goes from sig-
nifying an aesthetic category in *The System of Dante's Hell* to indicating a
political category, from the system that Baraka uses to organize his literary vision of hell to the system that is an actual hell on earth for Baraka.
As in his description of the liberation of his prose style, Baraka turns to the
imagery of slavery and emancipation to describe the alternatives he envi-
sions: "Either we will be extremists, and free men, masters of the earth, or
we will remain sick blind slaves, chained to the freezing winds that blow
up out of the vacuum caused by the white man's missing soul." In this new
activism the choice between freedom and slavery is clear. And the onus is
on the reader to act on the choice: "Your move . . ."
    In the epilogue at the end of *The System of Dante's Hell,* "Sound and
Image," Baraka anticipates this more radical statement of the Schomburg
piece. At the end of the novel he invites the reader to define hell: "What

is hell? Your definitions" (153). He continues with an example of hell as he perceives it in 1965, when he was about to make his dramatic change from the bohemian life of the Village to a new life in Harlem and Newark: "For instance, if we can bring back on ourselves, the absolute pain our people must have felt when they came onto this shore, we are more ourselves again, and can begin to put history back in our menu, and forget the propaganda of devils that they are not devils" (154). Baraka defines hell as what "our people" felt as they were brought over against their will to the Americas from Africa. Furthermore, hell is the propaganda that has portrayed "our people" as the devils, when in truth the promulgators of the propaganda are the actual devils. And it is they, Baraka implies, who are responsible for the political system that must be opposed, for it is their political machine that contributes to the creation of the underclass that fills his hell. The contemporary system perpetuates the slavery of the past.

The merging of aesthetic and political categories which depends on this redefinition of system is apparent in a subsequent work by Baraka, an unpublished play, "Columbia The Gem of the Ocean." A handwritten manuscript of the play is housed in the Schomburg collection along with several typed versions, some of which have annotated comments that indicate the typescripts were used in productions of the play. According to Pennington-Jones's bibliography, the play was first performed in 1973 at Howard University (16). This consciousness-raising work from Baraka's Black Nationalist period was put on in local school auditoriums and gymnasiums with, it would appear from the notes, much community involvement. The material on the play includes sketches of how to set up a high school gym for its production, which includes the projection of slides on four separate screens. Baraka provides a typed list of 139 slides that depict images from black and white life in the 1960s and into the early 1970s. The following examples from the list give an indication of the progression the play tries to highlight and bring into effect:

1.   Caricature of Nixon as a King
2.   Uncle Sam
5.   Wig stand fron of Scudder homes [*sic*]
6.   Men in front of bar
6a.   Women in club at table with liquor on it

7a.   one junkie with rag tied around his arm

8.   brother with do rag mad ready to fight

11.   negro man sitting with cracker women

14.   Muhammed Ali dressed like englishman

20.   two women eating pig feet

30.   negro trying to come through red, white, and blue bars

45.   Uncle sam with money belt around waist

49.   march on Washington

51.   Mrs. King looking in coffin

54.   cracker, hell angel type, making obscene gesture with finger

68.   Blk. men teaching

77.   Slaves with yokes and chains around their necks

88.   Two policemen and dogs dragging man off the street

93.   police helicopter

107. Marx

113. Nat. Black convention delegate giving Black power sign

117. Jesse Jackson—Richard Hatcher

130. Marcus Garvey

136. Malcolm

The slides were shown during the performance of the script itself behind and surrounding the actors, many of whom mime their parts, prompting Pennington-Jones to call it a "mime play" (16). The slides move from Richard Nixon to Malcolm X, from images of racist hatred to scenes of black political activism, and they serve as glosses on the message of the play. This is political theater with an edge, tinged with satire, humor, horror, and hope, produced to show blacks the progress that they have made in the move from Nixon to Malcolm. The satire emphasizes images of an underprivileged existence that can kill: alcohol, drugs, bad food, as well as racists with guns. Education, enlightened confrontation, even Marxist revolution, on the other hand, can lead the black community to a better place. The production ends on this hopeful note.

In "Columbia The Gem of the Ocean," a disembodied character identified as Black Voice argues with Uncle Sam over the meaning of America. The play opens with Uncle Sam pontificating while characters move across the stage back and forth behind him:

The America you are in is my America.
All this stuff you see is just reflection of me
I make all this and buy all these

These opening remarks are followed by an aside for the director:

(Niggers walking back & forth swiftly frenzied then slowly plodding.)

Presumably Uncle Sam gestures to the players behind him as he says, "I make all this and buy all these." The playwright then gives further indications of who these people are. I try here to respect Baraka's typography as accurately as possible:

"The <u>DRUNKS</u>"
(All become drunks)
"On 40 cent wine for the real
or 40 scotch for the fantasyridden"

"The <u>JUNKIES</u>"
(All become scratching addicts hanging & droopy eyed)

"The <u>PROSTITUTES</u>"
(Women solicit-some solicit U Sam)

"The <u>VIOLENT</u>"
(People crouch ease around sullenly"

"-<u>AGAINST EACH OTHER</u>"
(They have knife fights & chair fights & icepick fights)

"The <u>SELLERS OF HUMAN FLESH</u>"
(Pimp types emerge—some hanging on women steering them
to cracker)

"The <u>TOMS</u>"
(Shufflers shuffle—couple rush over sliding on their knees to boss)

"The <u>HYPNOTIZED</u>"
>   (Brother with portable tv, or he runs to sit down in front of one)

"The <u>REALLY HYPNOTIZED</u>"
>   (Nigger boushies in white chess-tight at the neck spring up.
>   Sister walking black fur + w/big fluffy wig)

"The <u>HYPNOTIZERS</u>"
>   (Preacher in silent frenzied monologue, stripped pants, big high hat,
>   eating chicken)

These products of Uncle Sam's America ("I make all this and buy all these") are schematized in a hierarchy that recalls the sort of moral structure outlined in Dante's *Inferno*. As we move from the top of this list of ten sins to the bottom, we move deeper and deeper into evil, the ten groups recalling the circles of Dante's hell. The broad categories of sin in Dante's depiction of the underworld are reflected in Baraka's hierarchy. As we have seen, Dante's hell, modeled on Aquinas's version of classical ethics, is divided into sins of incontinence, violence, and fraud. Baraka's breakdown of Uncle Sam's world moves from alcoholics to junkies to prostitutes, all hooked by sins of incontinence or lack of willpower. This is followed by gradations of violence: the violently sullen and those who are violent to each other. Here Baraka conflates different sections of Dante's scheme. Dante includes the sullen as the last and worst group of the incontinent sinners, in the fifth circle of hell, while he locates the violent farther down in the seventh circle. The medieval poet subdivides the seventh circle into three zones: the violent against others, themselves, and God, nature, and art, as he has Vergil explain in *Inferno* 11, just before the travelers enter the circle of the violent. Baraka's first group of violent sinners is simply angry, while the second contains the violent against each other—an interesting conflation of Dante's first and second zones of the seventh circle: the violent against others and the violent against themselves. Given the nature of the play and its political message of uplift, the violent against each other are clearly blacks who harm blacks, that is, intraracial violence rather than interracial. One could interpret Baraka's conflation of these categories as a rhetorical way of suggesting that black-on-black crime is a kind of racial suicide. To do violence to one's brother, in the black sense of the term, is to do violence to oneself.

Pimps fill the next section of the hell portrayed in "Columbia" in more or less the same location where Dante places them (first pouch of the eighth circle). We have moved into the area of sins classified under the broad category of fraud, that is, sins that abuse the faculty of intellect. Uncle Toms, hypocrites if you will, fall into this section, as Baraka sees it. But worse are those apathetic blacks, the Hypnotized, who spend their days in front of the TV. Like Gil Scott-Heron who threatened middle-class Americans with his claim, "The revolution will not be televised," Baraka agitated to take the Black Revolution into the neighborhoods and living rooms of white America, but not through the safe and distant medium of TV.[40] Here Baraka's interpretation of Scott-Heron's proto-rap piece focuses on the blacks who casually assume that they can get their politics over the television if they want to be involved at all. Worse still are those Really Hypnotized individuals who have given in to material comforts including the luxury of transforming the natural style of their hair. Finally, in the pit of Baraka's hell and, therefore, analogous to Dante's Satan, are the Hypnotizers. Not some embodiment of White America exactly, these figures include, rather, a preacher who talks too much and dresses too well, eating fried chicken all the while. The hypnotized and really hypnotized sinners in the circles just above are manipulated by the hypnotizers, much as Satan controls his minions in typical ideologies of hell. Baraka's picture is of a veritable hell on earth.

This is a much more succinct rewriting of Dante's system than the expanded treatment in *The System of Dante's Hell.* My point in introducing it here is to show that even as Baraka pledges to abandon Western culture, he still turns to Dante as a guide for his moral critique of the problems between white and black culture and of how those problematic tensions are internalized in black culture itself. He can't let go of a Dantesque systematization of sin. Elizabeth Hadley Freydberg finds this same contradiction in Baraka's nationalist theater. In "The Concealed Dependence upon White Culture in Baraka's 1969 Aesthetic,"[41] she argues that Baraka's plays *Junkies Are Full of (SHHH . . .)* and *Bloodrites* are "plays which undermine the spirit out of which they were born" (29). Specifically she notes that the plays are inspired by an "implied absolute opposition to white people, which guarantees that the work *will be drawn up in terms of whites* in some fundamental way, thereby defeating or at least weakening the very purpose for which the aesthetic was designed" (28). That is, the more radical its claim to an exclusive and exclusionary black culture, the less radical the aesthetic that governs that culture can actually be if it is couched in oppositional terms.

In a much later commentary on "system," Baraka maintains the term's political and revolutionary overtones. In remarks he made as a keynote speaker at the 1999 conference of black writers held in Atlanta, he urged his audience to establish an organization for the support of writers of color.

> We revolutionaries must criticize the enemies of the people, both the slave masters and their agents (and they come in all colors, genders and nationalities). But we must not be content merely to criticize the people's enemies. We must increasingly take up our time organizing alternative institutions, organizations, structures, networks, alliances, and collectives which can move forward and develop and create ever more productive answers to the questions of, How Do We Liberate Ourselves from all Oppression and Oppressors? How Do We Do Away With All Pests? We must answer Lenin's question, "What Is to Be Done?" with answers of organization and *systems* and concrete social development. ("The Role of the Writer in Establishing a Unified Writers Organization," 15–16, my emphasis)

Once again "system" has transformed in unexpected ways. Through Sinclair's translation, Baraka's adaptation of Dante's system comes to stand for the political and economic oppression that creates the hell on earth Baraka illustrates in his work. Here the author proposes vaguely another kind of system, a socialist one, which is needed to respond to the oppressive system that had created the hell on earth in the first place. His proposal recalls several of the principles of Kawaida, especially Ujima (collective work and responsibility) and Ujamaa (cooperative economics), which he had promoted aggressively as early as the 1970s.[42] Although still conceptualized in the context of slavery and oppression, in his statement of 1999 "system" has become part of the solution rather than the problem. Ever the revolutionary, Baraka urges his peers to think systematically in response to potential oppressors, who come, he notes, in all colors. And the systematic solution is the creation of a socialist system. Baraka is vague as to specifics, but the impulse, with his reference to Lenin, is clear. What kind of a system, then, might it be?

Long before Baraka was born, before Lenin, even before Marx's *Communist Manifesto,* a powerful voice from the very tradition that I believe Baraka has sprung from and that sanctions his interest in Dante, from the same tradition that produced Cordelia Ray's Colored Dante with its abolitionist overtones, said something similar about "system." Charles Bennett Ray, the father of Cordelia whom we discussed in chapter 1, invoked the category of "system" to inspire a large gathering of men of color who received extensive tracts of free land from the abolitionist Gerrit Smith. In an address of 1846, Ray urges the men to practice certain virtues or "elements of character," first among them "system," which he describes thus: "System, in your first movements, and subsequent labors, is most important. Without system you can effect but little, with it, you can accomplish any desireable and practicable undertaking. Mutual system, thoroughly arranged, and rigidly adhered to will accomplish infinitely more than separate labour, and will bring out all the advantages, profits, pleasures, and advancement, which are beginning to dawn upon Organized Industry" (13).[43] Here, *system* has a positive economic meaning, suggesting a form of cooperative labor and management among workers of color. Ray's list of what comes from systematic organization ("advantages, profits, pleasures, and advancement") is unabashedly upwardly mobile, but the logic is not strictly capitalist. This is a glimpse of a system that hardly had the chance to develop before the Civil War broke out, before the course of events that would create the context for a Colored Dante, Negro Dante, and the Black Dante of LeRoi Jones / Amiri Baraka.

The economics of color, the struggle of class combined with that of race, becomes even more visible in the chronology of Dante's reception as we move closer to our own day. One might expect a novel entitled *The System of Dante's Hell* to make the most extensive use of the Italian poet and his poem in the tradition that I am tracking. But we have to turn to the next major example in this history of reading Dante for our fullest imitation of Dante's poetry, built around a series of more deliberate and discernible allusions to the *Inferno*: Gloria Naylor's *Linden Hills* and the African American Dante.

CHAPTER 4
AFRICAN AMERICAN DANTE

The history of your women and your family and mine has a lot of different

colors in it. . . . Because the fact that I had never read Zora Neale Hurston and

wrote The Bluest Eye *and* Sula *anyway means that the tradition really*

exists. You know, if I had read her, then you could say that I consciously was

following in the footsteps of her, but the fact that I had never read her and

still there may be whatever they're finding, similarities and dissimilarities,

whatever such critics do, makes the cheese more binding, not less, because it

means that the world as perceived by black women at certain times does exist,

however they treat it and whatever they select out of it to record, there is that.

—Toni Morrison, "A Conversation:

Gloria Naylor and Toni Morrison" (1985)

In this chapter I examine the African American Dante presented in Gloria Naylor's novel *Linden Hills* (1985). Her protagonists are two young African American artists inspired by Amiri Baraka who follow in Dante's footsteps, although they actually eschew writing, as if they were wary of its potential to enslave them. They opt instead for a new oral tradition of poetry that takes its inspiration in part from Dante's poem. Naylor's careful rewriting of Dante's *Inferno* in *Linden Hills* features her creative adaptation of his poetic meter, *terza rima,* which she appropriates as a narrative device for her novel. In an interview from 1996, Naylor expresses frustration that no one has perceived, let alone understood "what I did as far as images and the *terza rima*. No one has gotten it yet. Granted, I bobble the *terza rima* just a tiny bit toward the end of the book, but for a good seven-eighths of it, I have re-created through images what he [Dante] did through rhyme schemes" (Fowler 155). In what follows I respond to her challenge by showing precisely how she uses her knowledge of the metrical pattern that shapes Dante's poem to create the narrative design of her novel. Naylor's meticulous rewriting of the medieval model was inspired by her study of Dante in John Ciardi's translation, which she read in an undergraduate course at Brooklyn College. Additionally inspired by Toni Morrison's imitation of Dante's poetic universe in *The Bluest Eye*, Naylor's is the fullest rewriting of Dante in the history of reception examined in *Freedom Readers*. The artistic creativity of the two protagonists of *Linden Hills*, Willie and Lester, in some ways anticipates subsequent responses to Dante by a variety of poets including N. J. Loftis, Dudley Randall, Askia M. Touré, Carl Phillips, and the Eternal Kool Project's *Inferno Rap*. These voices offer different versions of an African American Dante from the 1970s into the new millennium, from work of the Black Arts movement to high literary art to hip-hop. There is no one predominant way of sampling, as it were, Dante in these various African American versions of the poet. In fact, these artists together seem to offer a wide array of adaptations that recall all the previous rewritings of the poet we have considered up to now. The African American Dante is at once liberator, integrator, and separator, recalling the ways the poet is figured in the imitations of Cordelia Ray, William Wells Brown, Spencer Williams, Richard Wright, Ralph Ellison, and Amiri Baraka.

Gloria Naylor, *Linden Hills*

Gloria Naylor's second novel, *Linden Hills*, was published in 1985 to a ready audience that had enthusiastically received her first book, *The Women of Brewster Place*. The two works deal with many of the same themes, all of which come back to the author's overriding concern with the fate of blacks in white America. Race and class intersect in the narratives of each novel.

The first book tracks the lives of eight women living on a cul-de-sac in an urban ghetto on the outskirts of an unidentified city in the northern United States, a dead-end group marginalized in every sense of the word. *Linden Hills* is set in an exclusive black suburban development just beyond the edges of that same city and its troubled neighborhoods. It presents, in the words of Henry Louis Gates, Jr., Naylor's indictment of "the moral bankruptcy of the Black nouveau riche" (*Gloria Naylor* x). Whereas her first novel looks at the social conditions that contribute to an economic underclass in ghettoized urban American, *Linden Hills* examines the lives of those blacks who have made it, some pulling themselves up from the very neighborhood of the women who live on Brewster Place. Once they have made it, they have it made. Or so they think.

Two characters, Willie Mason and Lester Tilson, spend several days just before Christmas working in the tony suburb of Linden Hills to earn extra money for the holidays. Both are young twenty-year-old poets: Willie, a kind of hip-hop versifier who keeps his poems in his head, an iconoclast going against the grain who never got past ninth grade; while Lester is more traditional in his attempt at mastering the art. Both are from the ghetto beyond the hill, the Putney Wayne Projects of the women of Brewster Place. Willie still lives there, and his brief experience of Linden Hills is such that he is determined to stay in the city. Lester's family has already made the move from that inner-city neighborhood to the suburban hills. Two poets are wandering through another realm in which one of them lives, the one named Willie, recalling Dante-pilgrim's problems with his will. This begins a series of allusions to Dante's *Inferno.*

Linden Hills is a real estate development whose entire shape alludes to the infernal topography of Dante's lower world. The development covers a hillside that slopes down and away from the city at the top, with crescent drives (circles) from top to bottom, the poshest, wealthiest, most sought-after properties near the bottom of the hill where the original owner, Luther Nedeed, built his mansion and where his descendants, the ongoing developers of the area, still live. The current Nedeed, like his forefathers, presents long-term leases to upwardly mobile African Americans. He also runs a mortuary business with a morgue located in the basement of his mansion, which is at the bottom of the hill next to the local cemetery. It being an unusually cold December, the pond to the side of the Nedeed mansion is frozen solid. As one descends the circling streets of the hill, one moves deeper and deeper into a kind of black hell with a Lucifer of sorts frozen in the lowest circle. Luther Nedeed is as determined as members of the previous four generations of Nedeeds to make money, even if it means killing, literally and figuratively, those around him, including his own family. He is the real estate developer from hell, if you will, and Naylor plays this for all it's worth.

Naylor first read Dante in a "Great Works of Literature" course as a sophomore at Brooklyn College in 1977, when she enrolled in college after spending seven years on the streets of New York and in parts of the South as a Jehovah's Witness. That same year she also read her first novel by an African American woman, Toni Morrison's *The Bluest Eye*.[1] Its impact on her was immense, as she recounts in an interview with Morrison from 1985, just as *Linden Hills* was published. Below I shall consider Morrison's rewriting of Dante and propose how it might have influenced Naylor. In 1983, Naylor earned a master's degree in Afro-American Studies at Yale University, where she submitted a draft of what would become *Linden Hills* as her master's thesis. Since graduating from Yale, Naylor has held several teaching positions as a visiting professor but her energies have gone into writing. Five novels have come out over the last two decades, with *Linden Hills* the second volume of a loosely compiled quartet.[2]

Of all the artists of color under consideration in this study, Gloria Naylor is the most educated and she is the writer most steeped in the tradition of black literary culture. She encountered Dante first in a class with a university professor, who in turn would have learned about the Italian poet in school, and so on going back in time to those teachers and scholars of the nineteenth century who inaugurated the study of Dante in the United States. Her education puts her in a line that reaches back to those very first students of Dante in America who clustered around Longfellow at Harvard. Some early reviewers of *Linden Hills* were critical of what they saw as the empty and showy erudition behind Naylor's adaptation of the *Inferno*, implying that her education prevented her from seeing the dire situation of poor minorities in the United States in the mid-1980s.[3] But in truth Naylor's education did not cause her to forget the community she came from with its real-life Willie Masons, a community, we have seen, that also has a purchase on Dante. In the case of Naylor, and to a lesser extent Amiri Baraka, we have an example of someone who learned Dante in school, but whose experiences out of the academy put her in touch with that other version of Dante that has its origins in the abolitionists' practical reading and application of the medieval poet and politician. Her imitation of Dante bespeaks a familiar dichotomy of highbrow and lowbrow culture, of establishmentarian and radical responses to Dante, of aesthetic and political readings of the poet.

These two trajectories in Dante's reception come together throughout Naylor's novel. We glimpse them both in the only allusion to the actual text of Dante's poem in *Linden Hills,* easily recognizable to readers familiar with the original source. As the two main characters in the narrative stroll past their junior high school—Lester went on to senior high school, but Willie dropped out after ninth grade—which is situated at the end of the road that leads from the city to Linden Hills, the following scene develops.

They walked along the front of the school and passed the main entrance. There were three bronze plaques over the triple doors.

I am the way out of the city of woe
I am the way to a prosperous people
I am the way from eternal sorrow

Chico and the Raiders had spray-painted their insignia over the middle plaque:

Sacred justice moved my architect
I was raised here by divine omnipotence
Primordial love and ultimate intellect

"You know, Shit," Willie said, looking up at the last bronze plaque—

Only the elements time cannot wear
Were made before me, and beyond time I stand
Abandon ignorance, ye who enter here

—then down toward Linden Hills, "I could have done all right if I had gone to school."

"You're doing all right now."

"Naw, I mean I could have been a doctor or something. You know I have six hundred and sixty-five poems memorized up here—six hundred and sixty-five, and lots of 'em ain't mine. I have all of Baraka, Soyinka, Hughes, and most of Coleridge. And Whitman—that was one together dude. My mom says with a memory like that, I could have breezed through med school." (44–45)

The allusion to the inscription over the gate of hell is taken and recast from *Inferno* 3.1–9, where Dante and Vergil begin their descent into hell. A memorable and technical tour de force in the original where the gate seems to speak in the first person to the reader, allusive rewritings of Dante's poem often feature versions of the passage. The same passage marks the opening of the Dantesque imitation in Spencer Williams's film, *Go Down, Death!* Naylor's adaptation deserves our thorough analysis.

The text Naylor cites is taken from John Ciardi's popular version, completed in 1954 and reprinted frequently thereafter, a staple translation used in Great Books courses in the 1960s and 1970s. Ciardi's translation cornered the textbook market in the way that Sinclair's translation had in the 1950s when Amiri Baraka attended college.[4] Naylor makes several crucial changes to Ciardi's translation to shift the meaning of the inscription from that of entering hell to that of escaping an inferno of economic and social disadvantage. In the first line (on the first plaque) "into" the city of woe becomes "out of"; in the next line, "forsaken" is changed to "prosperous" people; the final line of the tercet changes "into" to "from." There is no direct change to the second tercet. In the third, "those" becomes "the" elements. Then the most telling alteration of all in the last line of the passage: Dante's famous verse, perhaps the best known in the entire *Divine Comedy*, "Abandon *all hope,* ye who enter here," becomes "Abandon *ignorance,* ye who enter here." The message is clear: education is the way out of the desperate life in the ghetto. More ambiguous is the suggestion that passing through the doors gives the student the means to move up to a better social class, from a "forsaken" people, Dante's hopeless sinners, to a "prosperous" people, the *nouveau riche* of the Linden Hills development. That new prosperity, we shall see, comes at a high cost.

Naylor's depiction of the gate of hell features different kinds of writing, each an intriguing example of written culture that has special meaning to her cultural moment in the 1980s. The bronze plaques over each door are set off in her text as indented quotations with a single Dantesque tercet marking each plaque. She makes no attempt to distinguish the font of the stamped lettering of the plaques with an altered typography as some versions and translations do, other than to forgo punctuation at the end of each verse. Nor does she try to recreate visually or linguistically the other type of writing mentioned in the passage: the middle plaque is covered with graffiti in spray paint left by a local gang. We're not told what the insignia of Chico and the Raiders looks like, but it's easy to imagine thick black swirling lines covering the plaque, without, however, obscuring it completely from view. That the actual design goes unremarked is an indication of the extent to which graffiti is an accepted and normal form of expression in the world of the protagonists. In the 1970s and 1980s, hip-hop culture was defining itself as a movement that emphasized graffiti, rapping, break dancing, and DJ work. Willie, and to a lesser extent Lester, are a part of that world. The juxtaposition of stamped lettering in bronze and graffiti in spray paint is a visual recreation of standard and vernacular modes of expression, regular speech and a form of dialect, as it were. Both modes of expression are treated equally in the passage: the narrator reads the first plaque and then observes the graffiti that covers the second plaque without adding any disparaging remarks about the gang's signature tag, and then moves on to read the third. In fact, Naylor's own authorial intervention on the texts of the first and third plaques parallels Chico's defacement of the second plaque.[5] That is, the author does to Dante what Chico does to the plaque.

More than merely juxtaposing modes of expression, the image of the bronze plaque covered with graffiti brings two cultures together, one European, learned, and monumental, but in danger of falling out of touch and out of date; the other African American, less tutored and angry, knowledgeable about the world in a different way, agitating to eclipse the primary culture. As we have seen in the various readings that compose this book, the rewriting of Dante by authors of color over the last two centuries is an exercise that inevitably juxtaposes European and American cultural values in productive ways. Naylor herself is equally a part of both traditions that come together in her imitation.[6] In fact, the author is engaged in a literary project that is analogous to what she portrays on the front of the school. Her work clearly exemplifies the Anglo-American tradition of the novel and by extension, as at least one critic has observed, the tradition of classical epic. The development of character, plot, voice, and narrative in *Linden Hills* is recognizable to readers schooled in the genre of the novel. At the same time Naylor adapts that European literary form to do justice to the African American material that she wants to transform into a literary work that will appeal to as wide an audience as possible. Other rhetorical traditions surface throughout the narrative of *Linden Hills*, several of which are integral parts of the African American experience. The preaching of the African American church and the speeches of Malcolm X, for example, help to define the literariness of Naylor's writing, as does the more confidential rhetoric of women's diaries, recipe books, and letters.[7]

Naylor maintains the balance between the high culture of the novel and the low culture of these other literary forms through her imitation of Dante. To be sure, it is Dante's text over the doors of the school that advertises the way out of the ghetto and thus positions itself to be perceived as the vehicle of high culture. But we've seen that Naylor has no qualms about visiting her own changes upon that text. Her Dante does not belong to a monolithic realm of unchangeable culture—medieval, Catholic, sempiternal. Rather, her African American Dante is descended from that figure to which writers of color have had recourse from the second half of the nineteenth century on as a kind of compromise between European cultural traditions, political and literary, and cultural traditions that are part of the African American experience. Like the bronze plaques above the school's entrance, the text of Dante functions as a kind of medium or mediating text through which authors negotiate the differences between European and African American culture. I said above that this juxtaposition is productive, by which I mean, following Amilcare Iannucci, that the "producerly" qualities of the *Divine Comedy* enable it to generate a variety of artistic responses, which can be poetic, cinematic, and in this particular case happens to be an ekphrastic description in prose of a work of art (7).

At other moments in the narrative of *Linden Hills,* Naylor also appeals briefly to two additional canonical authors, Milton and Shakespeare, in her search for extra literary compromises to bridge the various cultures in which she participates. Near the end of the novel, Willie responds to the enormity of what he has witnessed in Linden Hills by thinking to himself: "It would take an epic to deal with something like What has this whole week meant? He'd leave that to guys like Milton" (275). But Naylor, of course, has dealt with what the week has meant in the novel, cleverly putting herself at least briefly on a par with Milton, if not above him. Willie proposes Milton as a solution; Naylor uses Dante as her main source and solution with this brief aside to Milton. Shortly after this passage, in the final conversation between Willie and Lester, before, as it were, all hell breaks loose, Lester reflects on the possibility of a black Shakespeare, and Willie nominates himself with some qualifications:

> "And yet people wonder why black folks ain't produced a Shakespeare."
> "Well, I don't have any hopes of being that. But I think I can come pretty close. . . . do you remember us meeting any poets down here? You'd think of all the places in the world, this neighborhood had a chance of giving us at least one black Shakespeare." (282–83)

It may be that the respective receptions of Milton and Shakespeare can be configured in ways similar to Dante's over the course of African American cultural history. Milton's importance to Puritan culture had some impact on slaves and their owners, according to Carolivia Herron. And Shakespeare's own interest in the figure of the "other," as evidenced by the creation of a character like Othello, has given him currency with writers in the African American tradition (whether Colored, Negro, Black, or African American). Naylor herself rewrites *The Tempest* in *Mama Day,* and as Virginia Fowler has pointed out, she revises the conventional African American male appropriation of that Shakespearean play in interesting ways (92–93). *That* notwithstanding, Naylor clearly favors Dante as a model in *Linden Hills,* to the disapproval of several critics who berate her for depending on the Italian poet (Gomez, Erickson, Watkins), with one in particular taking her to task for not working harder "to utilize the endless and rich African mythology" at her disposal (Gomez 8).

Naylor is a part of two cultures—European and African American— and so is her main protagonist, Willie. When we move from the first plaque to the third, there is a shift in perspective from that of an omnipotent narrator who first directs the reader's viewing of the sequence of plaques, to Willie's point of view as he looks up and reads the third plaque as he and Lester pass by. The shift in perspective puts the focus on Willie as a reader, allowing Naylor then to turn the narrative's attention to him as a reader, autodidact, poet, and canon builder. Willie has his own list of canonical writers he studies, memorizes, and presumably performs: Baraka, Soyinka, Hughes, Coleridge, and Whitman. It is a canon characterized by remarkable variety despite its size.[8] First on the list is Baraka (he is not called Jones although he wrote most of his poetry under that name), the revolutionary black poet. The Nigerian writer Wole Soyinka, an author whose work is an example of postcolonial, global English literature, follows. One assumes that the next poet in line is Langston Hughes, the premier African American man of letters, a poet who was interested in the performance of his poetry, some of which he recorded to the jazz of Charlie Mingus and others. But the reference to Hughes is ambiguous. It's not inconceivable that it could be the modern English author Ted Hughes, named poet laureate of the United Kingdom in 1984, the year before *Linden Hills* was published. Ted Hughes, who died in 1998, was an iconoclastic poet whose deceptively simple poems on Crow and other allegorical beasts call to mind the African American oral tradition of Brer Rabbit and friends. Rounding out the list are the Romantic English poet-critic Samuel Coleridge and the major American poet of the nineteenth century, arguably the greatest American poet of all, Walt Whitman. Willie's canon, which brings together African American, African, English, and American cultures, is a venerable list to which Willie would add himself.

The Dantesque model encourages Naylor to have her protagonist entertain such fantasies. Once Dante and Vergil pass through the gate of hell they come to limbo and the noble castle of the virtuous pagans, or the virtuous heathen, as Sinclair's translation calls them, which Amiri Baraka follows. There Dante meets Vergil's companions, including four other writers—Homer, Horace, Ovid, and Lucan—who make him part of their company:

> And they honored me far beyond courtesy,
> for they included me in their own number,
> making me sixth in that high company.
> (*Inf.* 4.100–102)

And the group of six poets engages in an intense literary conversation, one assumes:

> So we moved toward the light, and as we passed
> we spoke of things as well omitted here
> as it was sweet to touch on there . . .
> (4.103–5)

Willie dreams of becoming the sixth poet in the group he has listed and then, as if he were encountering his canonical five in his daydreams, he drifts away while Lester continues to speak to him: "'Huh?' Willie had been lost in thought" (45). He may have been thinking of the same sort of unstated things Dante the pilgrim discusses with his canonical five in *Inferno* 4.

Willie shuns a formal education and remains in the ghetto where he chooses to perfect his oral poetry, inspired, as he says, first and foremost by Amiri Baraka. Naylor's character, although created some twenty years after *The System of Dante's Hell,* would fit right into the world of Baraka's novel, not among the many hypocrites who come, Baraka repeatedly observes, in lesser shades of black (brown, yellow, white), but among the authentic blacks whom Baraka's protagonist Roi hopes to emulate. Willie, it turns out, has much in common with Roi and Baraka, the man LeRoi Jones would become.

A brief digression on a work by Baraka not considered in the previous chapter confirms this connection with Naylor's narrative. Two years after *The System of Dante's Hell,* in 1967 Baraka published a collection of short stories with Grove Press, *Tales,* which opens with a story called "A Chase (Alighieri's Dream)." The piece, only four pages long, reads very much like the poetic description of a dream. The narrative focuses on a journey taken by the protagonist, who remains unnamed (it is easy, however, to picture Roi from *System* in the leading role), through the back streets of underclass neighborhoods in Newark. John O'Brien describes it in this way: "Rather than a short story in any traditional sense, it is more a verbal montage or prose poem in which one is bombarded by a series of rapid images of ghetto sounds, sights, and smells as they are filtered through the sensitive consciousness of a young black running through the streets of Newark" (89). As Baraka recounts in *The Autobiography of LeRoi Jones,* his family lived on the edge of the inner-city slums in a mixed neighborhood, part black, part white, with many Italians in the ethnic mix. At various points in both his autobiography and his novel, Baraka describes heading out to explore other parts of town, including the slums, in descriptive prose similar to the writing of "A Chase." While Baraka's family was not as well-off as the inhabitants of Naylor's Linden Hills, his parents had earned enough to move into a lower-middle-class neighborhood and to send their son to parochial schools and then on to Howard University. They were up and coming, a relatively prosperous family, compared with many of the people Baraka knew and observed in the neighborhoods of Newark. Hence the fear the protagonist experiences in "A Chase," as if he were being pursued through a dreamy Dantesque landscape, running from bad areas of the city back to his safer enclave. As the young protagonist moves across the landscape of the inner city, it opens up to reveal glimpses of the damned: "sprawled niggers dying without matches . . . enemies, strangers, fags . . . Black dead faces slowly ground to dust" (3). Baraka suggests here as he does in *System* that he is a young version of Dante and that he is moving through a version of hell. It is his inner city seen through the eyes of a young Dante, a Black Dante. And it could be Willie's world too, the world of Brewster Place from which he sees Linden Hills off in the distance and from which he sets out to visit the other worldly neighborhood.

As Willie and Lester make their way from one realm to the next, they pass by the doors of the junior high school. Lester wonders why schools need to be fenced off and separated from society by gates and chains. He answers his own question: "To get you used to the idea that what they have in there is different, special. Something to be separated from the rest of the world" (45). The exclusivity of education in an institutional setting convinces the learner that he or she is special too. Lester continues: "Then when you move to Linden Hills, or wherever, you're gonna stay put and help vote out radicals and heave a sigh of relief when you read that a Panther got it in the back from an L.A. cop" (45–46). Education enables upward mobility. Specifically, it may serve as a passport out of the tough life of the ghetto. But Lester is wary of the downside of that social movement, for African Americans who relocate to a supposedly better life in a subdivision outside the city run the risk of losing their ethnic identity. They run the risk of turning their backs on the politically engaged brother—if he is identified as a panther, of course, it is not an allegorical beast of the sort Dante encounters in *Inferno* 1—who stays at home in his original neighborhood to fight for a better life.

Even Lester's own family has fallen prey to this spiritual dislocation that accompanies relocation to the suburbs. Lester describes for Willie how his mother and sister are becoming more comfortable in their house on First Crescent Drive. They are eager to enter the world of suburban socializing marked by the upward mobility of others in Linden Hills: the Baptist who has become an Episcopalian; the professional who commits suicide when her career goes awry; the historian who ignores corruption in his quest for the Nobel Prize. Wayne Junior High School with its telling inscription over the doors has prepared the locals for a world in which worth is gauged in terms of material claims to real estate. But upward mobility in Linden Hills means, paradoxically, moving farther down the hill and moving closer to the mansion of the demonic Luther Nedeed. With Lester as his guide, Willie sets out to descend to the depths of this suburban hell. Now we need to follow him on his Dantesque journey.

Though Baraka's use of Dante in his *System of Dante's Hell* has drawn little analysis, critics have devoted significant attention to the Dantesque imagery and allusions in Naylor's rewriting of the *Inferno,* from Catherine Ward's article that came out soon after the publication of *Linden Hills,* to Nick Havely's more recent piece, with the result that there is no need to document the specific allusions to Dante in detail here.[9] I want, rather, to explore how Naylor uses her response to Dante as a means for engaging the discourse of race and how that discourse overlaps with her engagement with the European literary canon.

Once Willie and Lester pass by the school and enter into the world of Linden Hills, they begin their descent into hell: "They walked on in silence and finally reached the marble banister that separated the First Crescent Drive from Wayne J. H. S." (46). As they work their way down the hill over the next week, they encounter numerous inhabitants of the real estate development who are modeled, some more deliberately than others, on characters from Dante's *Inferno*. Naylor indulges the reader who knows the Italian poem by alluding to one's favorite chestnuts. Lester is Willie's Vergil, and as his Vergilian guide, he plays a formative role in shaping Willie's ideas about society. Both poets in turn take inspiration from Ruth Anderson, who now lives near Willie in the slums but who once lived deep in Linden Hills. She functions as a kind of Beatrice, who always lingers in the background of the narrative, a vague object of Willie's love and a direct focus of Lester's desire. It is Ruth who suggests to them that they have something to gain from Linden Hills. Willie juxtaposes her suggestion with another thought that establishes her status as Beatrice: "He was just sorry that she hadn't asked him to go into hell for her so he could really prove himself" (41). So they set out at her prodding in search of small jobs and a little spending money, but they find instead one tragedy after another that underscores the fragility of ethnic identity in the fabricated setting of Linden Hills.

Naylor uses the first episode of Willie and Lester at work to explore black masculinity, revealing that in Linden Hills class trumps everything: love, sexuality, even ethnicity. The goal of those who live there is to appear to be as wealthy as possible at all costs. In the poets' first job they help a caterer organize a lavish wedding reception on Second Crescent Drive. At their reception the newlyweds, Mr. and Mrs. Winston Alcott, are informed that they have been approved for a prestigious residence deeper down in the development; in other words, they have passed the curious, downwardly mobile grade of the place. Luther Nedeed himself is there to make the announcement that their mortgage for the new property has been approved. Willie and Lester deduce that the wedding has been arranged for the betterment of the groom's career and that by marrying he is leaving behind his true lover, a man, David. The conservative morality of Linden Hills dictated by the Nedeed family would never allow a gay couple to achieve the level of wealth to which Winston aspires, hence his

apparent decision to disavow his love for David. The estranged gay partners are the Paolo and Francesca of the novel, much like the pair in Dante's
second circle of the lustful, whose frustrated and illicit relationship leads
them to eternal unhappiness. The analogous location in the novel—Second Crescent equals second circle—marks an obvious link to Dante's
text, as does the pairing of the sets of two unhappy lovers. Moreover, in
the original source Dante uses three bird similes to describe the way the
sinners move in the second circle, one of starlings giving way to one of
cranes (*Inf.* 5.40–49), culminating in an image of doves (*Inf.* 5.82–87).
Naylor recreates this rhetorical signal with three similes of her own to describe the behavior of the socialites on Second Crescent Drive. The over-
dressed women at the reception, the social group to which the newlyweds belong, are "like glittering birds of paradise" (82); Willie comments
on the group as a whole, "They might look like birds of paradise, but they
sure ate like vultures" (84). Another character in this drama of betrayal
and tragedy is said to have "a face the shape and color of a brown egg" (84).
Finally, the act of reading plays a prominent role in revealing the lovers
in each respective couple. Paolo and Francesca are led to commit adultery when they read about the affair of Lancelot and Guinevere in the Ar-
thurian romance *Lancelot of the Lake* (*Inf.* 5.128–42). The nature of David's
attachment to Winston is revealed to Willie when David discreetly reads
from one of Whitman's erotic poems of homosexual love at the reception after Winston's wedding.[10] Willie knows the poem by heart and can
fill in the blanks, which he does as he unravels the relationship between
the two men for Lester. Although he claims not to understand this sort of
erotic attraction—despite the very close attraction he sometimes feels
for Lester—he realizes that something special has happened between the
two men (88–90). Only Willie's special knowledge of Whitman's poem
outs the lovers in the narrative. But in contrast to the gay men and the
couple in Dante's *Inferno,* Willie is not swayed by what he reads: "It gave
him a queasy feeling in the pit of his stomach to think that one man could
feel about another as he felt about Ruth" (89). Naylor will have the reader
know that Willie's own sexuality, his hip-hop masculinity, remains steady.

Like the pilgrim, Willie learns about life as he travels onward through
a realm of spiritual death. Winston Alcott's sin, interestingly, is never identified as the sin of homosexual love—far from it. His precise sin remains

unspecified, but the parallel with Paolo and Francesca from *Inferno* 5 suggests that the punishment for it ultimately is an unrequited love that doesn't allow for any peace. Winston forgoes a true love, for a false, hypocritical heterosexual relationship. And Luther Nedeed is responsible for putting everyone in his or her place. In the imitation he is analogous to Paolo's older brother and Francesca's husband, Giovanni Malatesta, who catches the lovers in the act of adultery and murders them. Francesca tells the pilgrim that Giovanni consequently is destined for a place at the bottom of hell. And indeed the reader's expectations of seeing Luther deeper below won't be frustrated. Willie, who looks on at the estranged couple and puts together the pieces of their broken life, is obviously analogous to Dante the pilgrim. But his role as the interpreter of Whitman's poem for the reader and for Lester makes him a kind of textual go-between, or, as Dante's text has it, a "Galeotto," a pimp, a literary enabler (*Inf.* 5.137). Ciardi translates the telling phrase thus: "that book, and he who wrote it, was a pander" (l. 134 in his version). Ciardi explains in his note, "'Galeotto,' the Italian word for 'pander,' is also the Italian rendering of the name of Gallehault, who in the French Romance Dante refers to here, urged Lancelot and Guinevere on to love" (64). Willie's hermeneutical and performance skills put him in the crucial position of animating the text and interpreting the scene. The hip-hop poet via Whitman gives Dante new life.

As they move deeper into the neighborhood, Willie and Lester encounter a kind of female Ulysses–Pier della Vigna in the character of Laurel Dumont whose drive for success leads her to commit suicide. Deeper still, they spend time with Dr. Braithwaite, the local historian of Linden Hills, who combines the role of Brunetto Latini, an older man who befriends the young poets and whose intentions they look upon with suspicion, and one of Dante's fraudulent hypocrites.

Naylor's imitation of Dante culminates with a tragedy at the end of the narrative which rewrites the episode of Ugolino and his children from *Inferno* 32–33, the longest story in the *Inferno*. Dante took a familiar contemporary event and altered it to suit the needs of his narrative, which required as grim a tragedy as possible for the deepest pit of hell. Accordingly, the poet rewrote the story of Ugolino to focus on the problem of innocent suffering. The political intrigues of the Pisan Count Ugolino were well known to Dante and his Tuscan contemporaries since Pisa was in an ongoing struggle with Florence, Genoa, and other neighboring city-states during the thirteenth and fourteenth centuries. In the world of Pisan politics Ugolino switched allegiances too easily, moving from the Ghibelline party, which sided with the Holy Roman emperor, to the Guelf party of the pope, and then back to his first alliance, flip-flops that earned him the enmity of many powerful Pisans. In 1289 the archbishop of Pisa had him locked up in a tower with four of his family members, two sons and two grandsons. After negotiations broke down, Ugolino and his four relatives were starved to death. Dante turns this historical event into a dramatic tragedy, reducing the ages of the characters to portray Ugolino as a father with four young sons. The poet's version leads the reader to question whether Ugolino cannibalizes the bodies of his children after they have died. Some readings of the episode have argued further that Ugolino fails to see the Christ-like nature of the sacrifice his children make for him once they realize the desperation of their situation.[11]

The Ugolino episode is the story through which English and American readers of Dante were most likely to encounter the poet in the eighteenth century as Dante was beginning to be known in translation. During the 1700s numerous versions of the Ugolino narrative were excerpted and completed, in poetry and prose, before complete translations of the poem were in circulation: Richardson (1719); Gray (1737); Joseph Warton (1756); the earl of Carlisle (1772); Thomas Warton (1781); Rogers (1782); Boyd (1785); and Jennings (1794). Readers were captivated by the gothic horror portrayed in the story's suggestion of cannibalism, and they were attracted to its portrayal of the tragic fall of a powerful political figure.[12] The first easel picture of a subject from Dante is Joshua Reynolds's "Count Hugolino and His Children in the Dungeon," exhibited at the Royal Academy in 1773. The earliest translation from the *Divine Comedy* completed in the United States is William Dunlap's version of the Ugolino episode, published in the *New York Magazine* in 1791. In the next century Rodin is said to have taken inspiration from Ugolino for his impressive statue *The Thinker*. Naylor's imitation falls into this tradition of depictions and rewritings of Ugolino.

The final job Willie and Lester must accomplish during the week's work in Linden Hills is to help none other than Luther Nedeed decorate his family's Christmas tree with candles and old-fashioned ornaments.

The assignment sounds simple enough, and they arrive as requested early on Christmas Eve. But they have already witnessed more than their share of tragedy over the previous days and have come to realize that Nedeed is the source, symbolic if not actual (they're still not sure), of the evil that they have encountered throughout his subdivision. They go to Nedeed's house reluctantly, but the money is good (he has offered to double whatever they have earned over the week), and they feel a sense of moral obligation to keep their promise to him. As Willie and Lester finish helping Luther decorate his tree, his wife emerges from the basement morgue of his house where Luther had locked her away because their son had not been born black enough. Having grown progressively more insane as her child starved to death in the makeshift basement dungeon, she emerges, demented, carrying the body of their young son wrapped in a funereal shroud made of a lace bridal veil. If Luther is shocked to see her, his two helpers are even more surprised. He sends them out quickly into the cold December night.

Thus culminates a second plot that runs parallel to the story of Willie and Lester. Luther's wife has been locked in the basement for an indefinite period, and throughout the novel the narrative shifts to her perspective. We learn only as she emerges that her name is Willa, suggesting a deliberate parallel between her character and that of Willie. We have learned over the course of the novel that she too is on a journey of sorts, as she travels back in time while locked away in the basement, by reading the notes jotted down in the Bible that belonged to the Mrs. Nedeed of the earliest generation, Luwana, and the cookbooks of the second Mrs. Nedeed, Evelyn, and the photograph albums of the third, Priscilla. She comes to understand that she is in a long line of mistreated Nedeed women, who have been abused to the point of losing their identities and lives. She also realizes that her child, whom she has named Sinclair and not Luther Nedeed V, is born "white" due to genes handed down in the Nedeed family, not through any fault of her own.

Once Willie and Lester are outside the Nedeed mansion, the tragedy comes to its dramatic conclusion as the child's funereal wrapping catches on fire and sends the entire house up in flames. Just before they realize the house is burning, as the final scene between Luther and his wife is unfolding, the two poets reflect on what they've witnessed.

What were the guidelines with which to judge what they had left behind that door? They stood there frozen in a space of time without a for-
mula that lost innocence or future wisdom could have given them. There
would have been no question of smashing in that door if their worlds
were still governed by the rules of cowboys and Indians, knights and
dragons—black and white. But their twenty years immobilized them in
a place where they were much more than boys, but a long way from
being men. (299)

They are poised between two realms like Dante-pilgrim when he confronts the ultimate evil in Satan at *Inferno* 34.25–27:

I did not die, and yet I lost life's breath:
imagine for yourself what I became,
deprived at once of both my life and death.

Like the pilgrim frozen between two worlds and two realms of existence,
Willie and Lester are immobilized in an ambiguous state, being neither
one thing nor another. They are caught between the status of boys and
men, but more ominously poised between good and evil as symbolized by
the outside and the inside of the Nedeed mansion. Moreover, they are in a
world no longer characterized by easy struggles between good guys and
bad guys. Their world is no longer simply, as Naylor puts it, black and
white. There is, therefore, nothing or little they can do about their predicament. Luther Nedeed and his wife die as the family mansion burns down
around them. And Willie and Lester realize that the inhabitants of Linden
Hills witness the tragedy but refuse to help or even call the fire department. Not until Willie breaks the living room picture window of a neighboring house do the police come; the firemen come even later. "They let it
burn," Willie keeps repeating as the narrative moves to its conclusion.
    The Nedeed family's isolationist dream of a utopian African Ameri-
can community implodes paradoxically as the material wealth all around
makes it look as if the dream has become a success. Naylor implies that
the mythic dream of racial purity is the spark that ignites the flame. She
has taken to heart the message of James Baldwin in his essay, "Stranger in
the Village," where he writes prophetically, "The time has come to realize

that the interracial drama acted out on the American continent has not only created a new black man, it has created a new white man, too. . . . The world is white no longer, and it will never be white again" (129). The impact of this new mixed reality creates the sociopolitical and economic changes that produce a Linden Hills. It accounts for the relentless obsession with race in Naylor's novel, as Nedeed and others ask repeatedly: Am I black enough or not? And this new mixed reality also accounts for the obsession with class and its intersection with race in the novel: Do I want to be rich if it means I have to act white? The Nedeed family has proposed that one can be black and rich, and yet Willie wonders about the cost of that plan. He has seen too many who have sold their souls to enter into the Nedeed suburban development, who have lost their sense of identity in their blind quest for a piece of the deceptive dream. Willie's brief encounter with them has given him a renewed sense of purpose. He decides that he does not have to keep up with the Joneses of Linden Hills and their deadly desire for material things. He suggests, rather, that he will continue in the role of griot for his community of Putney Wayne with his canon of black and white authors, inspired, as he says, by the poetry of Baraka-Jones, among others. Willie, like the pilgrim after whom he is modeled, learns from previous poets to steer clear of the sins of the present. But what sort of a person and poet he will become, and where he is headed under a full moon at the end of the novel is still not certain: "Then, they walked out of Tupelo Drive and into the last days of the year."

Multicolored, Multicultural *Terza Rima*

In an interview in 1993, Gloria Naylor referred to *Linden Hills* as her "masterwork" and indicated that critics hadn't yet understood much of what she did in the novel. Naylor was asked,

> *Do you believe that readers get from your work what you hope they will?*
>
> Well, what surprised me with *Linden Hills* is that no one quite got it. I don't think most people did. But then again, I haven't been analyzed that much. But as far as I'm concerned, that was my masterwork.

Linden Hills?

Yes. It really was. And I'm really waiting for people to go to *The Inferno* and go to my work and see what I did as far as images and the terza rima. No one has gotten it yet. Granted, I bobble the terza rima just a tiny bit toward the end of the book, but for a good seven-eighths of it, I have re-created through images what he did through rhyme schemes. And no one has seen it. And the colors, and how I play with colors, no one has gotten it yet. . . . I think that maybe in time—if I'm still around—in time someone will figure out what happened with that book and Dante's *Inferno*. Besides what's really obvious. In general, people have never gotten it, as far as what I do with colors. (155–56)[13]

To those critics who responded negatively to *Linden Hills,*[14] Naylor suggests that they have not fully understood her creative project, let alone the depth of her imitation of Dante. There are the obvious points of contact between the world she creates and the literary world of Dante's *Inferno,* such as the rewriting of the inscription over the gate of hell and the various parallels between her characters and those in Dante's *Inferno.* But in the interview she reveals that there is a much more profound dimension to her imitation of Dante, which depends on her adaptation of the rhyme scheme in the *Divine Comedy,* the *terza rima.*

Dante is credited with inventing a unique rhyme scheme, deriving it in part from other medieval poetic forms.[15] The innovative metrical pattern consists of tercets or three-line stanzas of verse, *terzine* in Italian. The standard verse is a hendecasyllabic line of eleven syllables, with exceptions allowed in the number of syllables when necessary and for the sake of variety. In each tercet the first and third lines rhyme, while the second line anticipates the rhyme of the first and third lines of the subsequent stanza, thus creating an ongoing, interlocking pattern of triplicate rhymes: ABA BCB CDC DED, and so on. The open-ended pattern could continue indefinitely, but the typical canto, another of Dante's formal poetic innovations, runs about forty to fifty tercets, or between 120 and 150 lines. Like much else in Dante's poem where form fits neatly with content, the triple rhyme scheme is a reflection of the Trinitarian underpinning of Dante's medieval universe. When the reader ascertains that the only word that rhymes with itself in the *Divine Comedy* is "Christ," it becomes apparent that each tercet is a poetic microcosm that reflects the macrocosmic reality of both the tripartite deity and its mystical unity as single godhead. Three-in-one is a principle that underlies both the design of the universe and the most basic unit in Dante's poetics.

Naylor claims to have recreated Dante's triple rhyme scheme through images and patterns of colors. Her remarks are worded in such a way as to suggest that she conflates images with colors, while her concluding comments in the interview cited above make it sound as if she is really more focused on the latter. Why such attention to the theme of color? Since "color" structures and determines the life of a person of color in Naylor's United States, why not make the general idea and theme of color one of the principal structural elements of her narrative, giving it a role analogous to that of the Trinitarian theology underlying the *terza rima* in Dante's poetics? In the brief exchange between Willie and the Reverend Hollis, Naylor demonstrates that she understands Trinitarian theology in general (168–70). I assume that she is aware of its fundamental role in Dante's poetics as well. Whereas for Dante the Trinity informs his art, for Naylor, the overriding artistic shape of her novel derives from color.[16]

Color is everywhere in *Linden Hills.* Each chapter contains dozens of references to the colors of objects, for example: dull brown shadow, smoky caramel skin, pale green kitchen, brown suede coat, pink silk ties, black limo, gray church, white satin, silver car, blue and white bathroom, pale blue silk, white tea roses, red gold ring, red fingernails, yellowing leaves, purple drapery, blue eyes, lilac-colored ink, maroon loafers, purple leaf sage, blue and orange sparks, red embers, and white clapboard house. At first these references appear to be casual but the sheer quantity of them begins to suggest otherwise. Moreover, there are other sorts of references to color that draw attention to themselves. There is nothing unusual about red mud in Georgia (216), or a red traffic light that turns green (173), or a woman at a wedding in a pink satin suit (83). But to speak of the white hot links in someone's brain (94), or insanity as a blue bubble (246), or the amber color of truth (280), raises questions about the discourse of color in Naylor's narrative. Why is truth, for example, an amber germ (289)? Why is the author so intent on depicting the world through which her characters move in terms of color?

Other statements, too, raise questions about the role of color in the novel. Naylor writes of the Nedeed family patriarch, the first Luther: "It was said that his protruding eyes could change color at will, and over the course of his life, they would be assigned every color except red" (3). Early in the novel, the reader is inclined to view this sort of sentence as merely descriptive, but over the course of one's reading it becomes clear that such statements function to keep the reader's attention focused on the issue of color. A similar moment unfolds as Lester and Willie help Chester Parker redo his deceased wife's bedroom, while they take bets on the color of the furniture underneath its protective sheets.

> ". . . two to one it's psychedelic pink with vinyl cushions 'cause she's [Parker's new wife] probably under thirty."
> "Naw, that wouldn't be his style of under thirty. It's brass with purple velvet cushions."
> "Okay, you're on."
> He yanked the dustcover off the bedroom furniture, and the vanity set they were betting on was chrome with a white leather seat. (129)

Here Naylor makes explicit the allegorical meaning of her exploration of color: Chester Parker's furniture is white underneath like the man himself. Another example of allegorizing color in this way occurs in the last chapter where Willie has finished wrapping presents for his family and friends: "Every scrap of ribbon and colored paper had been slowly folded and put away" (271). Willie is the character in the novel who copes with the challenges and difficulties of color most directly and ultimately most successfully, to the point that he can control it, use it, and put it away when necessary.

In addition to allegory, Naylor plays with the vocabulary of color. She takes pleasure in words or turns of phrases that refer to colors, whether or not they actually signify a specific hue. For example, she mentions the musical blues (11), whitewashing the wood (11), red-lining a residential district to keep it segregated (138), wintergreen gum (169), redwood fences (194), turnip greens (219), California oranges (226), goldfish (253), and blueprints (276, 289). These rhetorical colors are markers that testify to the author's strategy of enhancing the text with references to color.

All these colors, real and rhetorical, meld into achromatic black and white to focus the reader's attention on the discourse of color as applied to race in Naylor's America. The novel's opening paragraph mentions blacks and whites, and the first chapter continues with references to white farmers, black communities, the white god, true black power, and whiteness, among many other comments on race and color. The Nedeed family uses gold and silver (i.e., money) to give value to its blackness, to make Linden Hills "a beautiful, black wad of spit right in the white eye of America" (9). The Nedeed family patriarchs are introduced in the book's opening section as men obsessed with maintaining the racial purity of their line, with statements like: "He [the third Luther] knew how to stop that before it began. Even a goblet filled with the darkest liquid will let through light—if it's diluted enough . . ." (11–12). By not diluting the Nedeed line, allowing no white scions to emerge, the black patriarchs use their racial purity to lord it over the rest of Linden Hills with its pretensions to be an upperclass neighborhood.

Most importantly, Willie and Lester are introduced in language that highlights the issue of color and recasts it in terms of race. "Willie K. Mason was so black that the kids said if he turned just a shade darker, there was nothing he could do but start going the other way. . . . So the darkest boy in Wayne Junior High was tagged White Willie. He became friends with Lester Tilson in the seventh grade after helping him fight a ninth grader who had called Lester 'Baby Shit' because of the milky-yellow tone in his skin" (24). Here are Naylor's Dante and Vergil, one as black as can be—so black as to challenge Nedeed's sense of authenticity at points in the narrative—the other milky-yellow in complexion. The rhetorical absurdity of their nicknames is a reflection of the absurdity of the nomenclature of race and color in general in America. How absurd is it to call someone black when he or she isn't as black as the color itself? Why not try to reclaim the term and the color by subverting its meaning, if at all possible? Why not just call a black person white? To complicate the picture further, what do you call someone who is not really purely black or purely white? And what does "purely" even mean in such a question? Pure in hue, saturation, brightness? Pure genetically, pure culturally? This line of inquiry seems totally absurd.[17]

Naylor doesn't spend much time with the nomenclature of whites—in fact, Caucasians in general don't either—other than to refer to a blonde woman as "that pink job" (84). But she is very interested in exploring the shades of brown that characterize the variety of people of color. Her palette for people of color exhibits a remarkable range, moving from Lester's milky-yellow to Willie's blackness. People of color can be brown (18) or black (67), sable (82), dark (18), bronze, smoky caramel, golden-brown (31); or their skin can be like white chocolate, "the hidden essence of cocoa that was embedded in the deep-yellow cream of her skin" (98), pale-skinned (9), milky skin of a canary that appears green in certain lights (48), cream or ivory (152), coffee skin, brown sugar baby (217), light-brown skin (250). Further descriptors include: "dark-skinned dudes" (73); "denizens of the darker hue," a phrase that Lester ridicules (86); members of a congregation include "various shades of brown" (162); and Willie is "a darker-hued gentleman," another phrase Lester mocks (192). One upwardly mobile character, Maxwell Smyth, acts so Caucasian that he is white (105). Finally, the person of color at the center of the plot, the child without a voice, is simply "white," and his "whiteness" threatens "the destruction of five generations" of the Nedeed family (18).

There is no question that Naylor uses color in a coded way to focus the reader's attention on race as a category. And as she points out in her interview of 1993, she uses color as a formal device to lend shape to her novel. As far as I can tell, she actually does this in several ways, at least one of which could be said to approximate Dante's *terza rima*.[18] Each of the seven successive chapters in the novel adds colors to the mix, while at the same time each recapitulates most of the colors that have been mentioned through the previous chapter. Beginning with eight colors in the first chapter, there is a succession of eight, nine, ten, eleven, and twelve colors over the first five chapters. The sixth chapter highlights thirteen colors, while the seventh and final chapter recapitulates nearly every color that has been mentioned in the novel to arrive at a total of sixteen. Once it is under way in Dante's poem, the *terza rima* rhyme scheme builds on what has gone before to create a progression of rhyming words that point backward and forward simultaneously. Similarly, Naylor's array of colors, once beyond the first chapter, look backward and forward, recalling colors that have been mentioned and anticipating new ones that will subsequently be repeated. She opens the first chapter with numerous references to five basic colors: black, white, gold, silver, and brown. She also refers once each to lavender, ashy blue, and the "blues," for a total of eight different colors. In the second chapter, the same foundational palette is repeated: black, white, gold, silver, and brown. To these five she adds pink, red, green, and gray, to make nine. The third chapter recapitulates the nine colors of chapter 2 and adds one more to the mix, yellow. These ten colors, then, form the basis for the rhyming colors, as it were, in chapter 4, to which the author adds the color blue. Chapter 5 is built around multiple references to those eleven colors plus orange. Chapter 6 includes the dozen colors of the previous chapter and adds lilac. In chapter 7, the final section of the book, Naylor seems to go out of her way to mention nearly every color that has been described earlier in the book. In this final section of the narrative, it is easy to take a sentence like "All of Linden Hills stretched up in a magnificent array of colors" (283) as a commentary on the narrative design itself. It has become by the end of the book a carefully designed, multicolored "masterwork," to use her proud term for the novel in the interview of 1993.

Other organizational patterns contribute to the Dantesque imprint on the novel. The author, for example, frequently introduces colors in triads. These clusters may be intended to represent a loose approximation of one of Dante's tercets. Black, white, and gold constitute the defining triad in the first chapter, a grouping of colors that is fundamental for the thematic exploration of the economics of race and class in the novel as a whole. Naylor meditates throughout on how money further complicates the troubled relationship between blacks and whites in contemporary American culture (of the 1980s) and throughout U.S. history. The innumerable references to "black" and "white" begin with the novel's second sentence; "gold" comes into the picture soon thereafter on the second page: "And at the time none of the white farmers gave a flying squat what he called it, 'cause if some crazy nigger wanted to lay out solid gold eagles for hard sod only good enough to support linden trees that barely got you ten cents on the dollar for a cord of oak or birch—let him" (2). The patriarch of the Nedeed family buys seemingly useless land from white farmers and sets about to turn a profit on the deal. Black uses white as an investment for future gold. The opening sequence of black-white-gold (1–2) is recapitulated in the concluding triadic cluster of amber-white-black (19–20), with amber replacing gold in the equation. Luther is obsessed with Willa's imperfect coloring, "the amber flecks in the heavily lashed eyes" (19), one of the deciding factors in his rush to lock her away, as if her attempt at looking like she belonged among the wealthy of Linden Hills was all wrong, as if her amber eyes are an inappropriate match for their gold.[19]

A prominent feature of Naylor's array of colors is the way she ends a chapter with a sequence of colors that recapitulates a sequence marked at the beginning, as if to frame the entire chapter. These framing colors resemble somewhat the first and third rhyming lines in a tercet, whether Dante's original or Ciardi's version. This happens very noticeably in the book's first five chapters. "December 19th" opens with a reference to Putney Wayne in the past, "when white families had lived there" (23), and it ends with the first of many references to the Nedeed mansion at the bottom of Linden Hills, "the white clapboard house" (61). The first reference to a color in "December 20th" is an odd description of the clock that marks the time of Willa's imprisonment in the basement: "She was so terrified of those seconds, looming white and huge in that eternity of space between the numbers on the clock" (66). The concluding image of color in this chapter is equally strange: "With horror she [Willa] saw the answers forming through image after image strung out by white hot links webbing themselves among the crevices in her brain" (94). In "December 21st," the reference to "a black woman" (97) is balanced by "two slim volumes covered in black silk" (141). The next chapter opens with Willie dreaming of "a pale hand with bright red fingernails" (145), and it ends with a glimpse of the Dumont's "massive, stone Tudor with a red-cobbled roof" (199). The entire narrative is framed in this way with the achromatic colors of black and white. Blacks and whites dispute the exact location of Linden Hills in anticipation of the first full moon at the very beginning of the book (1–2). And Willie and Lester, "White" and "Shit," emerge from the tragic darkness at the bottom of the suburban development under the light of a full moon (304).

Despite the consistent focus on the color of race, class eventually trumps race in Linden Hills. "Linden Hills wasn't black; it was successful" (17), the narrator comments near the beginning of the book. It wasn't white either. But as for it being successful, it depends on how you define success. Examples of the function of class abound in the narrative. In the relentless quest for success, Maxwell Smyth is one of several characters "to make his blackness disappear" (102). An inhabitant of Linden Hills argues for a new housing project by saying, "It's not about black or white, it's about our civic duty" (137), which claim Luther Nedeed soundly rebuts, for in his world it is about being black and making money, as he goes on to explain. Naylor even uses the televisions of Willie and Lester to signal the intersection of race and class. The former owns a used black-and-white television (271), whereas the latter is able to have his color TV fixed as soon as its colors begin to fade (58). The money that guarantees mobility between classes can buy only colors that fade. Better to be financially poor and consistently monochromatic like Willie, who leaves Linden Hills in the book's last scene with his dignity intact and a poem in his head. Willie's authentic blackness is the novel's true color.

I do not claim to have unraveled all that Naylor has done with colors in *Linden Hills*. I do think, however, that I have understood why she uses color to structure the narrative of her novel in a meaningful way that reflects her understanding of Dante's poetic form. Whatever way a multicolored *terza rima* might look and how exactly Naylor displays it in *Linden Hills* is debatable. My goal has been to explore the theme of color, especially its lexicon, using her comment on Dante's rhyme scheme as my starting place. The main point to bear in mind is that Naylor established her link with Dante not only through various parallels to his content but also to his form. Her use of the theme of color as the primary link to Dantesque poetics is an ingenious way to bring form and content to bear on the crucial topic of color and, by extension, on the issue of race.

Margaret Whitt points out that "in *The Women of Brewster Place* Naylor uses the seven different notes of a musical scale to convey seven different stories." She goes on to say, "*Linden Hills* also has seven stories" (9), implying that there is a musical structure underlying *Linden Hills* too. I have presented the narrative of *Linden Hills* following Naylor to argue that the foundational structure instead is based on color and that its design is refracted through Dante's metrical scheme of the *terza rima*. Interestingly, however, when Sir Isaac Newton conducted his experiments on light in 1666, he designated the seven basic colors in the spectrum "by analogy with the seven notes of the musical scale" ("Colour," *Encyclopedia Britannica* 2009). In Newtonian optics the colors composing white light are analogous to the notes of the musical scale. In Naylor's view of the African

American world of the late twentieth century—her optics, as it were—authentic blackness absorbs white light and turns it into a new kind of illumination. As Willie uses Whitman and other canonical writers, so Naylor uses Dante to create a new kind of narrative device in her African American work. Merely to mask white with another color, like the furniture in the Parkers' house (129), is to create something superficial. Instead, Naylor's version of a transformed Dante is a profound adaptation of the Italian poet in this ongoing history of reception.

Toni Morrison, *The Bluest Eye*

A crucial link in the African American tradition of reading Dante binds Gloria Naylor's work to Toni Morrison's *The Bluest Eye*.[20] Naylor notes in several places that she was empowered to imagine herself as a writer through her encounter with Morrison's first novel. In an interview with Morrison, Naylor states, "And it said to a young black woman, struggling to find a mirror of her worth in this society, not only is your story worth telling but it can be told in words so painstakingly eloquent that it becomes a song" (Morrison, *Conversations* 189). She first read the novel, which was published in 1970, in a course at Brooklyn College in 1977, the same year she read Dante's *Inferno* (Fowler xii). The two works percolated in her imagination in interesting ways.

The Bluest Eye, in which Dante plays a small but significant part,[21] tells the story of an eleven-year-old African American girl, Pecola Breedlove, who wants to have the unattainable blue eyes that will make her truly beautiful, as she sees things. Pecola idolizes the blue-eyed Shirley Temple with her bouncy curls whose image she sees on a drinking cup in the foster home where she stays through several seasons in 1940–41. Pecola wants to be loved, and in the harsh world she experiences of racism and violence, being loved comes easier if you're white. Her desire for the bluest eye is the unstated yearning for the apparent safety and comfort offered by the parallel universe of the white citizens in Pecola's small Ohio town. Her foster sister, Claudia, on the other hand, is content with who she is, so much so that she eagerly dismembers the "blue-eyed, yellow-haired, pink-skinned doll" everyone assumed that she and every other "girl child treasured" (20).

The color blue signals "color" in the discourse of race as we have seen it elaborated in great detail in Naylor's *Linden Hills.* An omniscient narrator and Pecola's foster sister recount the story of the girl's demise: how she wants to have blue eyes; how her father rapes and impregnates her; how the community ostracizes her; and how she eventually goes insane. The protagonist's fate is juxtaposed with Claudia's similar yet different situation. Claudia, from a poor but stable family, despises her white dolls as she learns to love the image of herself as a black girl. She appreciates the profoundly simple lesson that true beauty comes from within and is not dictated by the strictures of racism.

Lorain, Ohio, the setting for *The Bluest Eye,* was Morrison's hometown during her youth. Her description of many of the places in the novel owes much to her memory of the way things were when she was growing up there. In an interview with Bessie W. Jones and Audrey Vinson, she speaks in some detail about the sociological arrangement of her neighborhood as a child: "I never lived in a Black neighborhood in Lorain, Ohio, because there weren't any at that time—it was too small, too poor, to have officially racist structures" (*Conversations* 172). Lorain is a smaller version of those industrial midwestern settings where blacks moving north in search of jobs coexisted temporarily with European immigrants before the latter established themselves financially over the course of a generation or two and moved into the more affluent and segregated suburbs. Blacks and Italians, as Amiri Baraka observes throughout his autobiography, share many experiences as newcomers to the northern United States in the first half of the twentieth century. To wit, the first thing the reader of *The Bluest Eye* sees once the narrator begins to tell her story are "Nuns" (9), most likely Italian ones. And the first character named in Claudia's story is a young Italian American girl, "Rosemary Villanucci, our next-door friend who lives above her father's café" (9). She stands out, Claudia goes on to suggest, for her white skin and the powerful arrogance it lends her. The reader learns immediately that *The Bluest Eye* is also about color and race. And it is the pairing of them that leads ultimately to the undoing of the protagonist.

Soaphead Church, a minor character in the novel, ekes out a living as a "Reader, Adviser, and Interpreter of Dreams" (167). He was born somewhere in the Caribbean as Elihue Micah Whitcomb and had settled in Lorain a decade before the time of the narrative. We learn that Whitcomb was the light-skinned son of a West Indian schoolmaster and a half-Chinese girl who died in childbirth. A mixed hybrid product of British colonial culture, he desperately sought to eradicate any elements of African and indigenous cultures in him. He had been taught from birth, trained, in fact, to favor whiteness over blackness. Educated in the classics of Western literature, his favorite author was Dante: "The works he admired most were Dante's; those he despised most were Dostoyevsky's. For all his exposure to the best minds of the Western world, he allowed only the narrowest interpretation to touch him. He responded to his father's controlled violence by developing hard habits and a soft imagination. A hatred of, and fascination with, any hint of disorder or decay" (169). Whitcomb, or Soaphead as everyone called him behind his back because of the pomade he used to slick his hair, had issues with his sexuality. The marriage to "his Beatrice" (169) failed due to various sexual problems alluded to in the narrative as his equating "lovemaking with communion" (170). By the time he had drifted into his position as an elderly spiritual adviser he was an obsessive-compulsive celibate, which gave him the reputation of having supernatural powers. In truth, he was a sexual pervert who preyed on the young girls in town.

Pecola seeks out Soaphead in search of a magical remedy for blue eyes. In the scene immediately preceding this decisive visitation, the narrative reveals how Pecola's father raped her, told from his own drunken perspective. Used by one man, Pecola is about to be taken advantage of by another—but in a different way. Soaphead deviously contrives to use her naïveté to rid himself of a nuisance, his landlady's old mangy dog on the back porch. Telling Pecola that God will send a sign in the behavior of the dog, he prepares a piece of poisoned meat, which she then feeds to the animal. Once the dog dies after a series of dramatic spasms, Pecola runs away convinced that her eyes will now be miraculously transformed.

If her father abuses her physically, Soaphead abuses her spiritually, "manipulating Pecola's faith in miracles" (Rubenstein 142).[22] His understanding of Dante prepares him intellectually for this climactic act in the narrative. Morrison takes the reader into Soaphead's warped mind for a theological disquisition on good and evil, with Dante as arbiter.

> With only occasional, and increasingly rare, encounters with the little girls
> he could persuade to be entertained by him, he lived rather peaceably

among his things, admitting to no regrets. He was aware, of course, that something was awry in his life, and all lives, but put the problem where it belonged, at the foot of the Originator of Life. He believed that since decay, vice, filth, and disorder were pervasive, they must be in the Nature of Things. Evil existed because God had created it. He, God, had made a sloven and unforgivable error in judgment: designing an imperfect universe. Theologians justified the presence of corruption as a means by which men strove, were tested, and triumphed. A triumph of cosmic neatness. But this neatness, the neatness of Dante, was in the orderly sectioning and segregating of all levels of evil and decay. In the world it was not so. The most exquisite-looking ladies sat on toilets, and the most dreadful-looking had pure and holy yearnings. God had done a poor job, and Soaphead suspected that he himself could have done better. It was in fact a pity that the Maker had not sought his counsel.

Soaphead was reflecting once again on these thoughts one late hot afternoon when he heard a tap on his door. Opening it, he saw a little girl . . . (172–73)

In what must be a frequent internal debate, Soaphead reflects on how Dante addresses the problem of good and evil in his *Divine Comedy*. Of course, this is not an orthodox reading of Dante, in fact, the narrator has warned the reader earlier that Soaphead always followed "the narrowest interpretation" of the great books (169). In the first place, the Italian medieval Christian accepts God's design of the universe as perfect. Moreover, following Augustinian teaching, he believes that evil is merely an absence of love, not a creation in its own right by God. Dante might agree with Soaphead's notion of the world as a triumph of cosmic neatness, but he would not claim that neatness for his own. Nor would he attribute it to Thomas Aquinas or any other church father whose doctrinal theology contributed to the articulation of the punishments of sin. The neatness, like the glory, is all God's. Soaphead's appropriation of Dante completely misunderstands this fundamental point.

Soaphead takes comfort in the Aristotelian and Aquinian features of Dante's representation of reality. Specifically, he is impressed with Aristotle's ethics refracted through Aquinas's design of hell, purgatory, and

heaven, and the consequent impact of that design on the poetic structure of the *Divine Comedy*. Amiri Baraka turns to Dante for an artistic *system*
to use in the design of his own work. Soaphead, however, is looking for
a moral system that coheres with his perverted view of the world. It is a
view that has no place for anything messy, no place for what the novel calls
elsewhere "funkiness," a synonym for authentic black culture, which white
wannabes try to wipe away: "The dreadful funkiness of passion, the funkiness of nature, the funkiness of the wide range of human emotions" (83).
Soaphead's world has no place for funkiness, which means it has no place
for blackness.

Pecola, then, hasn't come to any old fortune-teller; she has come to
the one person who understands her situation perfectly, because his own
life mirrors it in this essential way: he hates his blackness too. For this reason Soaphead is so responsive to her request, which he finds extremely
rational: "He thought it was at once the most logical petition he had ever
received. Here was an ugly little girl asking for beauty. . . . A little black
girl who wanted to rise up out of the pit of her blackness and see the world
with blue eyes" (174). This sets in motion the denouement of the plot, with
Soaphead's preparation of the poisoned meat and his instructions to Pecola.
When we see her next, she is engaged in a conversation with an imaginary friend about whether or not her eyes, already blue, are blue enough.
The Du Boisian double consciousness that was mentioned in chapter 2 in
the discussion of the retrospective first-person narrations of Ellison and
Dante is embodied in the schizophrenic conversation Pecola carries out
with her other self. She has two selves, one black and one white, and they
discourse on the color of the eyes that link them.

Soaphead too, as I have suggested, is split into two beings. His inability
to accept and value his hybrid colonial origins has created a mind that fails
to appreciate the hybridity in Dante's work, a mind that reads the *Divine
Comedy* as a moralizing straitjacket. He too suffers from a form of schizo-
phrenia, not very different in fact from that of the little Pecola. Moreover,
her tragic and psychotic babble is balanced by Soaphead's equally insane
theological banter before he meets her and as that banter is condensed in
his chilling letter to God after he has done his deed. While the letter to
God is a unique document in Soaphead's collection, the debate we hear

going on in his head happens over and over and over.[23] Morrison signals its repetition with the telling adverbial phrase "once again" (173). Soaphead had been waiting for Pecola to come forever. Or at least since he had first read Dante.

Dante Rap

While Du Boisian double consciousness can be used to account for the psychological state of Pecola and Soaphead, it can also be used as an aesthetic category. To wit, in chapter 2 we had occasion to consider the multiple perspectives of the narrative of the *Divine Comedy* (in comparison with Ellison's narrative in *Invisible Man*), built around the fiction that after his trip through the afterlife Dante the pilgrim will eventually return to Italy and begin to write his poem. The hermeneutic tension between the pilgrim who will become the poet and the poet who intervenes in his own voice at times in the course of the narrative is encapsulated in that provocative phrase of Charles S. Singleton mentioned in the discussion of hybridity in the book's introductory chapter: "The fiction of the *Comedy* is that it is not fiction."[24] Writing between 1307 and 1321, the year of his death, Dante took great pains to convince the reader that his journey really did take place over Easter week in 1300, and in the process focused consistently on his role as the artist. Baraka, too, develops *The System of Dante's Hell* around a similar tension between the protagonist as a youth and the more experienced voice of the novelist. The narrative of *Linden Hills,* however, isn't organized around the same principle of then and now, there and here, with a narrator who reflects on what he did earlier; rather, Naylor's narrative takes place and is recounted in real time over a six-day period just before Christmas one year in the 1980s. We can't see what Willie becomes after the novel's end, as we can with narrators in several of the other works that we've considered. But Naylor gives us enough hints to encourage speculation.

We are led to believe that Willie will continue to produce and perform his poems; and near the end of the novel we catch a glimpse of Willie's creative compositional process (275–77).[25] This prompts one to ask what kind of a poet Willie would be upon emerging from Naylor's narrative. One version of a latter-day Willie is a poet and activist of the Black Arts movement whose work extends from the 1970s to today, Askia M. Touré, born in 1938, originally named Rolland Snellings. Baraka recognizes him as one of the radical new poets of liberation in "The Revolutionary Tradition in Afro-American Literature" (*LeRoi Jones/Amiri Baraka Reader* 321). Touré's work is in dialogue with much of Baraka's, but a poem he published several years after Naylor's novel came out rejects Dante and, one assumes, Baraka's appropriation of the *Inferno* for the African American tradition. Here is the first half of Touré's "Infernos: A Griot-Song," which he dedicates with irony to Jimmy Carter and Pope John Paul II, leaders of the institutions he holds responsible for much of the people's suffering. The dedication suggests that he actually composed the poem in 1979–80, when both Carter and the pope were players on the world's stage.

> It is the *fire* that haunts
> us finally,
>   moves them inevitably —
> as popes or white-sheeted
> klansmen: we see
> the flames
> immolate martyrs, scorch
> righteousness; echoes
> of Mather's puritan
> (the Inquisition or
> Salem witchhunts)
> reflected in
> the ice-blue, missionary eyes.
>
> "Pagan savages";
> the World renamed,
> classified as prelude
> to annexation, genocide:
> multitudes sacrificed
> as funeral pyres for
> the wild fanatic's zeal.

It is the *fire* that haunts
us, finally
       as *metaphor:* the Aryan
deathwish rampant in
Hiroshima, Nagasaki;
Warsaw ghettoes scream
in tune to
helicopter Valkyries
scorching villagers
in Vietnam.
Why this zeal, this
Piromania?
Is it culture or insanity?
Hell, we understand struggle, politics,
perceptions of reality. Why
does
       all dialogue lead finally to
       charred Black bodies
       dangling
       in the American night?

We are warmblooded,
tropic peoples, loving
life,
       joy, ecstasy; a sensual
       rhythm/beauty, a
       heightened perception
       of creation, uniting opposites:
       life/death, joy/sorrow,
       love/hate, one eternal
       Yin/Yang ethic
       reverberating through
       emerald river valleys—
       Nile, Niger, Tigris—
       moist rainforests, rich
       savannah, fields and

meadows of our
       pyramidal lives.
What need we of
Dante's
       Inferno, "sin" or
       eternal damnation, all
projections of a nomad
psyche, barbequing
rivals in the dank heat
of pre-historic caves . . .
This hawk-eyed
       wanderer, the Aryan
       warrior plotting by chill campfires
       how Europe would arise,
       overthrow Egypt, thrust
       a Greek throwing spear
       into the heart of man.
   (*From the Pyramids to the Projects* 39—40)

Touré presents himself as an oral poet, a griot who sings for the good of the community. The style and mode of the griot-song create a kind of incantatory rap, the sort of genre that Willie might have produced. The theme of this specific song is the obsession the West has had with eradicating, slashing and burning, as it were, less powerful cultures it wanted to conquer. Fire, which figures prominently in Naylor's narrative, becomes the primary means of destruction in a chronology of death that begins with the Greeks, then proceeds to the Aryans, and Christians, both Catholic and Protestant, signaled by references to the papacy and Cotton Mather. Fire prompts images of the KKK, Nazi storm troopers, the atomic bomb, and the firebombing of villages in Vietnam, all presented as examples of white power being abused to the detriment of innocent victims. Like the dramatic sequence that leads up to Spencer Williams's citation of the film *L'inferno,* the culminating image in Touré's catalogue is a reference to lynching, emphasized by the author's italics: "*charred Black bodies / dangling / in the American night*" (40). In this context, the griot associates Dante with a Western tradition of death that he soundly rejects on behalf of his people.

In a reading that has points in common with that of Morrison's Soaphead, he sees Dante's text as nothing more than a guide to eternal damnation, a manual on how to classify and punish sin. While Soaphead delights in this orderly classification of evil, which he can use to counter the disorder around him, Touré is repulsed by it. And he is moved to pose the following question (without punctuation) in an inverted word order that draws attention to itself: "What need we of Dante's *Inferno.*"

Robert Rauschenberg emphasizes precisely this same grim sequence but comes to a different conclusion in a piece commissioned for *Life* magazine's issue of December 17, 1965: "Dante's *Inferno*: Drawings for Dante's 700th Birthday," also known as "A Modern Inferno." The editors of *Life* invited Rauschenberg to celebrate the septicentennial of Dante's birth because he had recently completed a set of inspired illustrations for Dante's *Inferno* in 1960. The mixed-media piece for *Life* is a six-page pullout panorama of the artist's vision of hell on earth (45–50). Characterized by Rauschenberg's signature transfer-drawings of photographs laid on white paper and rubbed with colored pencils and crayons, the images are visual citations, with the artist quoting and re-presenting images borrowed from other works in his style of collage drawing. Rauschenberg's visual response to Dante includes images from all the items in Touré's list (the Holocaust, atomic war, Vietnam). And there are many photographs documenting the civil rights struggle in the 1940s and 1950s, among them a shot of a Ku Klux Klansman in robes and hood displaying a hangman's noose from his car window on the way, one can only conclude, to a lynching. Dante provides Rauschenberg with a framework for responding to the evil inflicted on minorities and the underprivileged, with the suffering of African Americans in the foreground.[26]

Askia Touré, for his part, doesn't entertain this way of using Dante. One assumes that he is simply unaware of Dante's political critique of corrupt individuals within the hierarchical structures that institutionalized the damnation of sinners in the Middle Ages.[27] Moreover, he seems oblivious to the reception of Dante, the man and his work, which has occurred over the centuries in African American culture. His rhetorical question "What need we of Dante" may also imply a dig at Baraka's earlier project to rewrite the poet, perhaps reflecting discussions between the two of them on how to move cultural projects associated with Afrocentrism forward. By all accounts, the two men shared a mutual respect for one another when they were younger. In his rejection of the tradition I have been exploring in this book of a Dante that has special appeal for writers of color, Touré sees him as the emblem of a Eurocentric culture that rises to overthrow Egypt and the "warmblooded tropic peoples" of Afrocentrist revisionist history.

It may be that Askia M. Touré is too extreme a projection for Willie beyond the bounds of *Linden Hills.* It may be unfair to superimpose on Willie the Afrocentric rhetoric of Leonard Jeffries and others who propose categories like "warmblooded tropic peoples," given that Naylor is so broadly based in African American *and* European traditions. After all, Willie's canonical five includes Coleridge and Whitman. And Naylor herself makes a point of alluding to Eliot and Whitman in *Linden Hills,* putting them on a par with Baraka, Soyinka, Hughes, and Dante in her own canon of models. Perhaps Willie followed another path. Perhaps like Lester he graduated from high school and went forward with his education, like Lester's sister, or like Naylor herself. One can imagine various other models he might become in opposition to Touré.

In 1973 N. J. Loftis published a volume of poetry focused on uplift and black pride, *Black Anima,* which could perhaps be a model for the poetry that Willie might go on to compose.[28] The long poem that gives the book its title is divided into four parts: "Changes," "Hell," "Birth and Rebirth," and "Black Anima." Loftis writes about a descent into the underworld in which his poet-narrator encounters a variety of literary and political figures who appear to dispense advice on how to get by, but the issue is actually more profoundly a question of identity, specifically the identity of the black intellectual. It's a rather campy mix of sources and voices, including that of Frantz Fanon, the anthropologist-theorist of black culture, who serves as the narrator's guide through hell. With Fanon, the narrator catches sight of a magical encounter in the British Museum Library between Richard Wright and none other than Pushkin.

> And Pushkin said, "Here's Homer's hell,
>   the archetype is Egyptian
>   where the sun fell
> over Luxor scribbling its dread command
>   in Ikhnaton's brain.

And this is the hell of Dante
raining down revenge
    raining down justice
for the pain suffered on living land
"You see before you White and Black
    racism is dead here
We are beyond all that. . . ."
                  (54–55)

Against the backdrop of the museum's extensive collection of arti-
facts that cover the world's cultures, Pushkin, the Ethiopian Russian, provides an Afrocentric commentary on visions of the afterlife. In that context he promotes a traditional and not incorrect interpretation of Dante's
hell as a site of revenge and justice, but one wonders why he is the authority
to speak on Dante's hell. Ellison, we recall, ridicules writers of color who
claim a connection to Pushkin through ethnicity or ideology rather than art.
Pushkin, it turns out, was all the rage in certain circles in the 1970s, and
Loftis's rather uncritical reflections using the Russian poet would probably
have brought him under Ellison's fire.

Later in the poem the narrator and Fanon come to an entrance (64):

discussing what we'd seen
came to a red door marked:
BEWARE:
DANTE'S INFERNO

Beyond the door they move through several realms of sinners being
punished: absentee landlords who cheat their tenants, white politicians
"who . . . disseminated hatred and strife" (67), and John D. Rockefeller
and other thieves "balancing barrows filled with shit" (68). John D., as he
is called, concludes a brief conversation with the narrator with a very
Dantesque quip, "Tell Rocky a place awaits him here" (68). Loftis uses his
knowledge of Dante, which is hardly scant, to express his outrage at the
inequities of the world around him. He chooses three easy targets: landlords, politicians, and tycoons. The writing itself, while unremarkable, is
consistently striking for its humorous tone. You have to laugh to keep from

crying, says Langston Hughes, but who would have thought that you could use Dante in the process? This strand of the African American tradition—of which Naylor's Willie might well have become a part—succeeds in doing just that although it does not reach the level of the serious critical commentary that Ellison argues for.

Another potential model for Willie is Dudley Randall (1914–2000), an African American poet and publisher whose volume *A Litany of Friends* contains two poems that refer to Dante. "My Muse" makes a typical comparison between the poet's lady and Beatrice (38). This allusion to Dante in love situates Randall in a long and venerable tradition of Anglo-American poets.[29] More impressive is the final poem of the volume, "Detroit Renaissance," dedicated to Mayor Coleman A. Young, on rebuilding the city in the early eighties after two decades of white flight and urban deterioration (103). The poem opens:

> Cities have died, have burned,
> Yet phoenix-like returned
> To soar up livelier, lovelier than before.
> Detroit has felt the fire,
> Yet each time left the pyre
> As if the flames had power to restore.

The poet continues in this hopeful tone, envisioning a new civic space with its wealth embodied in its people, which includes a multicultural mix of citizens. On the one hand are the descendents of Africans, "Who built the pyramids," on the other are the various ethnic groups descended from Europeans, including those "Souls forged by Homer's, Dante's . . . style." In this utopian vision, Randall imagines a city where African Americans come together with later-generation immigrants from the Mediterranean, Greeks and Italians, and others to reconstruct a democratic space in a new America. The image of Dante invoked here is clearly of the poet as an instigator to action. The new *polis* needs its poets to inspire its citizens to act.

> Together we will build
> A city that will yield
> To all their hopes and dreams so long deferred.

With this concluding recommendation to the mayor, Randall has placed himself in that other tradition of appropriating Dante, which is in line with the work of Cordelia Ray: the Italian poet as a political activist. And he has situated himself as a worthy successor to Dante in this important civic work. This is a local application of Dante—to borrow Du Bois's phrase from the beginning of chapter 2—that would make sense to Willie.

But between Dante in love and Dante as activist, are there any other possibilities? Suppose Willie ended up writing poetry inspired more by Whitman than Baraka? Maybe he would have gone on to produce elegant, refined, passionate poetry like that of Carl Phillips, a poet and professor of creative writing at Washington University, who wears his allusions to Dante lightly. Phillips is an African American, but he defies the specific label, as if he were saying with Robert Hayden that he is a poet first and foremost.[30] All the other labels that one might apply—African American, gay, Europeanized—come later, if at all. In "One sees pictures of Dante," Phillips imagines the poet in exile catching sight of a young man working the edges of a field at harvest time, or perhaps he is a gleaner picking through the leftovers of a harvest. Here is the complete poem from *Cortège*:

One sees pictures of Dante:

in Byzantine profile, looking about
as visionary as the next unremarkable bird;
frozen in an encounter with Beatrice on a
significant bridge or some tumbledown
strada, about to lose her all over again.
My own picture is more plastic:
the maestro, leaning stiffly out
from the roofless cage of exile,
has his eye on the hands of a particular
young man just off of the roadside, lifting
the salvageable pieces of fruit
from the ground, and in a bucket he has brought
for the purpose, rinsing each separately

free of dirt, then paring away the soft,
inedible portions.
                It is another of those
afternoons when he can hardly endure
the ride home, he's that eager
to put it all down, that certain that each
of the man's beautiful gestures must
in some way concern the soul.

Phillips opens the poem with a typical image from Dantesque iconography, a profile view of the poet in a street scene that could be Henry Holliday's famous nineteenth-century painting of Dante encountering Beatrice and two of her angelic lady friends, with the Ponte Vecchio in the background. We have seen this picture before. But after evoking its tried and true images, the poet imagines Dante in a light heretofore unseen: "My own picture is more plastic." The unexpected erotic moment of Dante eyeing "a particular young man" who is picking over the fruit reminds one of Ginsberg's "A Supermarket in California," in which the narrator follows Walt Whitman up and down the store's aisles as he is "eyeing the grocery boys" (l. 25). Ginsberg's vision of Whitman and his love for the master prompt him to imagine America in the 1950s as a melancholic suburban landscape with a blue car in every driveway. It is a setting with little room for the Ginsbergs or Whitmans of countercultural America. Carl Phillips, however, imagines his Dante in exile sublimating that erotic moment into his overarching vision of the divine, for his Dante is "that certain that each / of the man's beautiful gestures must / in some way concern the soul" (37). Eros transforms into agape. The poet's own hands are eager to connect the man's gestures to the soul in his poem of divine love. The momentary glimpse of a different Dante morphs into a profound image of the poet hard at work on his sacred poem up to his last dying days in exile. Agape is sublimated into poetry.[31]

WRITING IN the 1980s as rap was coming into its own, Naylor portrays Willie as an up-and-coming rapper, a hip-hop artist dedicated to his craft who has memorized hundreds of poetic compositions. In fact, he claims to know 665 poems by heart (45), many of which are his own originals. In addition, as we saw above, he has memorized many works by his favorite authors, his canon including poems by Baraka, Soyinka, Hughes, Coleridge, and Whitman, "one together dude" (46). Willie's prodigious memory and his ability to compose in rhythmical verse—we see and hear him in action on pages 275–77—mark him as a rapper. So, let's take the leap and imagine what kind of rapper he might be in connection with Dante.

One well-known rap artist, Percy Carey aka the rapper M. F. Grimm, may have wanted his audience to associate his work with Dante when he entitled his second compact disc, *Digital Tears: Email from Purgatory* (2004). Grimm sings about his tough life as a thug on the streets, drug dealing and the rest, his paralysis from wounds received in a gunfight, his time in prison, and his ultimate search for redemption in ways that recall the typical narrative of sinner to saint. He also tells his story in an autobiographical graphic novel, *Sentences: The Life of M. F. Grimm.* Immediately following a frame in which he defends his love of reading when confronted by one of his gangsta friends, is one in which we read the tag DANTE blazoned on a wall of graffiti (33). The tag appears in a frame sandwiched by two others that include the protagonist's defense of his habit: "Oh, just cuz I do some gangsta shit means I should be illiterate?" And his interlocutor's response: "I just don't know why you'd read books if you don't have to. There's mad good shit on TV." Of course, "Dante" can be interpreted as merely the name of a graffiti artist, but perhaps it is a signal, not unlike that of Ellison's at the beginning of *Invisible Man,* to let the reader know something about the artist's allegiances. Dante would certainly be a good guide in the construction of this redemption narrative, in which the author goes to hell to emerge barely in the nick of time and to be given a second chance in a kind of purgatory. Although there is no direct connection to Dante's text as far as I can tell, one can use Grimm as a touchstone for what a narrative built around Dantesque rap might be like.

A fuller fusion between Dante and rap is found in a recent attempt to set some of the *Inferno* itself to the rhythms of rap music. In 2005 the Eternal Kool Project produced a one-track compact disc called the *Inferno Rap.* The liner notes state, "This is a unique, never before done approach to Dante Alighieri's *Inferno.* Lyrics written in the 14th Century, as translated in the mid 1800s by H Cary, are rapped by MicPwr, over a music track

composed by Mr Moe. It is a powerful depiction of a medieval Hell, performed by urban artists." I can discover nothing about these artists, thus
I am not even sure that they are artists of color. I submit *The Inferno Rap* as
my final example of Dante and African American art in this chapter following the logic (referred to at various points throughout *Freedom Readers*
and to be examined in more detail in the concluding chapter) that a Dante
of color has value on the grounds of literary aesthetics, even if the presen-
ter does not identify his or her race as African American. To invoke Ellison
on Pushkin once more: one should value any literary artistic connection
between Dante and African American culture on aesthetic grounds rather
than racial. In saying this I may appear to run counter to the course of
nearly all my examples thus far where every literary work heretofore,
from Cordelia Ray to Ellison to Baraka and all the poets mentioned above
in this section, are created by artists of color. The example of the man of
African descent in Dante's Regions from 1828, the wax museum in frontier Cincinnati, was a black man created by a white artist, which I adduced
as my symbolic starting place in this study. But after that first work the majority of our other examples were created by artists of color. Let's grant
again, even if momentarily, the possibility that the artist's race isn't the essence of what we seek in looking for an African American Dante.

    What can we learn from the artistic choices made by the members of
the Eternal Kool Project? The piece is almost seventeen minutes long, divided into four main parts. It begins with a voice over a rap beat reciting
Inferno 1.1–12 in Italian. This opening melds into the second part featuring
a rapper in English, presumably MicPwr, emphatically reciting the description of the gates of hell, *Inferno* 3.1–9, the passage that Naylor rewrites
so effectively. The translation is Henry Francis Cary's nineteenth-century
version (1814), read no doubt by Frances Trollope, Hiram Powers, William Wells Brown, Cordelia Ray, and most of the other figures of the nineteenth century we looked at in chapter 1. In fact, it is the version that Richard Wright had in his library, and given his mentoring of Ellison perhaps
it is a version that Ellison knew too. With Cary we have returned to our
beginnings in some sense. Cary's translation is a curious choice given the
many possible versions the rappers have at their disposal in 2005. But
Cary's translation is in the public domain, which makes it readily available
and free. Moreover, its blank Miltonic verse has its own incantatory effect

that the rap can play off of.[32] Cary's style is distinguished by its many en-
jambed verses that contribute to the Miltonic flowing syntax. In setting
Cary's lines to music, the rapper never recites them according to sense with
an overflowing hypermetric clause or phrase into the following line. Rather,
his style is to halt sharply at the end of each verse to create a staccato effect.
After an interlude of predictable infernal sounds (howls, growls, screams,
etc.), the third part of the rap begins, which presents *Inferno* 5 in its entirety. There is more howling at its end, some amplified satanic voices, omi-
nous bells tolling, birds, a young child laughing, then comes the fourth
and final part of the piece: *Inferno* 34 in its entirety.

The rap is framed effectively by *Inferno* 1 and 34; the snippet from
Inferno 3 serves to lead us into hell proper much as it functions for the
reader in Dante's original; *Inferno* 5, with its representation of the sin of
lust, is the part of hell that the rapper wants to emphasize. Uncontrolled
sexual desire is a common theme in contemporary rap, so the modern artists found a perfect source for their genre's needs in this portion of Dante's
text. MicPwr doesn't need to do anything to the text other than rap it out
fully against the beat. *Inferno* 34 leads the reader/listener out of hell to the
shores of Mount Purgatory at the very end of the *Inferno*. It works neatly
to bring the narrative to its conclusion. No murderers, no corrupt politicians, no hypocrites, no traitors. There are many other sinners the rappers
could have chosen to showcase, but the canto of the lustful with the narrative of Paolo and Francesca as its highlight is an understandable and legitimate artistic choice. It puts *The Inferno Rap* in a venerable tradition of adaptations that emphasize *Inferno* 5.[33]

Let this rap stand as a final example of an African American Dante.
This work of art raises questions about the interrelation of race, art, and
identity, in the context of reading Dante, which we need to explore further
in the conclusion.

CHAPTER 5
POETS IN EXILE

<hr>

The most illiterate among them [inhabitants of a remote Swiss village]
is related, in a way that I am not, to Dante, Shakespeare,
Michelangelo, Aeschylus, Da Vinci, Rembrandt, and Racine.

—James Baldwin, "Stranger in the Village" (1963)

I would like to submit one last example of a writer of color who turns to Dante in a moment of personal crisis. Consider the case of Edward Smythe Jones, who "in his over-mastering desire to drink at the Harvard fountain of learning tramped out of the Southland up to Cambridge. Arriving travel-worn, friendless, moneyless, hungry, he was preparing to bivouac on the Harvard campus his first night in the University city, when, being misunderstood, and not believed, he was apprehended as a vagabond and thrown into jail. A poem, however, the poem which tells this story, delivered him. The judge was convinced by it . . . and set him free to return to the academic shades" (Kerlin 163–64). The poem called "Harvard Square" ends on this note: "Cell No. 40, East Cambridge Jail, Cambridge, Massachusetts, July 26, 1910." But the familiar scenario of the black man harassed by the police and thrown in jail for no discernible reason is transformed into a magical encounter with the muse. The divine goddess of inspiration comes to the poet's aid with a brief lesson in literary history in which she compares his fate to Dante's—"I placed great Dante in exile"—suggesting that she has now done the same to Jones (Kerlin 165).[1] Dante's actual banishment from Florence sheds light on the figurative exile of Jones: the Negro in the white man's world; the southerner in the North; the backwoodsman in "the University city"; the autodidact amidst the hypereducated; and the would-be Dante at the very center of Dante's American home. This reference to the Florentine poet in exile with its political overtones breaks the mold of Dante as a hackneyed theme—as William Wells Brown and Cordelia Ray had done before Jones—and it prepares us for more radical adaptations of Dante to come.

Jones's personal crisis is part of a larger critical issue in the nineteenth and twentieth centuries, a veritable public political crisis, namely, the refusal of American society to honor its pledge of truth that "all men are created equal." For when he was writing in 1910, some citizens of the United States were more equal than others, as we know. That Dante is called upon to comment on the inequality of citizens of color in the United States might strike an untutored reader as a literary affectation. But I hope to have made a case throughout these pages for an interpretation of Dante's life and work, beginning with various Protestants in the sixteenth century, that emphasized his writings' applicability to political causes associated with reform. African American readers have been drawn to Dante consistently as they argued for and articulated their proper position as citizens in the United States, locating their cultural identity somewhere between the Europe of Dante and the America that they had come to inhabit. The *Divine Comedy*'s themes of freedom and reform especially appeal to this set of readers in its search for equality.

Cordelia Ray's appropriation of Dante, distinguishing her from the myriad of poetasters in the nineteenth century who were eager to embrace the Italian bard as nothing more than a love poet, goes so far as to see Dante as a civic activist, a constitutional lawyer, an agitator who used the courts to make his community better. Dante, for Ray and other writers and thinkers influenced by abolitionism like William Wells Brown, takes his place alongside Douglass, Garrison, Mazzini, Sumner, even Lincoln, as a man responding nobly to a great struggle. From the Colored Dante of Ray and Brown we moved to the Negro Dante of Spencer Williams, Richard Wright, and Ralph Ellison. Spencer Williams allows Dante to be the unique white presence in his segregated world, while Wright uses him as a marker of his migration to what he hopes will be a new and better life. For Ellison, Dante stands as the gatekeeper to a new literary world that enables him to integrate and Europeanize his vernacular American writing. For these Negro artists Dante represents not simply freedom in a political sense, though I believe he still bears that value for them too. For them, Dante is essentially an integrator who grants access to the heretofore closed society of the white powerful cultural elite. Like the celestial messenger of *Inferno* 9, who opens the gates of the city of Dis with little trouble, Dante comes to the rescue of these artists to open the way for their work as they move into new cultural contexts and traditions.

To create his Black Dante, Amiri Baraka goes a step further to allude to Dante as if the Italian poet were black. Much like Edward Smythe Jones, his predecessor in several crucial ways, Baraka finds a temporary soul mate in Dante. His predecessor's intrusion into Harvard Yard is an act of civil, intellectual disobedience with literary implications that prepares for Baraka's unruly adaptation of the Florentine poet. Specifically, the act of the earlier Jones is a direct challenge to the day's literary canon and to the system that perpetuates its study in 1910. His muse, in fact, establishes a new canon for him, outlined in the poem, from which he can take strength while in jail, which includes Homer, Dante, Byron, Keats, Shelley, Burns, Poe, Paul Dunbar, and, of course, Edward Smythe Jones himself. Much as Dante represents himself as having been accepted into the literary canon in *Inferno* 4.100–102, so Jones does in his own Dantesque moment. In both cases, it is a literary canon of the poet's own devising, the most important feature of which is the poet's self-inclusion. Similarly, LeRoi Jones/Amiri Baraka founds a new canon that also includes Dante, but his is more radical for it turns on Dante and reaches back to the writings of the slave, exchanging the Beats and other modern literary models for slave autobiographical narratives with Dante as the go-between.

We then considered Gloria Naylor's African American Dante. Naylor adapts the *Inferno* to the urban realities of African Americans in the 1980s, or rather, to the suburban realities of the rising black middle class in the final quarter of the twentieth century. It is a view of Dante as a literary model that seems, of the various Dantes under discussion, the least conscious of color, which is ironic given the novel's attention to the thematics of color. There is a sense that Dante's place in the canon of white European literature is not as much an issue for Naylor, as if the poem were an unproblematic part of her own tradition, for, indeed, it is. She doesn't need to advertise her claim on Dante with quite the tenacity of, say, Ellison. Whereas the Colored Dante of Ray and Brown appears to embody characteristics of Lincoln and other white abolitionists, Williams makes Dante the unique white presence in his film, and Jones would have us see a Black Dante, Naylor, the African American novelist, draws on the poem of the canonical white author with no reservations. It is as if she had said of the Florentine poet, to borrow from Frederick Douglass's quote in the epigraph to *Freedom Readers*: "I was glad to find him white, I have no prejudice against his color." But this is not to say that Naylor's reading is apolitical. Far from it. Her imitation of Dante, as seen, for example, in her rewriting of the inscription above the gates of hell from *Inferno* 3.1–9, while juxtaposing the hopefulness of education with the hopelessness of gangs, ultimately proposes a third course embodied in the marginalized figure of Willie, her character cast in the role of Dante the pilgrim. Naylor's novel questions the inappropriate adaptation of canonical education in an understated but thoroughly revolutionary mode. Willie's artistic middle course between formal learning and the lessons of the streets represents another and better way to be a poet and a citizen. At the end of the novel the marginal figure making his way through the circles of Linden Hills has come to its very center.

With few exceptions (several of the abolitionists, Robert Rauschenberg, perhaps the creators of *The Inferno Rap*), the writers and artists we have discussed in these pages are African American. But in order to write a Dante of color, does one have to be black? Are these rewritings of Dante ideologically black in some essential way, or is their defining characteristic merely that their authors are biologically black (however one might determine that)? This is to raise the hoary question of what constitutes blackness. And to ask, is a legitimate black identity racial or is it constructed in some way? While I have emphasized the work of people of color with a focus on the historical and cultural contexts in which those works were produced, the rewritings and adaptations of Dante in this broader tradition (for the sake of simplicity let's consider the film of Spencer Williams as another kind of text that rewrites the original) are thoroughly artistic undertakings. They are the products of imitation and negotiation with a model of literariness, Dante's *Comedy,* which is not out of Africa, to borrow a phrase, but comes straight from Europe. Anyone could use Dante in this way, and indeed many authors who are not of color do. Most recently, for one final example, Matthew Pearl.

Matthew Pearl's crime novel *The Dante Club* (2003) is inspired by that foundational moment for Dante Studies in the United States when scholars gathered around Longfellow to create a community of devoted readers of the Italian bard at Harvard College. It was the first and most famous of what were to be many such groups around the country, several of which were mentioned in chapter 1. Of note for my point above about race and art and for the general argument of *Freedom Readers* is that the first murder in the novel depends on a mysteriously transmitted passage from Dante's text, communicated by the initial victim in a whisper to the policeman who helps to solve the crimes. It is not Longfellow or one of the other Boston Brahmins in his circle who transcribes the crucial text; rather it is the African American police officer assigned to the case, Patrolman Nicholas Rey, "the first colored member of the police" (60). Rey wrestles with the whispered clue the dying victim passes on to him, but he eventually transcribes it and shares it with Longfellow and company. Without understanding the Italian text, Rey realizes that the criminal has left a valuable trace. He copies it out as carefully as he can sound it: "*Deenan see amno atesennone turnay eeotur nodur lasheeato nay*" (106). Finally, James Russell Lowell, fine philologist and scholar that he is, deciphers the text, which he realizes is a garbled version of *Inferno* 3.7–9: "Dinanzi a me non fuor cose create / se non etterne, e io etterno duro, / lasciate ogne." From the final tercet that marks the gates of hell, this is the very passage Naylor rewrites above the school's entrance and these are the same lines that *The Inferno Rap* uses to open its piece.

Pearl's designation of his detective's race says more about him and the hopeful moment we are now living at the beginning of our new millennium than it does about Dante's reception among African American artists or even about African Americans interacting with others in the Harvard milieu. In fact, Pearl, a graduate of Harvard College, has more in common with the members of the Dante Club than with the man of color he creates who is tangentially connected to them. But Pearl has this crucial detail in common with the various African American artists we have considered in *Freedom Readers*: he understands that the way into the text in the history of rewriting Dante is through the text itself. Maybe Patrolman Rey understood that truth more profoundly than the white members of the Dante Club could imagine. Located somewhere between Baldwin's illiterate Swiss villager (from this chapter's epigraph) and Longfellow's elite literary friends, Patrolman Rey realizes that Dante's text is the ultimate gate.

WHERE DOES that leave us in this study of Dante in black and white? In a review of Charles S. Singleton's translation of and massive commentary on the *Divine Comedy* published in six volumes between 1970 and 1975, D. S. Carne-Ross expressed concern about Dante's ability to continue to engage the modern reader. He worried that scholarship's tight grip might strangle the poem.

> We should also allow the poem to point *forward*. We pay the *Comedy* a dubious compliment if we suppose that its life and rage for truth were cut short at the year 1321. Instead of protectively putting it out of time's way, we should let it collaborate with, or struggle against, its own future and grant it what all other great poems possess, a genuine *Fortleben,* the power of entering into new relations of meaning beyond those its creator could have foreseen or intended. For a moment, remove the Aquinas map we have exhumed from the theological library, detach the *signa* from the *res* and let them stand in their own terminal right. For a moment, let the poem suffer the shock of its own dissolution. Then of course it must come together again, but subtly a change has taken place. . . .

Carne-Ross protests the way scholarship emphasizes the poem's fierce attachment to its own medieval "worldly domain," to cite again Edward Said's phrase from the introduction, only to disregard the contemporary world of the reader. The challenge, he implies in his review (and he takes Singleton to task for not meeting it), is to explore how the medieval work of art might speak directly to a contemporary audience. How can a medieval literary work like Dante's change the life of a modern reader? Perhaps the reception of Dante by artists of color, as unexpected and unusual as these adaptations and imitations are, exemplifies a kind of reading that follows precisely the course the reviewer proposes. For these writers perceived by some to be at the margins of the canon—Naylor, Baraka, Ray, and Brown, not to mention Wright, Ellison, Morrison, and the others who have come up in the course of this book, as well as the filmmaker Spencer Williams—show us how timely Dante's canonical poem remains for some of its readers.[2] The Dante they value is at times unruly, in various ways radical, and to varying degrees political, and he helps them make a case against injustice as he accompanies them on their journey toward freedom and civil rights over the course of the history of the United States. Dante speaks directly to these freedom readers whose interpretations time and again counter the scholarly strangulation of the poem.[3] I conclude by returning to the remarks of Carne-Ross:

> [The *Divine Comedy*] has been released from the timeless limbo to which scholarship would confine it and thus strengthened. It has been brought back into time and history, returned to the tradition (with all its hazards) to which we too belong.[4]

NOTES

Introduction

1. By comparison, one might consider the translation of the *Inferno* by Ciaran Carson, which casts the action in terms of the ongoing tension between Protestants and Catholics on the edges of Northern Ireland (xi–xii). In fact, Irish authors, most noticeably Joyce, Beckett, and Heaney, also seem attuned to Dante's "subversive power," to borrow the good phrase from the provocative, if brief, discussion of Pascale Casanova (*World Republic of Letters* 329).

2. Christian, *Black Saga* 410.

3. At times I also use the qualifier "African American" to refer to the entire tradition under examination. But chronological categories have their limitations. To cite only one example, Toni Morrison, whose novel *The Bluest Eye* I discuss in the context of its influence on Gloria Naylor's African American Dante in chapter four, wrote that work in the late 1960s at the time of Black Dante, and her protagonist is a girl in the 1940s whom some would call Negro or colored. Such obvious shortcomings aside, I believe this chronological framework is a helpful way to categorize the authors' responses to Dante. Another angle from which to approach the complexity of these categories is to consider how Italian scholars assimilate them into their critical discourse. See Martino Marazzi, "Preistoria e storia di 'afro-americano.'"

4. See Eldridge Cleaver's admonition in *Soul on Ice* 79–80.

5. See Havely, "Prosperous People"; Wallace, "Dante in English" 255; Cambon, *Dante's Craft* 145; and "Dante on Galway Kinnell's 'Last River'" 31; Boitani 263–68; Fabi, *America nera* 89; Mauro, *Storia dei neri d'America* 74. Walter Mauro recognizes Dante's impact on Jones/Baraka, but his observation that *The System of Dante's Hell* is situated in Harlem is incorrect.

6. In his essay "Connecting Empire to Secular Interpretation," *Culture and Imperialism* 43–61.

7. And it has remained such in new millennial discussions on globalizing literary studies. Wai Chee Dimock has argued for the ahistoricity of literature using

the global response to Dante as her case, with Mandelstam and Eliot as primary texts in her investigation. See Gayatri Spivak's short, albeit sympathetic, critique in *Death of a Discipline* 114n1. Influenced by Said's arguments about the colonial origins of comparative literature, Spivak pleads for a definition of globalism that is not "confined to Euro-U.S. debates" (114). In *The Translation Zone: A New Comparative Literature,* Emily Apter, like Dimock, makes a case for the value of translation in reading across national and historical literary traditions. She considers how their respective encounters with Dante shaped the thinking of two of the foundational figures of comparative literature, Erich Auerbach and Leo Spitzer (25–64), and how Edward Said's reception of their respective readings of Dante affected his own formulation about comparative literature (65–81). Finally, Pascale Casanova has situated Dante at the center of her attempt to come up with a new instauration of Goethe's dream of *Weltliteratur* (*The World Republic of Letters* 48–57).

8. One could add Werner Friederich's work as further example of the institutionalization of Dante in comparative studies. *Dante's Fame Abroad* was the second volume published in the University of North Carolina Studies in Comparative Literature series in 1950, followed several years later by his *Outline of Comparative Literature from Dante Alighieri to Eugene O'Neill.*

9. Said's position in *Culture and Imperialism* appears balanced somewhat, if unarticulated, by the painting used to decorate the cover of his final book of essays, *Reflections on Exile and Other Essays.* The choice of image suggests that he (or the staff at Harvard University Press) wanted to foreground the complexities of Dante as a political author. The painting *Dante in Exile,* by Domenico Peterlin, completed in the fateful year of 1865 as Italians gathered to celebrate their new state and the sixth centennial of the birth of their new nation's first hero, presents a pensive and somber Dante with book in hand stretched out on a hill overlooking the sea. Exile removes the urban poet from his city, which he can visit only in writing. It is precisely this politicized image of Dante in exile that appeals to writers of color. It may be, then, that Said's reading of Dante had come full circle by the end of his life: foundational author on the one hand, but radically antiestablishmentarian on the other.

10. Shakespeare is another important canonical author who could similarly be called upon to demarcate the passage of specific marginal writers from Colored to Negro to Black to African American and beyond, moving from the nineteenth century to today.

11. This is Bhabha's main theme in *The Location of Culture.*

12. Trans. Robert S. Haller, *Literary Criticism of Dante Alighieri* 100.

13. Charles S. Singleton, "The Irreducible Dove," *Comparative Literature* 9 (1957): 129.

14. See Havely's "'An Italian Writer against the Pope'?"

15.   Emerson is the first to translate *Vita Nuova* into English (ca. 1842); Lowell writes a famous biographical sketch on Dante for the *Appleton New American Encyclopedia* (1859); Norton is the first to publish a complete translation of *Vita Nuova* (1859); and Longfellow's translation of the *Divine Comedy* came out in 1865.

16.   Parenthetically, one might observe that this tradition develops at the expense of Francis Petrarch and his venerable literary reputation. Amedeo Quondam considers how and why Petrarch, the *princeps* of humanists (the first and best, Erasmus calls him), who had been without question the most popular, influential European literary figure, came to be, as Quondam's title has it, *Petrarca, l'italiano dimenticato,* the forgotten Italian. The process, which begins in the eighteenth century and then culminates decisively in the nineteenth, sees Dante replace Petrarch as the father of Italian letters. The political and ideological values that accrue to Dante in Risorgimento Italy enable him first to destabilize and then eventually to displace Petrarch in the Italian Pantheon, for the latter was associated with much of what the new and young Italy didn't want to be: aristocratic, cleric, lyric, prescriptive, classical, friendly to petty despots, as opposed to the way in which, rightly or wrongly, the followers of "giovine Italia" perceived Dante: a lay voice of liberty and unity and revolution dedicated to the recuperation of his "patria."

17.   See the definitive essay on the parallel between Dante's journey and Exodus by Charles S. Singleton, "In Exitu Israel de Aegypto."

18.   From St. Clair Drake's papers, housed in the Schomburg Center for Research in Black Culture, NYPL, box 22, folder 5, from an unpublished manuscript which appears to be a lecture he gave entitled "African-American Popular Culture and the Literary Tradition."

19.   McHenry mentions the Reverend Frank F. Hall's canonical list of authors to read, which includes Dante, for the members of the African American literary society, the Boston Literary and Historical Association, in 1902 (172). McHenry also refers to the African American author Sarah E. Tanner's inclusion of Dante in an essay on reading for *Women's Era* from 1895 (232).

20.   See, e.g., *Dante's Pilgrim's Progress; or, "The passage of the blessed soul from the slavery of the present corruption to the liberty of eternal glory,"* published in 1893.

21.   I cite from the Smalley edition (rpt. 1974).

22.   For the story of Nashoba, see Egerton; for Wright's life, see Stiller.

23.   Trollope actually knew Dante's poem in the original. Her son Thomas comments that she made her own translations, which as far as I know we no longer possess (*What I Remember* 123). For Cary's life and work, see R. W. King, *The Translator of Dante*; for a study of his translation of Dante in its cultural context and from the perspective of translation studies, see Edoardo Crisafulli, *The Vision of Dante: Cary's Translation of "The Divine Comedy."*

24. In contrast to these comments in praise of Wright, however, Trollope suggested that her friend had lost her mind in a confidential letter to Charles Wilkes, a lawyer who helped her with financial matters: "Poor Fanny Wright! I own to you that my firm conviction is, that the brain fever which attacked her last year has affected her intellect; there is no other mode of accounting for her words, or her actions" (letter of Feb. 14, 1828, Cincinnati, in Cincinnati Historical Society Library, Mss VF 4375).

25. There are at least four references to Dante in Trollope's book, two with citations from the appropriate passages in the original Italian (4, 44, 172, 312), one of which (44) is an interesting rewriting of *Inferno* 3.51.

26. For the definitive statement on Orientalism, but with no reference to Mrs. Trollope's early contribution, see Edward Said, *Orientalism*.

27. Although we have no direct evidence, scholars have come to the reasonable conclusion that she was the mastermind behind the scenes in the amusement scheme described below; see Kellogg 9, Smalley xxviii–xxxiv, and Tucker 90. The argument that the painter Frederick Franks may have been involved in the conceptualization of the exhibit seems far-fetched (Reynolds 49–50).

28. For more on the cenotaph, see the carefully documented essay by Graham Smith, *The Stone of Dante* 34 ff.

29. See Luigi Santini, *The Protestant Cemetery of Florence called "The English Cemetery,"* and Judi Culbertson and Tom Randall, *Permanent Italians: An Illustrated, Biographical Guide to the Cemeteries of Italy* 129–35.

30. In addition to wax, the figures were made of wood, cloth, plaster, and metal (Wunder 2:214). Some, not all, of the figures were moved to Dorfeuille's new museum in New York City in 1839, where they were destroyed by fire in 1840. We do not know the fate of the figures that were left behind in Cincinnati. For a more detailed look at the description of the exhibit in Powers's own letters and in the writings of his daughter, Louisa, see my essay "Flame-Coloured Letters and Bugaboo Phraseology," which covers some of the material discussed here but draws heavily on original documents in the archives of the Gabinetto Vieusseux in Florence.

31. Smalley xxviii–xxxiv, Tucker 90–95, and Dennett 20–21, 110–13, give the most extensive descriptions of the Dante exhibit. Dunlop laments the impact of the Dante spectacle on the exhibits of natural and local history in the original collection of the Western Museum (539, 548), which were increasingly neglected.

32. Wunder claims that Linus Everett is a relative of Edward Everett, who would become a friend of Powers in the years to come (1:62n61). Edward Everett is the recipient of several of Powers's most serious letters on slavery in the 1860s: Jan. 14, 1861 (*Copialettere* 1242), and Oct. 22, 1864 (*Copialettere* 1336). The Fondo Hiram Powers contains an extensive notebook compiled by the artist's daughter,

Louisa, which includes the copies of many letters to and from Hiram; I refer to this here and below as the *Copialettere.*

33. For more on the representation of blacks in nineteenth-century American sculpture, see Savage.

34. Powers himself uses this patronizing language in a letter to Edward Everett, Oct. 22, 1864, on the English reluctance to condemn the Confederacy: "There are many good men in the north who hate slavery as much as you do, and women too, to whom your noble Ladies appealed some years ago to do what they could for the *poor* slave. Where are those ladies now? And what are they doing for the *poor* African Slave?" (my emphasis, in *Copialettere* 1337–38).

35. As far as I can tell, this phrase is Everett's, not Trollope's. In his essay "Ohio Show-Shop" (91), Tucker attributes this phrase to a museum handbill and implies that Trollope wrote it. I can't find evidence of this specific handbill in the collections of the Cincinnati Historical Society where Tucker conducted his research. I am led to assume, therefore, that he mistook Everett's statement for something other than what it was. On the basis of the error, I believe, Wunder claims (without citing his references) that Linus Everett "was actually engaged to compose the descriptive pamphlet distributed after the exhibition opened to the public" (1:62n61).

36. On Aug. 10, 1829, race riots broke out in Cincinnati, which prompted the exodus of around one thousand blacks for points farther north and east. There had been antiblack rioting in 1826, and it would happen again in 1836. See Christian, *Black Saga* 95, 98, 119. In a letter to his wife of Aug. 11, 1836, Hiram Powers writes from Boston with concern about the riots in Cincinnati.

37. For Dante's notion of *contrapasso,* or the punishment fitting the crime, see his use of the word with the defining example of Bertran de Born at the very end of *Inferno* 28. See Marc Cogan's helpful discussion of "contrapasso," beginning with the passage in *Inferno* 28 (36–43 and 91–96).

38. See the sections on Paul Cuffe and others who promoted colonization in Bruce, *Origins of African American Literature* 129–74.

39. M. H. Dunlop decries the "Western Museum's shift from regionalism to grotesquerie" (539); and adds: "Drake's idea of a museum as a regional mirror became in Dorfeuille's and Powers's hands a tense and disharmonious mood, as their efforts at grotesquerie worked shattering effects on the Museum's connection to landscape realities. The mood expressed by their handiwork was profoundly dislocating and antiregional [*sic*], as night after night for thirty-eight years, the Western Museum's attic rocked to the shrieks of the damned while below, in the grimy display rooms, detailed representation of the untended Midwestern landscape gathered dust in the darkness" (548). Dunlop suggests that the Infernal Regions emphasized specifically the grotesque. "The experience of the grotesque is not

intellectual but emotional, and a complex of emotions at that. Grotesquerie is not fantasy; it is a troubling mixture of the comic and the terrifying that depends for some of its effect on the presence of a realistic framework. Contemporary accounts make it clear that the representation of suffering and torment that was The Infernal Regions aroused in its audience emotions characteristic of the grotesque: the effect was a combination of the comic with 'terror and astonishment' plus a considerable element of the 'loathsome and disgusting'" (541).

40. Dante's vision of hell as a model for haunted houses at carnivals is portrayed in the 1935 film *Dante's Inferno,* starring Spencer Tracy. The film was the screen debut of Rita Hayworth, who appeared in a minor role as a dancer.

Chapter 1. Colored Dante

1. William J. Kennedy's discussion of readings of Petrarch in the Renaissance in the context of the Reformation and Counter-Reformation has stimulated my thinking on Dante as a reformer. In various commentaries Petrarch, too, emerges in a surprising light. See Kennedy, *Authorizing Petrarch* 67–81. See also Martin McLaughlin's comments in "Petrarch: between two ages, between two languages" (36–38), on the 1503 Venetian edition of Filelfo's commentary on Petrarch's *Canzoniere* in Oxford's Bodleian Library, in which a Catholic reader troubled by Petrarch's criticism of the papacy has tried to scorch sonnets 137–38 off the page.

2. Dante as reformer also appealed to writers from New England who wrote, some more directly than others, under the influence of Calvinism; see Verduin 2005.

3. For Kirkup's recounting of his discovery of the Bargello portrait, see his letters to Dante Gabriele Rossetti in Toynbee, *Dante in English Literature* 2:639–42. For a description of the uncovering and restoration of the Bargello fresco in the context of Florentine and Italian politics in the 1840s, see Barocchi and Bertelà, especially 3–8. For an influential account of the discovery written for an American audience, see Botta 114–16.

4. On the swell of women, scholars, and general readers, who began reading Dante at this time, see La Piana 137–38, 141–42, and 148–49.

5. For discussion of the Whig appropriation of Dante, see Braida 77–87, Crisafulli 265–325, and Milbank 8–28; for a general orientation to the topic of Dante in Reformation England, see Havely, "Dante in Reformation England." As Crisafulli points out, the majority of readers accepted the Whig, i.e., neo-

Ghibelline, paradigm that promoted Dante as precursor to the Reformation (288). But Braida finds other readers, mainly "connoisseurs of Italian literature" (64), who are beginning to argue for nonpolitical readings of Dante in the 1830s and beyond.

6. See Verduin 1996, 40 and 50, who refers to Lears 155–59, and Turner, *Without God* 251–54, for further discussion of this point.

7. From James Turner's biography, *The Liberal Education of Charles Eliot Norton*: "In the Turnbull Lectures delivered at Johns Hopkins in 1894, he [Norton] attributed the vogue of Dante to a combination of 'the materialism of our existing state of civilization' and 'the general dissolution of the old forms of religious faith'" (335). The original speech is catalogued as "Dante, Lecture I," typescript, box 13, Miscellaneous Papers, Norton Papers, Houghton Library, Harvard University (*Liberal Education* 458n35).

8. Even though they are unaware of Ray's specific interpretation, as far as I can tell, writers to follow in the tradition of reading Dante that I am mapping here—Richard Wright, LeRoi Jones/Amiri Baraka, Toni Morrison, Gloria Naylor, among others—will respond to him similarly.

9. Among the passages in the *Divine Comedy* frequently cited: *Inf.* 7.46–48, *Purg.* 16.100–102, and *Par.* 9.127–38, on papal greed; *Purg.* 32.149 on the papal court as a harlot; *Par.* 18.127–36 on the political abuse of excommunication; *Par.* 29.81 ff. on misinterpretations of Scripture.

10. Havely points out some shortcomings in Boswell's work in "Dante in Reformation England" (128).

11. Boswell notes: "The insular English took more than a cursory interest in Continental popular culture, and they noted Dante's use of the vernacular, citing it to validate English as a likewise respectable means of literary expression. They praised his contributions to Tuscan eloquence even as they invoked him as an authority on hell (along with Homer and Virgil), on purgatory, and on bad popes. Following the publication of *De Monarchia* (Basel: Oporinus, 1559; reprinted 1566), Dante's name began to figure largely in the battle between Roman Catholics and Protestants for the soul of England; thereafter, Dante's fame as a poet was nearly eclipsed by his renown as a political polemicist. He had written *Monarchia* . . . to promote the cause of the Holy Roman Emperor in his struggle with the pope for temporal power; and Protestant sympathizers were quite happy two hundred years later to recycle Dante's invective against the pope in defense of the 'true' faith. After all, if they could quote 'one of Rome's own' in scathing denunciation of the Holy Father, they might lay claim to intellectual objectivity and plausibly defend themselves against allegations that they were inventing papal chicanery.

That he had been excommunicated and his books burnt at the behest of the bishop of Rome because of his use of unvarnished truth was proof enough for them that Dante was a proto-Protestant" (xv).

12. See Anthony K. Cassell's brisk report of the early fortunes of the *Monarchia* in the introductory section to his translation (41–43).

13. Hermann Oelsner may have been the first to note this connection (*Influence* 42).

14. See Havely's careful reconstruction of how Foxe and other Protestants took refuge on the Continent at various moments in the mid-1500s ("Dante in Reformation England" 137). See also Toynbee's article on Foxe's role at Oporinus's publishing house, "John Foxe and the *editio princeps* of Dante's *Monarchia*."

15. Citations from Foxe are from *Foxe's Book of Martyrs Variorum Edition Online* (2nd ed.). Accessed Oct. 6, 2007. <http://www.hrionline.ac.uk/johnfoxe/index.html>.

16. Havely cites this same passage in Foxe in "Dante in Reformation England" 134. Stephen Greenblatt's comment "There are surprisingly few references to Dante, hostile or otherwise, in the controversies between Catholics and Protestants . . ." may not be incorrect (it depends on how one calculates a "few" references), but it is misleading (*Hamlet in Purgatory* 49). Dante, perhaps more the author of the *Monarchia* than the poet of the *Purgatory,* is surprisingly prominent in the debate. In addition to Havely's essay, David Wallace provides a good starting place in his brief commentary on the reception of Dante in sixteenth-century England in "Dante in England" 425–27.

17. For Bellarmine's life and bibliography, I have consulted the unsigned article in *Encyclopedia Britannica* (1911), 3:694–95.

18. The full title of the appendix refers to the work of Perrot, which was apparently written in Italian: *Appendix ad libros de Summo Pontifice quae continent responsionem ad librum quondam anonymum cujus titulus est Aviso piacevole dato alla bella Italia.* The section on Dante runs from pages 1026 to 1034, chapters 14–19, in the 1608 Paris edition. Bellarmine also includes shorter sections on Petrarch (1034–38) and Boccaccio (1038–40).

19. Robert Hollander's note in his translation of the *Inferno* proves Bellarmine's count wrong (130); if one includes unnamed popes, the Protestants were reading this detail in Dante accurately all along!

20. Sumner refers to Dante at various points during this first trip, e.g., writing with verve to William Wetmore Story in 1839: "I have already seen life in considerable variety. I am about to retire to *convent* to live with some Franciscan monks in a beautiful place, which hangs over the Alban lake. —'far from the madding crowd's ignoble strife.' I shall overhaul their library, study Dante, & drink

their wine. Don't report me to the Temperance Society" (*Letters* 1:64–65). From that same trip abroad, Sumner provides his friends back home with a steady record of his reading, claiming at one point to have read "nearly all the Italian classics, poets, & prose-writers, from Dante & Mach. To Alfieri & Manzoni" (*Letters* 1:75). Once back in the United States, Sumner can comfortably use citations from Dante to embellish his letters with humor and point. "I trust *Minos* will teach the Lockport judge some of the duties of the bench. Where would Dante doom him?" (*Letters* 1:105). This sort of casual allusion to Dante in the 1840s and 1850s is an indication of his familiarity with Dante and the relative familiarity he assumed his correspondents already had with the poet's writings.

21. *His Complete Works* 48. Sumner cites Dante from the translation of Thomas Brooksbank, *Dante's Divine Comedy. The First Part: Hell* 106.

22. To Samuel Gridley Howe, Nov. 10, 1858.

23. See Mary Hensman's *Dante Map,* in the British Library, 11420. cc.14, and at the John Rylands University Library, Manchester, R17263. The handsome map opens out to approximately 2×3 feet, with a depiction of the Italian peninsula on the left-hand side and north-central Italy on the right. A small pamphlet accompanies the map in which the author-cartographer explains that she distinguishes places mentioned in Dante's writings from places he was likely to have visited in exile (v–vi).

24. See Henry's *Life of Calvin* 1:229–30, and Withrow's comments in "The Ladies of Port Royal," where he links Dante, Luther, and Pascal for their efforts at standardizing their respective languages (131).

25. "A Poet among the Poets," *Catholic World* 23.133 (April 1876): 17.

26. For Thomas and his project, see Gilbert F. Cunningham, "*The Divine Comedy" in English* 102–8.

27. For other examples of pro-Italian sentiment in the *North Star,* see the poems by unnamed authors, "Rome Shall Be Free," from Sept. 7, 1849 (2.37, p. 4), and "To Pius IX," in which the pope is referred to as "the Nero of our time," Sept. 14, 1849 (2.38, p. 4). Also see the poem by Fanny Kemble, actress and abolitionist, on Italy's struggle for freedom in the issue of Jan. 28, 1848 (1.5, p. 4).

28. Adams's speech is found in Foner and Branham, *Lift Every Voice* 460–62.

29. I have followed the biographies of Denis Mack Smith and Roland Sarti. For general comments on the reception of Dante by Mazzini and others mentioned below, see Caesar's anthology, *Dante: The Critical Heritage, 1314(?)–1870.*

30. My translations from Mazzini's *Scritti letterari,* here and following.

31. For a discussion of alternate interpretations of Dante at the time of Mazzini, see Thompson, "Dante, the *Risorgimento,* and the British" 106–12; on Mazzini's political reading of Dante, see Ciccarelli 77–80.

32. Garrison's preface to Douglass's narrative runs from p. vii to p. xiii in the Dover edition. For a brief history of the publication of Douglass's autobiography, its changing titles, and accompanying paratexts, see Logan's preface, *Life and Times* 15–16.

33. In *Darkest Italy* and in his essay "Imagined Italies," John Dickie lays the groundwork for a more detailed comparative analysis of the Italian Mezzogiorno in the nineteenth century and the American South. While he doesn't actually address the U.S. version of the "southern question," much of what he says is applicable to a discussion of the two historical situations of the respective "Souths" in the second half of the nineteenth century. Two books came out in 2002 that take up precisely that challenge: the contributions to the edited volume by Dal Lago and Halpern, *The American South and the Italian Mezzogiorno,* and Don H. Doyle's *Nations Divided.* The question one could explore—which I do not have space to do here—is the extent to which Dante features in both sets of representations of southern identity. A starting place on the Italian side is with Antonio Gramsci's work on Dante, specifically his reading of *Inferno* 10, in his critique of power and politics. On the southern U.S. side of the question, one could consider the detailed response of the Agrarians— especially Allen Tate and Robert Penn Warren—to Dante. Their adaptations of Dante owe much to Eliot and modernism, but the Italian's extensive influence on them is also refracted through a filter not unlike that discussed in *Freedom Readers.* They read Dante as a highly politicized author whose text they sometimes use to shed light on the difficult question of race in their own historical moment. One could do much with the influence of Dante on Warren's *All the King's Men* and Tate's chilling poem on a voyeuristic experience of a lynching, "The Swimmers."

34. On Mazzini and slavery, see Epstein 54–57. Garrison probably first learned of this specific letter by Mazzini in the pamphlet *Letters on American Slavery,* in which the letter is dated March 21, 1859 (14).

35. See Wicks on Italians in exile, such as Foscolo, Mazzini, Panizzi, and Rossetti, who turned to Dante as a touchstone and comforter. Isabella is good on the politicized nature of the triangular relationship Mazzini constructed among Foscolo, Dante, and himself (497–500).

36. The autograph is in a private collection in Italy.

37. In another work Mazzini cites the line from Dante again and adds to it the phrase "from exile" (using a variant spelling of the word in Italian) thus making clear the connection in his mind: "Da martirio / E da esiglio venne a questa pace" (*Living Thoughts of Mazzini* 115). In addition, in this passage either he remembers the verb form incorrectly, *venne* for *venni,* or the typographer made an error.

38. See the full note on the topic by Robert Hollander in his translation of the *Inferno,* p. 130.

39. In a letter of Sept. 8, 1847, before the establishment of the Roman Republic, Mazzini urged the pope to bring Italy together under papal rule and leadership (Smith, *Mazzini* 51–52). But he was more often critical of the papacy as in a letter of May 1, 1854, to the Reverend Dr. Beard of Manchester, England: "Blessed be your efforts . . . if you do not forget, whilst at work for the emancipation of the black race, the millions of white slaves, suffering, struggling, expiring in Italy, in Poland, in Hungary, throughout all Europe; if you always remember that free men only can achieve the work of freedom, and that Europe's appeal for the abolition of slavery in other lands will not weigh all-powerful before God and men, whilst Europe herself shall be desecrated by arbitrary, tyrannical power, by czars, emperors, and popes" (*Letters on American Slavery* 13).

40. He recruited soldiers to fight with him in Kansas, including one Hugh Forbes who had fought with Garibaldi in Italy (*All on Fire* 476). For more on Forbes, see *Life and Letters of John Brown* 430–32.

41. The full title of Cournos's book is *A Modern Plutarch: Being an Account of some Great Lives in the Nineteenth Century, together with some Comparisons between the Latin and the Anglo-Saxon Genius*; the section on Garibaldi and Brown is at 177–220. Seymour Drescher mentions the collocation of the two men in journalism of the late 1850s and 1860s, noting that in Europe there was understandably much more focus on Garibaldi (261–62).

42. Wendell Phillips, *Speeches, Lectures, and Letters* 304–5.

43. For an edition that Sumner might have consulted, see I. A. Wright's version, *Dante, Translated into English Verse* (1854).

44. The author of the letter may have known that "Young America" was actually the name assumed by the radical group of young politicians in the Democratic Party in the 1850s. The man who coined the term, Edwin de Leon, did use it in conjunction with references to various revolutionary political movements in Europe at the time. See Rossi, "Mazzini and Young America" 91–104. Mazzini makes the link in a letter of March 21, 1859: "I am very much pleased at . . . response . . . coming from Young America, to whom Young Italy looks for sympathy and support in her approaching struggle . . ." (*Letters on American Slavery* 14).

45. For the link between Garibaldi and Lincoln, see the article by H. Nelson Gay, "Lincoln's Offer of a Command to Garibaldi." Gay suggests that Garibaldi's demand that Lincoln emancipate the slaves as a condition for his possible assumption of a major position in the U.S. army may have had some impact on Lincoln's eventual decision to do so.

46. McHenry analyzes the paper's role in meeting "the changing needs of black readers" (106) in *Forgotten Readers* 103–14; see also the discussion in Penn 35–47, valuable for its early recognition of the paper's importance.

47. See, for example, "The Two Sicilies," on the growing tension between the English and the Neapolitans (1.12, p. 4); "The Trembling Eye Lid," on the political intrigues of "Romish priests" (1.8, p. 4); "General Intelligence," with a section on Italy (1.43, p. 1); and ". . . against Color," a passionate meditation on the historic lack of prejudice in countries like Italy "where colored persons have not been held as slaves" (1.27, p. 1). Dante is mentioned twice in *Colored American,* both times in passing, in passages that are not remarkable: "In conversation, Dante was taciturn" (1.1, p. 4); "Yet he [Boccaccio] became one of the three great masters of the Tuscan dialect, Dante and Petrarch being the other two" (2.35, p. 2). Despite the superficiality of the references, they do show some familiarity with Dante.

48. For the complicated textual tradition of the four editions/versions of *Clotel,* the best guide is provided by the "Bibliographical Descriptions and Publisher Information" in the scholarly apparatus that accompanies the electronic version published by the University of Virginia Press at <http://rotunda.upress .virginia.edu/clotel/descriptions.html>.

49. See Joan E. Cashin's comments in the introduction to her edition of *Clotel; or, The President's Daughter* (ix).

50. He mistakenly calls the poem "The Lament of Dante."

51. Fabi gives a careful description of the changes among the various versions of the novel in *Passing* 21–26.

52. This passage occurs in installment 4 of the serialized novel on March 2, 1861.

53. Kapai 745. Blount's analysis of two sonnets is an exception to the underestimation of Ray's powers (esp. 229–31), as is the reading by Walters 50–58.

54. La Piana lists nearly fifty poems between 1881 and 1905 (150–51).

55. First published in the *AME Church Review* 1.3 (1885): 251, Ray's poem was reprinted in 1910 in a collection of her work called simply *Poems,* republished in *Collected Black Women's Poetry.*

56. A popular book that came out in 1879, shortly before Ray published her poem in 1885, Wicksteed's *Dante: Six Sermons,* may have caught Ray's attention for its references to Dante's skills as a statesman; see the opening chapter, especially 4 and 16–20.

57. Wolseley has more on the history of "colored" journalism; as does McHenry, esp. 54–55, 80–81, 103–14, and 137–38.

58. "Its ducal palaces, its grand Duomo, its fine galleries of art, its beautiful Arno, its charming environs, and its many associations of great historical personages, especially of Michelangelo, Dante, and Savonarola, give it a controlling power over mind and heart" (*Life and Times of Frederick Douglass* 589).

59. The Kentucky artist Joel Hart sculpted the bas-relief for Parker's tomb-stone; we don't know exactly who composed the epitaph. For a reproduction, see the entry under "Joel Tanner Hart" at <http://www.florin.ms/libr.html>. Accessed Nov. 30, 2008. The wording of the epitaph, which also gives the birth and death of "The Great American Preacher," has points in common with Douglass's original impression recorded in his travel diary. "I could but recall as I looked upon his grave the many heroics rendered the cause of human freedom by him, freedom not only from physical chains but the chains of superstition" (*Tour of Europe and Africa* 57; accessed June 2, 2010). In his entry, Douglass notes the simplicity of the grave, an initial impression that is edited to sound more negative in the finished autobiography in which he complains about "his simple grave. It did not seem well that the remains of the great American preacher should rest thus" (*Life and Times* 589). Perhaps Douglass's popular autobiography inspired others to remedy the apparent neglect of Parker's tomb, and in the process someone invited Douglass to write the epitaph himself?

60. See the entry on Parker in Mason Lowance's *Against Slavery: An Abolitionist Reader* 273–90.

61. See the article by Nancy Farrell, "The Slave That Captivated America."

62. Cathy Ingram, the curator of the Frederick Douglass National Historic Site at Cedar Hill, reported that the Dante piece is no longer in the collection; letter to the author, Dec. 20, 1999. The passage from the Washington *Press* is in *The Frederick Douglass Papers* 5:399. There is a similar description of Douglass's study from the Cleveland *Gazette*, Sept. 10, 1892, in vol. 5:500.

63. Under the name "Dante," the U.S. Federal Census provides the following data:

"Dante"	1880	1890	1900	1910	1920	1930
total citizens	39	0	243	169	460	446
Italians	1	0	50	?	284	440
non-Italians	38	0	193	?	176	6
white	37	0	185	169	151	4
black/colored	1	0	8	0	25	2

The table shows that there is a marked increase in the name among blacks in the 1920 census. The 25 black Americans named Dante listed in 1920 were born between 1847 and 1913, with the majority of them (17) born in the 1870s, 1880s, or 1890s. That is, most of the black males listed in the 1920 census with the name Dante were born in the decades following the Civil War during the explosion of interest in the Italian writer. It is worth noting that alternate spellings of Dante yield much more data. For example, in the 1910 census, in which no black has the name Dante, there are 15 individuals whose race is listed as "colored" with the following variants of Dante, among others, as their names: Dantee, Dant, Dantus, Danta, and Dantty. I consulted the census online at ancestry.com; accessed April 7, 2008.

Chapter 2. Negro Dante

1. Herbert Aptheker provides a brief account of the publication history of the talk, which was published posthumously, in his edition of Du Bois's *The Education of Black People* ix–xi.

2. This line occurs in the concluding paragraph to "Of the Training of Black Men," originally published in *The Atlantic Monthly* (Sept. 1902), reprinted as chap. 6 in *The Souls of Black Folk* 55–67. Du Bois goes on to list these other European authors: Balzac, Dumas, Aristotle, and Marcus Aurelius.

3. See the full discussion of this moment in Du Bois's life by David Lewis 67–72. Cook and Tatum provide a careful reading of Du Bois's use of Cicero in this section of *The Souls of Black Folk* without, however, making the same points I do (107–14). I agree with them that this "is one of the most moving chapters in a book that has many" (114).

4. Ernest Hatch Wilkins passionately argues for the importance of Petrarch's *Coronation Oration*: "The oration delivered by Petrarch on the occasion of his coronation on April 8, 1341, illuminates more clearly than does any other existing document the gradual transition from the Middle Ages to the Renaissance. With all its mingling of elements old and new it is the first manifesto of the Renaissance" ("Petrarch's *Coronation Oration*" 300).

5. For more on the importance of Cicero's oration for Petrarch's seminal work, see Dennis Looney, "The Beginnings of Humanistic Oratory" 136–38.

6. For a brief review of how *Renaissance* transforms from a literary term to a more generic cultural label in this context, see Powell, *Black Art and Culture* 50–51.

7. See his unpublished typescript, "Aaron Douglas (1899–), An Autobiography," in the Aaron Douglas Collection, Special Collections, Fisk University (box 1, folder 1, p. 1).

8. The epigraph to the introduction of *Freedom Readers* refers to this park and its Dante monument but from the time frame of 2007, when its name unofficially

had become "Malcolm X Park" rather than Meridian Hill. The blogger wiredog expresses his incredulity of any possible connection between Malcolm X and Dante, the ultimate DWEM, "dead white European male." By now, dear reader, you have seen that there is a multitude of direct links between Dante and African American culture (for Malcolm X, some indirect connections to come in chaps. 3 and 4).

9.   There are at least four documents that refer to Dante in the Jean Toomer Archives in Beinecke Library, Yale University, box 48. In folder 1010, there is an undated note for an essay in progress on spirituality and literature: "The person, on reading a masterpiece of poetry, drama, or philosophy would also be conscious-that-there-is-method in the Divine Comedy, that there is method in Dante . . ." In folder 1007, three different unnumbered documents are connected with a lecture he gave to the Catholic Poetry Society of America, "Poetry and Spiritual Rebirth," on April 15, 1947. In one document he collects his thoughts on poetry: "Poetry as a reward of those who in some measure possessed their possessions. Dante, Saint John of the Cross, Blake, Whitman, Herman Melville." He invokes a version of this canon in another note: "Poetry as an expression of things seen, felt, and realized by those who have undergone new birth. Dante—his great poem a record of experience, plus impure additions. Blake. Whitman. St. John of the Cross. Brothers [*sic*] Lawrence. Herman Melville. Others." In another document he essentially repeats this same idea and list.

10.   Aaron Douglas did the illustrations for Johnson's work, which Powell describes as one of "several quintessential 'New Negro' publications" he illustrated (229). For a detailed description of the images, see Kirschke 98–101, and see plates 52–59 for reproductions of some of Douglas's illustrations. See also Powell's discussion in *Black Art and Culture in the 20th Century* 41–54.

11.   See the articles by Clayton and Cripps (*Amos 'n' Andy . . .*) for discussions of the controversy surrounding the TV show. Also see Ely's *The Adventures of Amos 'n' Andy*. Ely studies both the radio and the TV shows and the friction on the TV set when the white radio players tried to coach the black actors: "Some veteran black performers [like Spencer Williams] were not happy with the idea of 'a white man teaching a Negro how to act like a white man acting like a Negro'" (206). The citation is from Alvin Childress who played the part of Amos on the television show.

12.   Adrienne Lanier Seward organized the retrospective and provided the program notes. Thomas Cripps has devoted much attention to Williams, but he has relatively little to say about the film that concerns me most, *Go Down, Death!*

13.   But Lee does give Williams his due in a blurb in *American Movie Classics Magazine* 77 (Oct. 1994) in connection with the Second Annual AMC Film Preservation Festival: "The films of Oscar Micheaux and Spencer Williams are important

to preserve because they document black filmmakers who are the grandfathers of black cinema. They're the people who paved the way, and it's important that we know about their work and that the viewer can see it" (5).

14. Thomas Cripps's essay "The Films of Spencer Williams" is an early attempt (1978) to address the indifference to Williams's work; Jacqueline Stewart of Northwestern University is currently writing what will be the definitive study of his work and career.

15. Williams's obituary claims erroneously that he was born in the British West Indies: *Hollywood Reporter* (Dec. 18, 1969). For an image of his tombstone in Los Angeles National Cemetery with Louisiana as his birthplace inscribed on it, see <http://www.findagrave.com>, memorial number 6268549; accessed Nov. 21, 2009.

16. For a biographical sketch of Williams, see Jones, *Black Cinema Treasures* 31–35, and Cripps, *Black Film as Genre* 90–99. Clayton discusses Williams's role in the controversial television show, as does Ely. Spencer Williams the actor and director is to be distinguished from the composer of "Basin Street Blues" and other pieces written for Josephine Baker at the Folies Bergère in Paris.

17. Discussions of *Go Down, Death!* give 1944 as the date of completion, but information in the AMPAS Library archives suggests that the film wasn't completed until 1946; however, this later date could be merely marking a re-release (Weisenfeld 276).

18. See Judith Weisenfeld's study *Hollywood Be Thy Name* for a detailed discussion of the relation between Williams's films and religion, 88–129.

19. Sack produced or presented or helped out with the funding for at least twenty-seven race films in the 1930s and 1940s, including several by Spencer Williams and one by Oscar Micheaux, *God's Stepchildren*. However, Arthur LeMont Terry claims to have interviewed a cameraman for Williams, Jack Whitmore, who said, "Spencer paid for that film with his own money" (103).

20. Cripps discusses the dynamics of the different audiences, urban vs. rural, in *Black Film as Genre* 98–99.

21. I have yet to find any reference to Williams's use of Dante in the critical literature. Even Franco Minganti, in his fine introductory survey of African American cinema, seems to be unaware of the filmmaker's Italian source.

22. At least one other author, Sue Brown Hays, was moved to use the sermon as a source in a novel of the same name, *Go Down, Death*. The housewife protagonist in plantation Mississippi of this white female novelist (apparently her first and only novel) overhears her maid singing a version of Johnson's "sermon" and asks to learn more about it. Lyrics from the song the maid sings are given at pp. 47 and 176.

23. A lobby card in the Edward Mapp Collection at the Academy of Motion Picture Arts and Sciences Library in Beverly Hills, California, emphasizes this dichotomy. The card contains this text: "Alfred N. Sack reverently presents *Go Down, Death! The Story of Jesus and the Devil.*" The poster contains a still from the film's first jitterbug scene with three couples dancing. Their clothes have been colored in with very bright reds, yellows, and greens. A devil (perhaps from the publicity posters for *The Blood of Jesus*) is positioned in the bottom left corner, Jesus in prayer is in the upper left, and Christ crucified is at the upper right corner. In the lower right, there is a ribbon, "Sack Mark of Merit Attraction," and the phrase "A Spencer Williams All-Negro Production."

24. I believe that G. William Jones (*Black Cinema Treasures* 50) is mistaken when he says of this image in *The Blood of Jesus*: ". . . some unusual scenes which literally interpret the story of Jacob's ladder (which Director Williams borrowed from French director Georges Méliès' 1916 film entitled *Going to Heaven*)." I find no reference to a film of Méliès by that name, nor does the cut look at all like the work of Méliès. Jones's mistake, if I am correct in calling it such, has now entered the critical literature and is being repeated by subsequent scholars. See, e.g., Terry, *Genre and Divine Causality* 105, 189.

25. John Welle's essay ably discusses the Italian film in its national cultural context.

26. Texas, where Williams did much of his work, leaves its mark in this topographical detail: Georgia is not known for its canyons! In an analogous move, Williams uses Ferde Grofé's *Grand Canyon Suite* at a climactic moment in the film's soundtrack.

27. I thank Michael Syrimis for the astute suggestion that the seemingly poor quality of the filming with many tableau shots and the static camera may be an act of reverence on the part of Williams for the silent film as a genre represented by *L'inferno.*

28. Dante the poet also must often choose where to assign a sinner who is guilty of multiple sins; he assigns Dido, for example, to the circle of the lustful (*Inf.* 5.85) rather than the wood of the suicides. Sometimes, as in the case of Dido, the poet's choice is more in line with aesthetic rather than moral criteria.

29. Comparative examination of the cuts used by Williams and the version distributed in the United States reveals several incongruent passages. The version for U.S. distribution does not have the scene of the devils from cantos 21–22 poking their pitchforks at the surface of the boiling pitch in the fifth pouch of the eighth circle, which Williams uses; I assume he found the scene in the Italian version of the film, or the French or German.

30. For a reproduction of the film's publicity broadside in Italy, see the cover of Casadio, *Dante nel cinema*. For a poster used to publicize the film in England, see Havely, *Dante's Modern Afterlife* plate 6.

31. Nick Havely, *Dante's Modern Afterlife*, "A Note on Film and Video" 12.

32. I thank Barbara Hall, librarian in the Special Collections Department at the AMPAS Library in Beverly Hills, for her assistance in locating these censorship reports. The radical nature of the Ohio board's cut is not clear from the basic information provided in the entry on *Go Down, Death!* in Gevinson 392.

33. Matilde Serao, Italian critic and novelist, acknowledged the filmmakers' debt to the illustrator shortly after the film came out in 1911: "A great show . . . and if Doré used his pencil to design the best graphic commentary on the divine poem, this cinematographic piece has brought Doré's work back to life" (Brunetta, *Storia del cinema italiano* 144). See Welle's discussion of the same passage (386–87).

34. P. 2 of the brochure created by Adrienne Seward.

35. For items in Wright's library, see Fabre, *Richard Wright* 35.

36. See Benston, "Facing Tradition" 108n8. At the end of the lengthy passage to which Benston refers, Wright's narrator says, ". . . that same city which had lifted me in its burning arms and borne me toward alien and undreamed-of shores of knowing" (31). In his search for the Dantesque source Wright may have had in mind, Benston is probably conflating several passages, whether intentionally or not doesn't matter. Dante refers to Vergil as his "father" at *Inferno* 8.110, and he attributes a fatherly presence to his guide at several other points in the text; but in the passage where Dante invokes the image of a burning city he actually compares Vergil to a "mother" who leaps out of bed to save her baby from the flames (*Inf.* 23.38). This is perhaps, then, to borrow from Benston, an anxiety-ridden echo of the European literary tradition in which the father image is conflated with and then supplanted by the mother—as if to say that Dante as Mother rescues Wright from the fires of some undefined hell.

37. Butler reads the passage as a mix of Dante, spirituals (North Star as guiding light for the slaves on the Underground Railroad), and *The Great Gatsby*; see "Metaphor" 139–40. Wright had described the migration north without these specific Dantesque allusions in his earlier work of 1941, *12 Million Black Voices* 92–100; see Stewart's comments on Wright and the great migration in *Migrating to the Movies* 245–46.

38. Robert Penn Warren meditates on a similar flashback at the beginning of *Who Speaks for the Negro?* 11–12. The imaginary glimpse of the lynching rope becomes a topos in southern literature and journalism in the twentieth century.

39. Clayton interviewed Williams, who said, "We [he and Gosden] couldn't get together on this use of dialect . . . He wanted me to say 'Dis here' and 'Dat

dere' and I just wasn't going to do it. He said he ought to know how *Amos 'n' Andy* should talk but I told him Negroes didn't want to see Negroes on TV talking that way. Then I told him I *ought* to know how Negroes talk. After all, I've been one all my life. He never came back on the set" (Clayton 70).

40. Butler "Dante's *Inferno*," Cooke, L. Jackson, Slade. Piero Boitani was one of the first critics to explore the thematic connections between Ellison and Dante in *Prosatori* 175 ff. Hortense J. Spillers points to the symbolic connection between Dante's underground and Ellison's dreamy setting in the prologue (71–72). I would argue more forcefully than she that Ellison was aware of the dreamlike nature of the landscape in *Inferno* 1. Following Butler, William W. Cook and James Tatum review some of the numerological similarities between the *Comedy* and *Invisible Man* (173–75).

41. See the Modern Library edition, *Three Days before the Shooting* . . .

42. Box 151, folder 10.

43. Some of the language and imagery in this note is recycled near the end of the surreal section in *Invisible Man*'s prologue, where Ellison writes, "I longed for water and I heard it rushing through the cold mains my fingers touched as I felt my way . . ." (12).

44. Box 146, folder 4. Lawrence Jackson reports that Ellison's wife, Fanny, produced the typescripts of *Invisible Man* (327); see similar claims in Rampersad 246 and 253. In contrast, Rampersad cites one of Ellison's letters from 1955 in which he is doing his own typing of the sequel novel (310).

45. The bar where the narrator of *Invisible Man* takes Mr. Norton is called the Golden Day (70–95), an allusion to the book on nineteenth-century American literature by Lewis Mumford.

46. For the definitive treatment of Ellison and classicism, see Patrice D. Rankine's *Ulysses in Black*. I see my reading of Ellison's use of Dante as complementary to his interpretation of Ellison's classicism. There is more that needs to be done with Ellison's language and classicism.

47. Box 152, folder 3.

48. In a reading of this essay's final scene, Richard Purcell elaborates on his brilliant insight that the image of Ellison descending to a tenement basement apartment recalls Dante's encounter with Farinata and Cavalcante in *Inferno* 10. Ellison listens in on four black coal shovelers arguing over "which of two celebrated Metropolitan Opera divas was the superior soprano!" (519–20). Like the sinners of *Inferno* 10, he is a politicized heretic who can't believe his ears that lower-class workmen, black ones no less, could also be opera buffs. The very embodiment of vernacular criticism, these men are doing their part to make the language transcendent. See Purcell's dissertation, "Ralph Ellison and the American Pursuit of Humanism."

49. See also his very direct comments in the essay "Alain Locke": "Speaking of language, whenever anyone tells you that you're outside the framework of American culture, and when they deflect you into something called 'black English,' remember that the American version of the English language was born in rebellion against proper English usage, and the music of the African voice and the imagery coming from the people who lived close to the soil and under the condition of slavery added greatly to that language" (*Collected Essays* 449).

50. See Lawrence Jackson's detailed description of how Ellison carefully studied "The Waste Land" at Tuskegee (151–54).

51. See T.S. Eliot, *The Waste Land: A Facsimile and Transcript of the Original Drafts Including the Annotations of Ezra Pound* 4.

52. Eliot's address at Washington University in St. Louis on June 9, 1953, later turned into an essay, "American Literature and the American Language," explored some of the unique features of American literary and linguistic culture in contrast to British. I have no record that Ellison knew this piece, but he would have agreed with its main argument. Also in 1953, Melvin B. Tolson published what is arguably the most ambitious modernist poem by a poet of color, *Libretto for the Republic of Liberia*. The influences of Eliot and Pound are great, and not surprisingly there is an interesting nexus of Dantesque allusions; see Brunner 142–59, esp. 150–51; and Cook and Tatum 246–47. But for all Tolson's modernistic density, his gesture to Eliot and company is ultimately much less satisfying than Ellison's.

53. The two men met at the PEN International Writers Conference in London in July 1956. Rampersad assumes that Eliot would have had little to say to Ellison (328–29). In any case, we have no record of their conversation.

54. Box 151, folder 8.

55. I allude to Harold Bloom's influential study of literary influence, *Anxiety of Influence*.

56. It can also be an act of violence, Ellison implies, in the scene where Invisible Man insults the white leader of the Brotherhood, Brother Jack, by calling him "great white father" and then in slave vernacular "Marse [i.e., Master] Jack." Jack attacks him "lapsing into a foreign language" (465), emphasizing the critical impasse in which the two men find themselves, unable to communicate peacefully. See Boyagoda 73.

57. Box 172, folder 1, Speeches, Sept. 19, 1979. Speech delivered at the Ralph Waldo Ellison Festival, Brown University.

58. Trans. Robert S. Haller, *Literary of Criticism of Dante Alighieri* 100.

59. Box 151, folder 6.

60. In several interviews Ellison mentions Pushkin but only to dismiss the African connection. He holds the position that Pushkin is great because of his lit-

erary excellence and not his ethnicity (*Conversations* 111, 328–29). Ellison was fairly knowledgeable about canonical Russian literature in general and is likely to have been familiar with the image of the poet. In an interview of 1965 he notes, "I look at it [my material] through literature; English, French, Spanish, Russian— especially nineteenth-century Russian literature" (*Collected Essays* 742).

Chapter 3. Black Dante

1. For my understanding of Baraka's life and thought, I am indebted to the works of many critics referenced below, especially Sollors, Harris, and Watts. Lloyd W. Brown's early essays on Baraka's encounter with Dante and his chapter "The System of Dante's Hell" in *Amiri Baraka* remain useful.

2. The student is William Roscoe Thayer (Verduin 41–42).

3. Interview with D. H. Melman in *Conversations with Amiri Baraka.*

4. For an accounting of these periods, dates, and titles, and some reflections on the limitation of such chronological categories, see the "Editor's Note" in *The LeRoi Jones / Amiri Baraka Reader* xv–xvi. Baraka's Marxist fourth period continued unabated into the new millennium with a shift to more of a focus on domestic issues; see, e.g., *Bushwhacked!*

5. For a brief review of the various alternative presses and magazines associated with Baraka in his Beat and Transitional periods, see Clay and Phillips, *A Secret Location on the Lower East Side.* For a discussion of publishing during his Black Nationalist phase, see Julius E. Thompson, *Dudley Randall, Broadside Press, and the Black Arts Movement in Detroit.*

6. According to Steven Watson, the reference is in Ginsberg's journals in the Ginsberg Collection at Stanford University; see Watson 38 and 341n89.

7. Harry Gantt's operation was based at 360 Cabrini Boulevard, New York 40, NY. There is a vast amount of bibliographical material connected with *System* in the Special Collections at Syracuse University Library. The collection contains papers and materials of Baraka (five boxes) and the Grove Press. The boxes of materials connected with Baraka are divided into sections that deal with his correspondence, memorabilia, writings, and *Yugen* magazine records. The Syracuse University Library is the historical archive for Grove with hundreds of boxes connected with the press. As regards *System,* the files include reports of copyrights, translations, contracts, letters between literary agents and the press about negotiations, Grove Press royalty master form (a sort of credit and debit record keeper), royalty statements, lists of who received review copies, advance copies, publicity shots for the book, invoices for proofs, galley production, offsetting, and more.

All the information is there if one wanted to do a detailed study of the complicated textual history of *System*.

8. For a facsimile of the first edition's dust jacket, see the web site of the main library at the University of Virginia: <http://www2.lib.virginia.edu/exhibits/rec_acq/lit/baraka.html>. Accessed Nov. 21, 2009.

9. I have learned much about Baraka's life, or rather how he wants to present it, from his *Autobiography*. His ex-wife's autobiography, *How I Became Hettie Jones*, often provides a different take on their time in the Village.

10. Hudson, *From LeRoi Jones to Amiri Baraka* 35, quoting Baraka. For a fuller picture of Kawaida, see Baraka's description: "7 Principles of US: Maulana Karenga & The Need for a Black Value System" in his *Kawaida Studies* 9–22.

11. See the comparative table that follows shortly in the text. In an unpublished three-page typescript, "Note on one Side (The Study)," Baraka lists all the items in his view as he sits at his typewriter. Among them: "on the other side, of the case top my 4 trans. of Dante, from which the System came out of" (3). He refers to the three volumes of Sinclair's translation plus a fourth unidentified book; it may refer to a copy of the *Vita Nuova*. From box 1, Writings, Amiri Baraka/LeRoi Jones, Special Collections, Syracuse University Library.

12. Various printings treat Baraka's note on the heretics differently. The reprint by Lawrence Hill Books relegates the note to the bottom of the same page rather than highlighting it by positioning it at the top of the following page as happens in the first edition. The *LJ/AB Reader* paraphrases the note in its excerpt of the Heretics.

13. In a short piece, "Black Writing," originally published in *American Dialog*, he comments: "A book—no matter what you have to say in it—is just a commercial object and Negro Material is not the commercial object that gets the best sales. But even so, there are always exceptions. Baldwin books sell. Ellison, and some others" (*Home* 162).

14. Di Prima attributes this claim to A.B. Spellman: "It was in one of these sessions that A.B. made the remark that 'Roi wanted to be the Black Ezra Pound'" (*Recollections* 240).

15. Guy Davenport is reported to have made this observation in conversation.

16. See Aldon L. Nielsen, *Writing between the Lines* 86. Moreover, Nielsen cites the passage from Baraka sloppily, making several errors in his transcription. On the other hand, Nielsen makes many good points in his reading of Baraka's *System*. Better still is his chapter on Baraka's literary relations with the Beats and others, "LeRoi Jones as Intertext," in which he tracks the references to Baraka and his work in the writings of O'Hara, Ginsberg, Blackburn, di Prima, Olson, and Dorn, among others. Finally, Nielsen's more recent essay, "Fugitive Fictions," is an important reassessment of Baraka's fiction, published and unpublished.

17. See Posnock for the more plausible reading of the scene as set in a Boy Scout camp (84–85). J. R. Goddard, "Poet Jailed for Obscenity; Literary Magazine Hit," article in *Village Voice,* Oct. 26, 1961, pp. 3, 16, says: "The play by Jones which the government has called obscene turned out to be a graphic but very grim view of homosexuality at some kind of military base. Written under a John Hay Whitney Foundation Fellowship, it was part of the poet's long work, 'The System of Dante's Hell'" (16).

18. "'Eighth Ditch,' especially when read in the context of the rest of *System,* seems, like the novel, to be 'about' the difficulties of coming into one's own cultural tradition if it is about anything" (Scott, *Closet Case* 279).

19. Having ignored the publication of the original in 1919, Italian critics responded vigorously to the publication of an Italian translation in 1994 of Miguel Asín Palacios's controversial book *La escatología musulmana en la Divina Comedia* [*Dante e l'Islam*]. Renewed investigations of the relationship between Dante and Islamic culture by Maria Corti, Carlo Ossola, among others, have focused on astronomy, astrology, and mysticism, but one recurrent issue in the debate revolves around Dante's portrait of Muhammad. As Jan M. Ziolkowski points out in his introduction to the special issue of *Dante Studies, Dante and Islam* (7–9), Asín Palacios's book deals with Muhammad's representation in an important text in the Islamic tradition from the early Middle Ages, the *Liber Scale Machometti.* Corti, following Asín Palacios, suggests that the *Liber* may have had an impact on Dante's understanding of the law of divine punishment in hell, the "contrapasso," and on the "sowers of discord" in *Inferno* 28, the section of the poem where Dante clarifies the doctrine of divine retribution by naming it (69–71). Dante would have had access to this text through a Latin translation, undertaken by a Tuscan notary in Toledo at the court of Alfonso X. The notary, Bonaventura of Siena, was a friend of the Florentine diplomat to Alfonso's court who would become Dante's mentor in the 1290s, Brunetto Latini, remembered impressively in *Inferno* 15. Corti (66) proposes that it is inconceivable that Brunetto wouldn't have shared his knowledge of this work with his protégé in Florence, especially upon learning that his student was contemplating a poem about a journey through the afterlife. For that is precisely the topic of the *Liber,* a journey through heaven and hell undertaken by Muhammad himself. Among the places visited in this tour of the Islamic hell is the area where those are punished "qui seminant discordiam," (who sow discord). According to this line of argument, Dante's notion of contrapasso derives from Arabic cultural traditions that can be traced to the *Liber.* That is, Dante's law of contrapasso as well as his image of "sowers of discord" may derive from an Islamic work on Muhammad. If so, in incorporating that work into his own poem, Dante in turn alters it significantly by placing Muhammad himself among the sowers of discord.

Moreover, the Italian poet constructs a grisly contrapasso for the founder of Islam and his first followers, based on the law of contrapasso that he finds in the *Liber.* See the special issue of *Dante Studies* 125 (2007), *Dante and Islam,* for a series of articles around the broader topic of Dante and Islam.

20. See Darieck Bruce Scott's 1999 Stanford dissertation, "Closet Case."

21. Hudson calls "The Heretics" an example of Baraka's "Negro-versus-black theme" (*From LeRoi Jones to Amiri Baraka* 115).

22. Many southern towns had a neighborhood called something like "the Bottom," a place known for the sort of activities one might associate with the bottom of hell. By naming his murderer Jim Bottoms, Spencer Williams takes advantage of the same pun: as his life ends, he heads to the bottom of hell.

23. Some other allusions to the Dantesque forest: "The day . . . where had it gone? It had moved away as we wound down into the mass of trees and broken lives" (122); "Once past you knew that your life had ended. That roads took up the other side, and wound into thicker dust. Darker, more insane, nights" (126); "The old wood" (134).

24. Hudson notes that the novel is built around "sketches of psychological-spiritual states [that] only informally parallel Dante's schema" (*From LeRoi Jones to Amiri Baraka* 112). In a negative review, Gilman claims that "there is absolutely nothing Dantean about Jones' vision" (12). Wolff says, "But the suit Jones has borrowed from Dante fits badly" (A18). An unidentified reviewer for *Newsweek* notes of Baraka's *System,* "Its relationship to Dante is entirely spurious" ("Out of Touch"). There are many more critics who chastise the modern author for failing to follow Dante as closely as his title suggests he will; see Hogan, McMurtry, Prescott, and Redding.

25. Two-page undated press release prepared by Grove Press to advertise the publication of Baraka's *System* (Syracuse University Library, Special Collections, Grove Press, Editorial Files, box 140, *System*).

26. "As, listen to the beginning of Sonny Rollins' *Oleo,* new version, to get a sense of the first part of *Dante,* or Cecil Taylor's *Of What* to discover the total rhythm form I collect my words around" (press release, p. 2).

27. In regard to Baraka's poetry, Nathaniel Mackey has considered "Black music in its dual role of impulse (life-style or ethos as well as technique) and theme in Baraka's work, exploring its usefulness as a sort of focal point or thread pulling together disparate strands of Baraka's thought" ("The Changing Same" 121).

28. I find Baraka's claim in an interview of 2003 that he didn't follow Dante's *Inferno* playfully disingenuous: "You see the Dante—which escaped me at the time . . . it shows you how you can be somewhere else and even begin to take on other people's concern—I wasn't talking about Dante Alighieri. See? I 'thought'

I was, but I was really talking about Edmund Dante, The Count of Monte Cristo." See the interview with Kalamu ya Salaam, "Amiri Baraka Analyzes How He Writes" (1).

29. "For me, Lorca, Williams, Pound and Charles Olson have had the greatest influence. Eliot, earlier (rhetoric can be so lovely, for a time . . . but only remains so for the rhetorician)." In the autobiographical note as a contributor to Donald M. Allen, ed., *The New American Poetry* 425.

30. In 1967 Robert Hayden could refer to Baraka as "the most controversial Negro writer in America" (208). He continues in the introduction to a selection of Baraka's poems in the anthology *Kaleidoscope,* "As the leading 'Poet of the Negro Revolution,' Jones [Baraka] attacks both 'Whitey' and 'Uncle Tom' with equal vehemence, but the result is more often angry abuse than it is impassioned poetry" (209). This way of putting it, "controversial Negro writer" and "Negro Revolution," probably grated on Baraka's ears. The point was that by 1967 he wasn't a Negro; he was black and had already begun to identify himself as a black poet. Baraka responded to this charge with broadsides of his own against Hayden and the poetry of what he called "white-out," that is, the writing of blacks who wrote to seem like whites. Hayden had made himself an easy target through various of his published comments like the one above. In addition, in 1966 at the First Black Writers' Conference held at Fisk University in Nashville, Tennessee, Hayden made the statement by which he would be forever branded, that he was "a poet who happens to be a Negro" (Hatcher 78). As Jones turned into Baraka he was becoming a black man who happened to be a poet. Smethurst reports that Baraka was invited to attend the conference in 1966 but did not go; he was, however, one of the leaders among the Black Arts poets in attendance in 1967 (332–33).

31. See Baraka's essay "The Revolutionary Tradition in Afro-American Literature," *LJ/AB Reader* 318–20.

32. Watts considers the relationship between Baraka and Ellison in *Amiri Baraka* 437–43. Posnock explores Baraka's antagonistic relationship with Baldwin, eventually reconciled by the end of Baldwin's life in chap. 7 of *Color and Culture.*

33. Cited and discussed in Posnock (248), who argues that Baraka fails to break away from his sources of inspiration with *System*; Nielsen reports that Baraka said something similar to him in a private interview (*Writing between the Lines* 78).

34. Rafia Zafar finds analogous contradictions, or so they seem at first glance, in the earliest African American writing: "Early narratives represent borrowings from the literary arsenal of the white Protestant majority. . . . Taking on an established genre, early black writers tried to make it their own; along with riffs on

other forms, these accounts helped to construct an African American literary tradition" ("Capturing the Captivity" 32).

35. In his *Autobiography,* Baraka makes it clear that he wanted to free himself from a way of life he calls "white-out" (120) and "elitist hedonism" (177), as much as from a literary style. Norman Podhoretz anticipated Baraka's dilemma in an essay of 1958: "Bohemianism, after all, is for the Negro a means of entry into the world of the whites, and no Negro Bohemian is going to cooperate in the attempt to identify him with Harlem or Dixieland" (119). Indeed, Baraka leaves the bohemian world behind to go to Harlem.

36. Maryemma Graham, in her introduction to the *Complete Poems of Frances E. W. Harper* (New York: Oxford University Press, 1988), has made this same claim in a different context: "Dunbar's *Sport of the Gods* is at the beginning of the tradition in modern black literature, which novelizes the slave narrative tradition and makes a place for it in the discourse of urban black writers" (xliii). She continues in a note: "Examples of this include . . . Baraka's *System of Dante's Hell*" (lvi).

37. See Barolini's essay "Medieval Multiculturalism and Dante's Theology of Hell" for a discussion and appreciation of the radical nature of Dante's structure of hell. *Dante and the Unorthodox,* edited by James Miller, focuses primarily on the poet's challenge to church doctrines on gender and sexuality.

38. In *Home* 251–52.

39. Amiri Baraka/LeRoi Jones Collection, Schomburg Center for Research in Black Culture, NYPL, folder 1971.

40. For a text of Gil Scott-Heron's piece, see *The Norton Anthology of African American Literature* 61–62.

41. *Black American Literature Forum* 17.1 (1983): 27–29.

42. See Madelyn Hart's thesis for a discussion of the impact of Kawaida principles on Baraka's rhetoric in the 1970s (17–30).

43. The Reverend Charles Bennett Ray, Theodore S. Wright, and Dr. J. M'Cune Smith, *An Address to the Three Thousand Colored Citizens of New York . . .* For a discussion of Smith's radical proposal for land redistribution, see John Stauffer, *The Black Hearts of Men* 138–46.

Chapter 4. African American Dante

1. Virginia Fowler's volume in the Twayne series is an excellent introduction to Naylor's life and work. I have depended on it and several published interviews with Naylor for these details on the artist's life.

2. See the bibliography for titles of her novels.

3. Gomez, Erickson, Watkins.

4. Rita Dove, a contemporary of Naylor's, credits this same translation with setting her on her literary path. In high school an English teacher took her to a book signing by Ciardi: "I didn't know who John Ciardi was, but I was sufficiently impressed to buy a copy of his translation of Dante's *Inferno,* and for the first time in my life the author's photo on the back of a book meant something. . . . that experience first put the notion into my head that writing could be a viable vocation" (*Conversations with Rita Dove* 122).

5. Nick Havely makes this point in "'Prosperous People' and 'The Real Hell' in Gloria Naylor's *Linden Hills*" (214–15).

6. Naylor's image of graffiti on the second plaque recalls how Greek and Latin classical authors and their classicizing imitators in the medieval and Renaissance periods used the image of vines growing over and around a column to depict the uneasy relationship between the literary traditions of epic and romance, of canonical and vernacular literary forms. For a further investigation of the image of column and vine, see the epilogue to my book *Compromising the Classics* 170–73.

7. Nick Havely, again, provides this insight on Malcolm X; see "Prosperous People" (215–16). For the comparison with epic, see Moore (1421–23).

8. Naylor feels no compunction to include a female voice among Willie's models. In fact, she comments in various interviews that she herself keenly felt the lack of literary models who were female and black until she read Toni Morrison. While Willie's canon is not Naylor's canon exactly, it resembles the models she draws direct inspiration from in *Linden Hills*: Dante, Whitman, Stevens, and Eliot. Naylor's own literary tendencies, even her biography, resemble that of her character Willie, to a large extent.

9. Additional critics who deal with Naylor's intertextual relationship with Dante, as well as with other authors, include Berg (in chap. 2 of her dissertation and in her essay on Whitman), Bouvier, Fowler, Goddu, Homans, Moore, Sandiford, and Saunders. Berg's dissertation provides the most thorough comparison between Naylor's text and the Dantesque source.

10. On Naylor's use of Whitman especially in regard to "a gay man passing for straight," see Price 98 ff.

11. See Shapiro; also Freccero, "Bestial Sign."

12. Tambling comments that Blake's portrait of Dante (1800–1803) contains an Ugolino figure that appears to highlight the problem of power relationships (41).

13. Interview with Virginia Fowler, Sept. 6, 1993 (Fowler, *Gloria Naylor* 143–57).

14. Henry Louis Gates, Jr., suggests that Naylor may be more at home and therefore a more convincing novelist with working-class material: "If *Linden Hills* is

widely seen as less successful than *Brewster Place,* it is perhaps because her grasp on the mores of the Black bourgeoisie seems less sure than is her understanding of the lives of the Black under- and working classes" (Gates and Appiah, *Gloria Naylor* x).

15. Freccero reports that some critics link the rhyme scheme to the poetic forms of sonnet, *sestina,* and *sirvente* ("The Significance of the *Terza Rima*" 261).

16. I take Naylor's claim that she maintained her imitation of *terza rima* for seven-eighths of the narrative loosely. Since *Linden Hills* is divided into seven chapters, the first an introduction to the history and topography of the suburban development, the following six dedicated in turn to days in the calendar from December 19th to the 24th, either she meant she maintained her version of *terza rima* till the last chapter (which would actually be six-sevenths) or she meant to the last chapter or thereabouts. I assume her to mean that she maintains a certain structural pattern built around color until the novel's penultimate section, loosely understood, where she alters it slightly.

17. Omi and Winant give examples of the absurdity of classification by race (181–83).

18. One should first try to determine Naylor's understanding of *terza rima,* which most likely derives from the meter as it is presented in Ciardi's version. In a prefatory note to his *Inferno,* Ciardi accounts for his decision not to use an exact version of Dante's meter because "English is a rhyme-poor language. It was obvious to me that the price of forcing that third rhyme into place in English was ruinous to the language" ("Translator's Note" xxi, 2003 ed.). He reports various experiments in versification to approximate Dante's verse form before coming up with his solution: "Then I hit on what I may as well call dummy *terza rima,* which is to say, I kept the three line unit but rhymed only the first and third lines" (xxii). Ciardi's version of Dante's meter, then, lacks the third linking rhyme that connects with the tercet that follows. Naylor's loose approximation of the Italian rhyme scheme respects Ciardi's version of it. For a more detailed discussion of Ciardi's take on *terza rima,* see De Sua, *Dante into English* 110–16, and Cunningham, *The "Divine Comedy" in English* 225–33.

19. Another triad that occurs early in the first chapter is embedded in this sentence that calls attention to itself: "Putney Wayne's son had sold a quarter of his pasture to a shoe factory and the smoky cinders blew over the entire field, settling in the sheep's wool and turning the grass an ashy blue" (5). Most of the time Naylor is very explicit in naming the colors she wants to focus the reader's attention on, but sometimes as she does here she alludes to the color through an image. The phrase "grass an ashy blue" announces the colors green, gray, and blue, all of which subsequently recycle throughout the narrative.

20. In the vast critical corpus that surrounds Toni Morrison's work, I have not found an essay that addresses her intertextual relationship with Dante in *The Bluest Eye,* although Nick Havely mentions it briefly at the end of his essay on *Linden Hills,* "Prosperous People" (219).

21. Critics have commented on the Dantesque implications of Morrison's later sequence of novels, *Beloved, Jazz, Paradise.* I leave it for others to explore them. See, e.g., the respective essays by D. Quentin Miller and John Domini, as well as the point Kubitschek makes in *Toni Morrison* 116.

22. Gurleen Grewal speaks of Soaphead's metaphorical rape of Pecola in *Circles of Sorrow* 32–34. Grewal argues that Soaphead's colonial origins are central to the "connections that the text makes between capitalism and colonialism" (26).

23. John N. Duvall proposes that Soaphead's letter stands for a letter from Morrison to Ellison as she elaborates in her rape scene a feminist revision (following Michael Awkward's reading) of the Trueblood rape in *Invisible Man.* He sees the letter as part of the complicated process in which Morrison engages to construct an authorial identity at the beginning of her career. Duvall also reads the death of the old dog as similar to Cholly's orgasm when he rapes Pecola. See *The Identifying Fictions* 28 ff.

24. "The Irreducible Dove," *Comparative Literature* 9 (1957): 129.

25. I agree here with John Noell Moore, who states in one of the better essays on *Linden Hills* and intertextuality that "Naylor issues us an invitation to continue the narrative, to write Willie's poem on the landscape of our imaginations where story weds past, present, and future" (1429).

26. See the discussion by Dora Apel in her *Imagery of Lynching* 193–94, with a reproduction of Rauschenberg's work, plate 8. For a description with images of the Dante illustrations, see Mary Lynn Kotz, *Rauschenberg: Art and Life* 98–101.

27. Al Young is another African American poet who rejects Dante but he does so specifically for the Italian poet's treatment of Muhammad. See his poem "Erudition" from *Straight No Chaser,* where he writes (2):

And all the worlds and mine
get centered by and by
by clever pundits of the printed world
O hallelujah Dante knew his Popes
and Florentines but Islam no

To even think Muhammed
infernalized seems almost as negligent

as Pope Gregory's error in sending
back to Cathay with Marco Polo
not the 100 scholars Kubla Khan requested
to sell his cultured court on Christian grace
but dispatched instead two peevish priests
who didn't withstand the rigors of the trip

28. I have been able to find out very little about Loftis's life and work. He wrote criticism and poetry into the 1990s while he was teaching around New York City.

29. From an earlier moment in this extended tradition of reading Dante, William Stanley Braithwaite (1878–1962) makes a similar passing reference in an unpublished poem in manuscript in the Schomburg Center for Research in Black Culture, NYPL, MG 84, box 3, folder 8:

Between Dante and Beatrice
The action 'tis said was Platonic:
But between Abelard and Héloise,
The treatment was electronic.
But I wish, by Jupiter, the gods would give
These charming praters a dose of a tonic!

30. See my more detailed report of Hayden's controversial claim that he was "a poet who happens to be a Negro" (Hatcher 78), at the end of the section above on Amiri Baraka, "A New Narrative Model."

31. Another poem by Carl Phillips focuses on Dante on his deathbed: "Two Versions of the Very Same Story," in *From the Devotions* 65. The poem is inspired by Borges's short prose piece, "*Inferno 1, 32,*" in *Labyrinths* 237, a meditation prompted by the verse that describes the leopard that leaps out and impedes the progress of Dante-pilgrim up the mountain of enlightenment in the opening allegory of the *Divine Comedy*. Phillips approaches Dante through the imagined world of Borges who sees the Italian poet from the point of view of an allegorical beast. This mediated Dante is far removed from the oral Dante of Naylor's African American hip-hop protagonist.

32. R. W. King points out that Cary's diction, while noticeably Miltonic, actually differs from Milton's in various crucial ways (301 ff.).

33. For more works in that tradition, see Nick Havely's essay "Francesca Observed."

Chapter 5. Poets in Exile

1. "I placed great Dante in exile, / And Byron had his turns; / Then Keats and Shelley smote the while, / And my immortal Burns! / But thee I'll build a sacred shrine, / A store of all my ware; / By them I'll teach thy soul to sing / 'A place in Harvard Square.'" For more on Jones, see *Blacks at Harvard* 152–58.

2. When taken as a collective way of responding to Dante and the *Divine Comedy,* these artists of color anticipate recent interpretations of Dante's work that emphasize its edgy transgressiveness. I am thinking in particular of Edoardo Sanguineti, *Dante reazionario*; the volume edited by James Miller, *Dante and the Unorthodox*; and the essay by Teodolinda Barolini, "Medieval Multiculturalism and Dante's Theology of Hell," which she has developed in recent lectures that, one assumes, are the harbinger of more published work in this direction.

3. I have not found any reader of color who responds to the extraordinary passage in *Paradise* 19—in fact, I have found surprisingly few readers, period—where Dante questions Christian doctrine for barring good and just non-Christians from entering heaven. His first example is a man born on the banks of the Indus River (67 ff.), while with his second he implies that an Ethiopian who is good but not a Christian will go further than hypocritical Christians (103 ff.). For a discussion of the passage, see Brenda Deen Schildgen, *Dante and the Orient* 92–109. As my examples in *Freedom Readers* make clear, the vast majority of readers' responses are to the *Inferno.*

4. "Dante Antagonistes," in *Instaurations* 128. This sounds somewhat like Wai Chee Dimock's description of Dante's impact on Mandelstam in her essay "Literature for the Planet" as not timeless but "timeful" (Gunn 27).

BIBLIOGRAPHY

Manuscript Collections and Archives

Baraka, Amiri/LeRoi Jones Collection. Manuscripts, Archives and Rare Books Division. Schomburg Center for Research in Black Culture. The New York Public Library, New York, New York.

Baraka, Imamu Amiri/LeRoi Jones. Special Collections. Syracuse University Library, Syracuse, New York.

Braithwaite, William Stanley, Papers. Manuscripts, Archives and Rare Books Division. Schomburg Center for Research in Black Culture. The New York Public Library, New York, New York.

Douglas, Aaron, Collection. Special Collections. Fisk University Library, Nashville, Tennessee.

Douglass, Frederick, Papers. Manuscript Division. Library of Congress. Washington, D.C. <http://www.memory.loc.gov/ammem/doughtml/dougres.html>.

Drake, St. Clair, Papers. Manuscripts, Archives and Rare Books Division. Schomburg Center for Research in Black Culture. The New York Public Library, New York, New York.

Ellison, Ralph Waldo, Papers. Manuscript Division. Library of Congress, Washington, D.C.

Grove Press Archives. Special Collections. Syracuse University Library, Syracuse, New York.

Marsh, George Perkins, Collection. Special Collections. Bailey-Howe Library, University of Vermont. <http://bailey.uvm.edu/specialcollections/gpmorc.html>. The University of Vermont has created an online research center, which contains letters from the Powers-Marsh correspondence. The letters, dating from 1847 to 1871, are housed in several different collections: the Marsh Collection at the Special Collections Department, Bailey-Howe Library, University of Vermont; the Powers Papers at the Archives of American Art, Smithsonian Institution, Washington, D.C.; and the New-York Historical Society, New York, New York.

Norton, Charles Eliot, Miscellaneous Papers. Houghton Library, Harvard University.

Powers, Fondo Hiram. Archivio Storico. Gabinetto Scientifico Letterario G. P. Vieusseux. Florence, Italy.

Powers, Hiram, Collection. Cincinnati Historical Society Library, Cincinnati, Ohio.

Powers, Hiram, Papers. Archives of American Art. Smithsonian Institution, Washington, D.C.

Toomer, Jean, Papers. The James Weldon Johnson Memorial Collection. Beinecke Library, Yale University.

Trollope, Frances, Collection. Cincinnati Historical Society Library, Cincinnati, Ohio.

Works Cited and Consulted

Alighieri, Dante. *La Commedia di Dante Alighieri Illustrata da Ugo Foscolo.* Ed. "An Italian." 4 vols. London Pietro Rolandi, 1842.

———. *La Commedia secondo l'antica vulgata.* Ed. Giorgio Petrocchi. 4 vols. In *Le opere di Dante Alighieri.* Milan: Mondadori, 1966–67. Text reproduced in Singleton.

———. *Dante for the People: Selected Passages from the "Divine Comedy" in English Verse.* Trans. Gauntlett Chaplin. London: J. Clarke, 1913.

———. *Dante's Divine Comedy. The First Part: Hell.* Trans. Thomas Brooksbank. In the Meter of the Original with Notes. London, 1854.

———. *Dante, Translated into English Verse.* Trans. I. C. Wright. Illustrated with engravings on steel, after designs by Flaxman. 4th ed. London: Bohn, 1854.

———. *The Divine Comedy. Inferno. Purgatorio. Paradiso.* 3 vols. 1946. 1948. Trans. John D. Sinclair. New York: Oxford University Press, 1961.

———. *The Divine Comedy.* Trans. with commentary Charles S. Singleton. 6 vols. Bollingen Series 80. Princeton: Princeton University Press, 1970–75.

———. *The Inferno.* Trans. Ciaran Carson. New York: New York Review of Books, 2002.

———. *The Inferno.* Trans. John Ciardi. 1954. New York: Mentor Books, 1982.

———. *The Inferno.* Trans. John Ciardi. 1954. New York: New American Library, 2003. "Translator's Note." ix–xxiii.

———. *Inferno.* Trans. Robert Hollander and Jean Hollander. Intro. and notes Robert Hollander. New York: Doubleday, 2000.

———. *The Divine Comedy: Inferno.* Trans. Robert M. Durling. Intro. and notes Ronald L. Martinez. New York: Oxford University Press, 1996.

————. *Literary Criticism of Dante Alighieri.* Trans. and ed. Robert S. Haller. Lincoln: University of Nebraska Press, 1973.

————. *The Trilogy, or Dante's Three Visions.* Trans. J. W. Thomas. 3 vols. London: Bohn, 1859–66.

————. *The Vision; or Hell, Purgatory, & Paradise of Dante Alighieri.* Trans. Henry Francis Cary. New York: Hurst, 1844.

Allen, Donald M., ed. *The New American Poetry.* New York: Grove Press, 1970.

Anderson, Eric, and Alfred A. Moss, Jr. *Dangerous Donations: Northern Philanthropy and Southern Black Education, 1902–1930.* Columbia: University of Missouri Press, 1999.

Anderson, James D. *The Education of Blacks in the South, 1860–1935.* Chapel Hill: University of North Carolina Press, 1988.

An Anthology of Verse by American Negroes. Ed. Newman Ivey White and Walter Clinton Jackson. Intro. James Hardy Dillard. Durham, N.C.: Trinity College Press, 1924.

Apel, Dora. *Imagery of Lynching: Black Men, White Women, and the Mob.* New Brunswick, N.J.: Rutgers University Press, 2004.

Apter, Emily. *The Translation Zone: A New Comparative Literature.* Princeton: Princeton University Press, 2005.

Asín Palacios, Miguel. *Dante e l'Islam.* Ed. and intro. Carlo Ossola. Trans. R. Rossi Testa and Y. Tawfik. 2 vols. Parma: Pratiche, 1994.

Assassination of Abraham Lincoln . . . Washington, D.C.: Government Printing Office, 1867.

Awkward, Michael. " 'The Evil of Fulfillment': Scapegoating and Narration in *The Bluest Eye.*" Gates, *Toni Morrison* 175–209.

————. "Roadblocks and Relatives: Critical Revision in Toni Morrison's *The Bluest Eye.*" McKay, *Critical Essays on Toni Morrison* 57–68.

Baker, Houston A., Jr. *The Journey Back: Issues in Black Literature and Criticism.* Chicago: University of Chicago Press, 1980.

[James Baldwin.] *Modern Critical Views.* Ed. Harold Bloom. New York: Chelsea House, 1986.

Baldwin, James. "Stranger in the Village." *Collected Essays.* New York: Library of America, 1998. 117–29.

Baraka, Amiri. [LeRoi Jones.] "Amiri Baraka Analyzes How He Writes." Interview with Kalamu ya Salaam. *African American Review* (Summer–Fall 2003): 1–29.

————. *The Autobiography of LeRoi Jones.* New York: Freundlich Books, 1984.

————. *Bushwacked! A Counterfeit President for a Fake Democracy: A Collection of Essays on the 2000 National Elections.* Newark: Unity and Struggle Publications, 2001.

————. *Conversations with Amiri Baraka.* Ed. Charlie Reilly. Jackson: University Press of Mississippi, 1994.

————. *Daggers and Javelins: Essays, 1974–1979.* New York: William Morrow, 1984.

————. "A Dark Bag." *Poetry* 103.6 (March 1964): 394–401. *Home: Social Essays* 121–32.

————. *The Dead Lecturer. Three Books by Amiri Baraka (LeRoi Jones).* 1963. New York: Grove Press, 1975. 7–79.

————. "La Dolce Vita." *Kulchur* 4 (1961): 85–90.

————. *Home: Social Essays.* New York: William Morrow, 1966.

————. *Kawaida Studies: The New Nationalism.* Chicago: Third World Press, 1972.

————. *The LeRoi Jones/Amiri Baraka Reader.* Ed. William J. Harris. New York: Thunder's Mouth Press, 1991.

————. "The Role of the Writer in Establishing a Unified Writers Organization." *Defining Ourselves: Black Writers in the 90s.* Ed. Elizabeth Nunez and Brenda M. Greene. New York: Lang, 1999. 15–24.

————. *6 Persons. The Fiction of LeRoi Jones/Amiri Baraka.* Foreword Greg Tate. Ed. and intro. Henry C. Lacey. Chicago: Lawrence Hill Books, 2000. 227–462.

————. *The System of Dante's Hell.* New York: Grove Press, 1965. Republished London: MacGibbon and Kee, 1966; Darmstadt: Joseph Melzer Verlag, 1966; Amsterdam: Mevlenhoff/de Bezige Bij, 1968.

————. *The System of Dante's Inferno. The Trembling Lamb.* Ed. John Fles. New York: Harry Gantt for the Phoenix Book Shop, 1959. 29–48.

————. *Tales.* New York: Grove Press, 1967.

————, ed. *The Moderns: An Anthology of New Writing in America.* New York: Corinth Books, 1963.

Baraka, Amiri, and Diane di Prima, eds. *The Floating Bear: A Newsletter.* Intro. and notes adapted from interviews with Diane di Prima. La Jolla, Calif.: Laurence McGilvery, 1973.

Barański, Zygmunt G., and Martin McLaughlin. *Italy's Three Crowns: Reading Dante, Petrarch, and Boccaccio.* Oxford: Bodleian Library, 2007.

Barlow, H. C. "The Sixth-Centenary Celebrations of Dante's Birth." Grant, *T. S. Eliot: The Critical Heritage* 621–24.

Barolini, Teodolinda. "Medieval Multiculturalism and Dante's Theology of Hell." *The Craft and the Fury: Essays in Memory of Glauco Cambon.* Ed. J. Francese. *Italiana* 9. West Lafayette, Ind.: Bordighera Press, 2000. 82–102.

Barr, Stringfellow. *Mazzini: Portrait of an Exile.* New York: Holt, 1935.

Bay, Mia. *The White Image in the Black Mind: African-American Ideas about White People, 1830–1925.* New York: Oxford University Press, 2000.

Bellarmine, Robert. *Appendix ad libros de Summo Pontifice quae continent responsionem ad librum quondam anonymum cujus titulus est Aviso piacevole dato alla bella Italia. Disputationes* 1013–46.

————. *Disputationes . . . de Controversiis Christianae Fidei adversus huius temporis Haereticos.* (On Controversies of the Christian Faith.) 4 vols. in 3. Paris: Officina Tri-Adelphorum Bibliopolarum, 1608.

"Bellarmine, Roberto." *Encyclopedia Britannica.* 11th ed. 1911. 3:694–95.

Bellows, Henry W. "Seven Sittings with Powers the Sculptor, Part III." *Appleton's Journal of Popular Literature, Science, and Art* 1.13 (June 26, 1869): 402–4.

Benston, Kimberly W. *Baraka: The Renegade and the Mask.* New Haven: Yale University Press, 1976.

————. "Facing Tradition: Revisionary Scenes in African American Literature." *PMLA* 105.1 (1990): 98–109.

————, ed. *Imamu Amiri Baraka (LeRoi Jones): A Collection of Critical Essays.* Englewood Cliffs, N.J.: Prentice Hall, 1978.

Berg, Christine G. " 'Giving sound to the bruised places in their hearts': Gloria Naylor and Walt Whitman." In Felton, *The Critical Response to Gloria Naylor* 98–111.

————. "Methods of Intertextuality in Gloria Naylor's *Linden Hills.*" Diss. Lehigh University, 1997.

Bhabha, Homi K. *The Location of Culture.* London: Routledge, 1994.

Blacks at Harvard: A Documentary History of African-American Experience at Harvard and Radcliffe. Ed. Werner Sollors, Caldwell Titclomb, and Thomas A. Underwood. New York: New York University Press, 1993. On E. S. Jones, see 152–58.

Bloom, Harold. *Anxiety of Influence: A Theory of Poetry.* 1973. Oxford: Oxford University Press, 1997.

Blount, Marcellus. "Caged Birds: Race and Gender in the Sonnet." *Engendering Men: The Question of Male Feminist Criticism.* Ed. Joseph A. Boone and Michael Cadden. New York: Routledge, 1990. 225–38.

Bogle, Donald. *Toms, Coons, Mulattoes, Mammies, and Bucks: An Interpretative History of Blacks in American Films.* 4th ed. New York: Continuum, 2001.

Boitani, Piero. *Prosatori negri americani del Novecento.* Rome: Edizioni di storia e letteratura, 1973.

Borges, Jorge Luis. *Labyrinths: Selected Stories & Other Writings.* Ed. Donald A. Yates and James E. Irby. Preface André Maurois. New York: New Directions Press, 1964.

Bosfield, Angela Charlene. "Three Ways to Picture Hell: An Aesthetic Approach to Richard Wright's *Native Son,* Ralph Ellison's *Invisible Man,* and LeRoi Jones's *The System of Dante's Hell.*" Diss. Concordia University (Canada), 1978.

Boswell, Jackson Campbell. *Dante's Fame in England: References in Printed British Books 1477–1640*. Newark: University of Delaware Press, 1999.

Botta, Vincenzo. *Dante as Philosopher, Patriot, and Poet*. New York: Scribner's, 1865.

Bouvier, Luke. "Reading in Black and White: Space and Race in *Linden Hills*." Gates, *Gloria Naylor* 140–51.

Boyagoda, Randy. *Race, Immigration, and American Identity in the Fiction of Salman Rushdie, Ralph Ellison, and William Faulkner*. New York: Routledge, 2008.

Braida, Antonella. *Dante and the Romantics*. New York and Basingstoke, Hampshire, UK: Palgrave Macmillan, 2004.

Braida, Antonella, and Luisa Calè, eds. *Dante on View: The Reception of Dante in the Visual and Performing Arts*. Burlington, Vt.: Ashgate, 2007.

Brown, Hallie Q. *Homespun Heroines and Other Women of Distinction*. Xenia, Ohio: Aldine, 1926.

[Brown, John.] *The Life and Letters of John Brown, Liberator of Kansas, and Martyr of Virginia*. Ed. F. B. Sanborn. 1885. New York: Negro Universities Press, 1969.

Brown, Lloyd W. *Amiri Baraka*. Boston: Twayne, 1980.

———. "High and Crazy Niggers: Anti-Rationalism in LeRoi Jones." *Journal of Ethnic Studies* 2.1 (1974): 1–9.

———. "Jones (Baraka) and His Literary Heritage in *The System of Dante's Hell*." *Obsidian* 1.1 (1975): 5–17.

———. "LeRoi Jones (Imamu Amiri Baraka) as Novelist: Theme and Structure in *The System of Dante's Hell*." *Negro American Literature* 7.4 (1973): 132–42.

Brown, Sydney M. *Mazzini and Dante*. Bethlehem, Pa.: Lehigh University Press, 1927. Rpt. from *Political Science Quarterly* 17.1 (March 1927): 77–98.

Brown, William Wells. *The American Fugitive in Europe: Sketches of Places and People Abroad*. New York: Negro Universities Press, 1855.

———. *Clotel; or, The President's Daughter: A Narrative of Slave Life in the United States*. 1853. Ed. and intro. Joan E. Cashin. Armonk, N.Y.: M. E. Sharpe, 1996.

———. *Clotel; or, The President's Daughter: A Narrative of Slave Life in the United States*. 1853. Ed. and intro. Robert S. Levine. Boston: Bedford/St. Martin's, 2000.

———. *Clotelle: A Tale of the Southern States*. New York: Redpath, 1864. Accessed Nov. 4, 2007. < http://rotunda.upress.virginia.edu:8080/clotel/>.

———. *Clotelle; or, the Colored Heroine. A Tale of the Southern States*. 1867. Miami: Mnemosyne, 1969.

———. *Miralda; or, the Beautiful Quadroon. A Romance of American Slavery, Founded on Fact*. *The Weekly Anglo-American* 21–35 (Dec. 1860–March 1861). Accessed Nov. 4, 2007. <http://rotunda.upress.virginia.edu:8080/clotel/>.

Bruce, Dickson D., Jr. *The Origins of African American Literature, 1680–1865*. Charlottesville: University Press of Virginia, 2001.

Brunetta, Gian Piero. *Storia del cinema italiano 1895–1945.* Rome: Riuniti, 1979.

————. *Storia del cinema mondiale. Gli Stati Uniti.* Vol. 2. Turin: Einaudi, 2000.

Brunner, Edward. *Cold War Poetry.* Urbana: University of Illinois Press, 2001.

Butler, Robert J. "Dante's *Inferno* and Ellison's *Invisible Man*: A Study in Literary Continuity." *CLA Journal* 28 (1984): 57–77.

————. "The Metaphor of the Journey in *Black Boy*." *Readings on "Black Boy."* Ed. Haley Mitchell. San Diego: Greenhaven Press, 2000. 131–40.

Caesar, Michael, ed. *Dante: The Critical Heritage, 1314(?)–1870.* London: Routledge, 1989.

Callahan, John F. *In the African-American Grain: Call-and-Response in Twentieth-Century Black Fiction.* 1988. Middletown, Conn.: Wesleyan University Press, 1990.

Calvesi, Maurizio. *Treasures of the Vatican: St. Peter's Basilica, the Vatican Museums and Galleries, the Treasure of St. Peter's, the Vatican Grottoes and Necropolis, the Vatican Palaces.* Intro. Deoclecio Redig de Campos. Trans. James Emmons. Geneva: Skira, 1962.

Cambon, Glauco. "Dante on Galway Kinnell's 'Last River.'" *Dante's Influence on American Writers, 1776–1976.* Ed. Anne Paolucci. New York: Griffin House, 1977. 31–40.

————. *Dante's Craft: Studies in Language and Style.* Minneapolis: University of Minnesota Press, 1969.

Capouya, Emile. "States of Mind, of Soul." Review of Baraka's *System of Dante's Hell. New York Times Book Review* 70 (Nov. 28, 1965): 4.

Carey, Percy. [M. F. Grimm aka G. M. Grimm.] *Digital Tears: Email from Purgatory.* CD. Day by Day Entertainment, 2004.

————. [M. F. Grimm.] *Sentences: The Life of M. F. Grimm.* Illustrated by Ronald Wimberly with Lee Roughridge. New York: Vertigo, 2007.

Carne-Ross, D. S. "Dante Antagonistes." *Instaurations: Essays in and out of Literature Pindar to Pound.* Berkeley: University of California Press, 1979. 116–32.

Cary, Henry Francis, trans. Dante Alighieri. *The Vision; or Hell, Purgatory, & Paradise of Dante Alighieri.* New York: Hurst, 1844.

Casadio, Gianfranco, ed. *Dante nel cinema.* Ravenna: Longo, 1996.

Casanova, Pascale. *The World Republic of Letters.* Trans. M. B. DeBevoise. Cambridge: Harvard University Press, 2004.

Cashin, Joan E. "Gender, Race, and Identity: An Introduction to William Wells Brown's *Clotel*." Brown, *Clotel; or The President's Daughter* ix–xix.

Cassell, Anthony K. *The* Monarchia *Controversy: An Historical Study with Accompanying Translations of Dante Alighieri's* Monarchia, *Guido Vernani's* Refutation of the "Monarchia" Composed by Dante, *and Pope John XXII's Bull* Si fratrum. Washington, D.C.: Catholic University of America Press, 2004.

Christian, Charles M. *Black Saga: The African American Experience*. Boston: Houghton Mifflin, 1995.

Ciccarelli, Andrea. "Dante and the Culture of Risorgimento: Literary, Political or Ideological Icon?" *Making and Remaking Italy: The Cultivation of National Identity around the Risorgimento*. Ed. Albert Russell Ascoli and Krystyna von Henneberg. Oxford–New York: Berg, 2001. 77–102.

Cifelli, Edward M. *John Ciardi: A Biography*. Fayetteville: University of Arkansas Press, 1997.

Clark, Rufus W. *The African Slave Trade*. Boston: American Tract Society, 1860.

Clay, Steven, and Rodney Phillips. *A Secret Location on the Lower East Side: Adventures in Writing, 1960–1980*. New York: New York Public Library and Granary Books, 1998.

Clayton, Edward T. "The Tragedy of Amos 'n' Andy." *Ebony* 16 (Oct. 1961): 66–73.

Cogan, Marc. *The Design in the Wax: The Structure of the "Divine Comedy" and Its Meaning*. Notre Dame, Ind.: University of Notre Dame Press, 1999.

Collins, Grace E. "Narrative Structure in *Linden Hills*." Felton and Loris, *The Critical Response to Gloria Naylor* 80–88.

Collins, James J. *Praying with Dante*. Companions for the Journey Series. Winona, Minn.: St. Mary's Press, 2000.

The Colored American. New York, 1837–42. General ed., Charles Bennett Ray, 1837–42. Organized by volumes within years, numbers within volumes.

"Colour." *Encyclopedia Britannica*. 2009. Encyclopedia Britannica Online. Accessed Nov. 25, 2009. <http://www.britannica.com/EBchecked/topic/126658/colour>.

"Columbian Reading Union." *Catholic World* 57 (1893): 294–96.

Cook, William W., and James Tatum. *African American Writers and Classical Tradition*. Chicago: University of Chicago Press, 2010.

Cooke, Michael J. "The Descent into the Underworld and Modern Black Fiction." *The Iowa Review* 5.4 (1974): 72–90.

Cooksey, Thomas L. "Dante's England, 1818: The Contribution of Cary, Coleridge, and Foscolo to the British Reception of Dante." *Papers on Language and Literature* 20.4 (1984): 355–81.

Cooper, Anna Julia. *A Voice from the South*. Intro. Mary Helen Washington. The Schomburg Library of Nineteenth-Century Black Women Writers. New York: Oxford University Press, 1988.

Corti, Maria. "Dante and Islamic Culture (1999)." Special issue *Dante and Islam*. *Dante Studies* 125 (2007): 57–75.

Cournos, John. *A Modern Plutarch: Being an Account of some Great Lives in the Nineteenth Century, together with some Comparisons between the Latin and the Anglo-Saxon Genius.* London: Thornton Butterworth, 1928.

Cripps, Thomas. "*Amos 'n' Andy* and the Debate over American Racial Integration." *American History, American Television: Interpreting the Video Past.* Ed. John E. O'Connor. New York: Ungar, 1983. 33–54.

———. *Black Film as Genre.* Bloomington: Indiana University Press, 1978.

———. "The Films of Spencer Williams." *Black American Literature Forum* 12 (1978): 128–34.

———. *Making Movies Black: The Hollywood Message Movie from World War II to the Civil Rights Era.* New York: Oxford University Press, 1993.

———. *Slow Fade to Black: The Negro in American Film, 1900–1942.* New York: Oxford University Press, 1977.

Crisafulli, Edoardo. *The Vision of Dante: Cary's Translation of "The Divine Comedy."* Leicester, U.K.: Troubador Publishing, 2003.

Culbertson, Judi, and Tom Randall. *Permanent Italians: An Illustrated, Biographical Guide to the Cemeteries of Italy.* New York: Walker, 1996.

Cunningham, Gilbert F. *The "Divine Comedy" in English: A Critical Bibliography, 1901–1966.* New York: Barnes and Noble, 1967.

Dal Lago, Enrico, and Rick Halpern, eds. *The American South and the Italian Mezzogiorno: Essays in Comparative History.* London: Palgrave, 2002.

"Dante and His English Translators." *Westminster Review* 75 (1861): 108–24.

Dennett, Andrea Stulman. *Weird and Wonderful: The Dime Museum in America.* New York: New York University Press, 1997.

Dent, Gina, ed. *Black Popular Culture.* Seattle: Bay Press, 1992.

De Sua, William J. *Dante into English: A Study of the Translation of the "Divine Comedy" in Britain and America.* Chapel Hill: University of North Carolina Press, 1964.

Dickie, John. *Darkest Italy: The Nation and Stereotypes of the Mezzogiorno, 1860–1900.* New York: St. Martin's Press, 1999.

———. "Imagined Italies." *Italian Cultural Studies: An Introduction.* Ed. David Forgacs and Robert Lumley. New York: Oxford University Press, 1996. 19–33.

Dimock, Wai Chee. "Literature for the Planet." *PMLA* 116.1 (2001): 173–88.

Di Prima, Diane. *Recollections of My Life as a Woman: The New York Years: A Memoir.* New York: Viking, 2001.

Di Scala, Spencer M. *Italy from Revolution to Republic: 1700 to the Present.* 1995. Boulder, Colo.: Westview Press, 1998.

Domini, John. "Toni Morrison's *Sula*: An Inverted Inferno." *High Plains Literary Review* 3.1 (1988): 75–90.

Douglass, Frederick. *Frederick Douglass Diary (Tour of Europe and Africa).* <http://www.memory.loc.gov/ammem/doughtml/dougFolder1.html>. Accessed June 2, 2010.

———. *The Frederick Douglass Papers.* Ed. John V. Blassingame. 5 vols. New Haven: Yale University Press, 1979–92.

———. *Life and Times of Frederick Douglass.* Intro. Rayford W. Logan. 1962. Toronto: Collier Books, 1969.

———. *Narrative of the Life of Frederick Douglass.* Preface William Lloyd Garrison. New York: Dover, 1995.

Dove, Rita. *Conversations with Rita Dove.* Ed. Earl G. Ingersoll. Jackson: University Press of Mississippi, 2003.

Doyle, Don H. *Nations Divided: America, Italy, and the Southern Question.* Athens: University of Georgia Press, 2002.

Drake, St. Clair. "African-American Popular Culture and the Literary Tradition." Unpublished ms. in Schomburg Collection, New York Public Library, box 22, folder 5.

Drescher, Seymour. "Servile Insurrection and John Brown's Body in Europe." *His Soul Goes Marching On: Responses to John Brown and the Harper's Ferry Raid.* Ed. Paul Finkelman. Charlottesville: University Press of Virginia, 1995. 253–95.

Du Bois, W. E. B. *Darkwater: Voices from Within the Veil.* 1920. New York: Schocken, 1969.

———. *The Education of Black People: Ten Critiques 1906–1960.* Ed. Herbert Aptheker. Amherst: University of Massachusetts Press, 1973.

———. "Galileo Galilei." *The Education of Black People* 17–30.

———. *The Souls of Black Folk.* 1903. New York: Dover Books, 1994.

Dunlop, M. H. "Curiosities Too Numerous to Mention: Early Regionalism and Cincinnati's Western Museum." *American Quarterly* 36.4 (1984): 524–48.

Dupree, Robert S. *Allen Tate and the Augustinian Imagination: A Study of the Poetry.* Baton Rouge: Louisiana State University Press, 1983.

Duvall, John N. *The Identifying Fictions of Toni Morrison: Modernist Authenticity and Postmodern Blackness.* New York: Palgrave, 2000.

Eady, Cornelius. *You Don't Miss Your Water.* New York: Holt, 1995.

Edwards, Brent Hayes. *The Practice of Diaspora: Literature, Translation, and the Rise of Black Internationalism.* Cambridge: Harvard University Press, 2003.

Egan, Maurice F. "Calderón de la Barca." *Catholic World* 33 (1881): 474–87.

Egerton, John. *Visions of Utopia: Nashoba, Rugby, Ruskin, and the "New Communities" in Tennessee's Past.* Knoxville: University of Tennessee Press, 1977

Eliot, T. S. "American Literature and the American Language." *To Criticize the Critic and Other Writings.* New York: Farrar, Straus & Giroux, 1965. 43–60.

————. *Four Quartets.* 1943. New York: Harcourt Brace Jovanovich, 1971.

————. *The Waste Land: A Facsimile and Transcript of the Original Drafts Including the Annotations of Ezra Pound.* Ed. Valerie Eliot. 1930. New York: Harcourt Brace Jovanovich, 1971.

Ellison, Ralph. *Collected Essays.* Ed. and intro. John F. Callahan. Preface Saul Bellow. New York: Modern Library, 2003.

————. *A Collection of Critical Essays.* Ed. John Hersey. Englewood Cliffs, N.J.: Prentice Hall, 1974.

————. *Conversations with Ralph Ellison.* Ed. Maryemma Graham and Amritjit Singh. Jackson: University Press of Mississippi, 1995.

————. *Invisible Man.* Preface Charles Johnson. 1952. New York: Modern Library, 1994.

————. *Juneteenth.* Ed. John F. Callahan. New York: Random House, 1999.

————. *Modern Critical Views.* Ed. Harold Bloom. New York: Chelsea House, 1986.

————. *Three Days before the Shooting . . .* Ed. John F. Callahan and Adam Bradley. New York: Modern Library, 2010.

Ely, Melvin Patrick. *The Adventures of Amos 'n' Andy: A Social History of an American Phenomenon.* New York: Free Press, 1991.

Epstein, Steven A. *Speaking of Slavery: Color, Ethnicity, & Human Bondage in Italy.* Ithaca: Cornell University Press, 2001.

Erickson, Peter. "Shakespeare's Naylor, Naylor's Shakespeare: Shakespearian Allusion as Appropriation in Gloria Naylor's Quartet." *Literary Influence and African-American Writers: Collected Essays.* Ed. Tracy Mishkin. New York: Garland, 1996. 325–57. Rpt. in Gates, *Gloria Naylor* 231–48.

Eternal Kool Project. *The Inferno Rap.* CD. Eternal Kool Project, 2005.

Fabi, M. Giulia. *America nera: La cultura afroamericana.* Rome: Carocci, 2002.

————. *Passing and the Rise of the African American Novel.* Urbana: University of Illinois Press, 2001.

Fabio, Sarah Webster. "Who Speaks Negro? What Is Black?" *Negro Digest* (Sept./Oct. 1968): 33–37.

Fabre, Michel. *Richard Wright. Books and Writers.* Jackson: University of Mississippi Press, 1990.

Farrell, Nancy Clow. "The Slave That Captivated America." *Cincinnati Historical Society Bulletin* 22.4 (Oct. 1964): 221–39.

Farrison, William Edward. *William Wells Brown: Author and Reformer.* Chicago: Chicago University Press, 1969.

Felton, Sharon, and Michelle C. Loris, eds. *The Critical Response to Gloria Naylor.* Westport, Conn.: Greenwood Press, 1997.

Ferris, William H. *The African Abroad or His Evolution in Western Civilization . . .* New Haven: Tuttle, Morehouse & Taylor Press, 1913. Rpt. New York: Johnson Reprint Corp., 1968.

Floating Bear: A Newsletter. Ed. Diane di Prima and LeRoi Jones. Intro. and notes adapted from interviews with Diane di Prima. La Jolla, Calif.: Laurence McGilvery, 1973.

Foner, Philip S., and Robert James Branham, eds. *Lift Every Voice: African American Oratory, 1787–1900.* Tuscaloosa: University of Alabama Press, 1998.

Fowler, Virginia C. *Gloria Naylor: In Search of Sanctuary.* New York: Twayne, 1996.

Foxe, John. *Foxe's Book of Martyrs Variorum Edition Online (2nd ed.).* Accessed Oct. 6, 2007. <http://www.hrionline.ac.uk/johnfoxe/index.html>.

Francini, Antonella. "Premessa." *Semicerchio, revista di poesia camparata.* Special issue: *Rewriting Dante. Le riscritture di Dante. Russia, USA, Italia* 36 (2007): 5–10.

Franck, Adolphe. *Réformateurs et publicistes de l'Europe.* 2 vols. Paris: Michel Lévy, 1864.

Freccero, John. "Bestial Sign and Bread of Angels: *Inferno* xxxii–xxxiii." *Dante: The Poetics of Conversion* 152–66.

———. *Dante: The Poetics of Conversion.* Ed. Rachel Jacoff. Cambridge: Harvard University Press, 1986.

———. "The Significance of *terza rima.*" *Dante: The Poetics of Conversion* 258–74.

Freydberg, Elizabeth Hadley. "The Concealed Dependence upon White Culture in Baraka's 1969 Aesthetic." *Black American Literature Forum* 17.1 (1983): 27–29.

Friederich, Werner P. *Dante's Fame Abroad, 1350–1850.* Chapel Hill: University of North Carolina Press, 1950.

———. *Outline of Comparative Literature from Dante Alighieri to Eugene O'Neill.* Chapel Hill: University of North Carolina Press, 1954.

Gaja, Katerine. "'Scrivendo nel marmo': Lettere inedite tra Elizabeth Barrett Browning e Hiram Powers." *Antologia Vieusseux* 25–26 (2003): 31–65.

———, ed. *Hiram Powers a Firenze.* Mostra documentaria in occasione del bicentenario della nascita. Florence: Edizioni Polistampa, 2005.

Ganim, John M. *Medievalism and Orientalism: Three Essays on Literature, Architecture and Cultural Identity.* New York: Palgrave Macmillan, 2005.

Garrison, William Lloyd. *Letters.* Vol. 6. *To Rouse the Slumbering Land, 1868–1879.* Ed. Walter M. Merrill and Louis Ruchames. Cambridge: Belknap Press, Harvard University Press, 1981.

Gates, Henry Louis, Jr. "Criticism in the Jungle." *Black Literature and Literary Theory.* Ed. Henry Louis Gates, Jr. New York: Methuen, 1984. 1–24.

Gates, Henry Louis, Jr., and K. A. Appiah, eds. *Gloria Naylor: Critical Perspectives, Past and Present.* New York: Amistad, 1993.

————, eds. *Toni Morrison: Critical Perspectives, Past and Present.* New York: Amistad, 1993.

Gaudenzi, Cosetta. "Exile, Translation, and Return: Ugo Foscolo in England." *Annali di Italianistica* 20 (2002): 217–33.

Gay, H. Nelson. "Lincoln's Offer of a Command to Garibaldi: Light on a Disputed Point of History." *The Century Magazine* 75 (1907): 63–74.

Gevinson, Alan, ed. *Within Our Gates: Ethnicity in American Feature Films, 1911–1960.* American Film Institute Catalog. Berkeley: University of California Press, 1997.

Gilman, Richard. "The Devil May Care." *Herald Tribune Review* Dec. 26, 1965: 12.

Ginsberg, Allen. *Howl and Other Poems.* Intro. William Carlos Williams. 1956. San Francisco: City Lights Books, 1976.

Goddard, J. R. "Poet Jailed for Obscenity; Literary Magazine Hit." *Village Voice* 7.1 (Oct. 26, 1961): 3, 16.

Goddu, Teresa. "Reconstructing History in *Linden Hills.*" Gates, *Gloria Naylor* 215–30.

Gomez, Jewelle. "Naylor's Inferno." Review of *Linden Hills. Women's Review of Books* 2 (Aug. 1985): 7–8.

Graham, Hugh Davis. *Civil Rights Era.* New York: Oxford University Press, 1990.

Grant, Michael, ed. *T. S. Eliot: The Critical Heritage.* London: Routledge, 1997.

Greenblatt, Stephen. *Hamlet in Purgatory.* Princeton: Princeton University Press, 2001.

Greenwood, Emily. *Afro-Greeks: Dialogues between Anglophone Caribbean Literature and Classics in the Twentieth Century.* Oxford: Oxford University Press, 2010.

Grewal, Gurleen. *Circles of Sorrow, Lines of Struggle: The Novels of Toni Morrison.* Baton Rouge: Louisiana State University Press, 1998.

Gubar, Susan. *Racechanges: White Skin, Black Face in American Culture.* New York: Oxford University Press, 1997.

Gunn, Giles. "Introduction: Globalizing Literary Studies." *PMLA* 116.1 (2001): 16–31.

Gurney, Emilia Russell. *Dante's Pilgrim's Progress; or, 'The passage of the blessed soul from the slavery of the present corruption to the liberty of eternal glory.'* London: Elliot Stock, 1893.

Hahn, Thomas, ed. *Race and Ethnicity in the Middle Ages.* Special issue of *Journal of Medieval and Early Modern Studies* 31.1 (2001).

Hall, Stuart. *Race: The Floating Signifier.* Video recording. Northampton, Mass.: Media Education Foundation, 1997.

Harper, Frances E. W. *Complete Poems of Frances E. W. Harper*. Ed. and intro. Mary-emma Graham. The Schomburg Library of Nineteenth-Century Black Women Writers. New York: Oxford University Press, 1988.

Harper, G. M. "Dante as a Guide through life." *Carroccio* 13 (1921): 266–68.

———. "If Dante Were Alive." *Sewanee Review* 29 (1921): 258–67. Rpt. in *Spirit of Delight* 174–90.

———. "Lesson from Dante." *Spirit of Delight* 191–98.

———. *Spirit of Delight*. New York: Holt, 1928.

Harris, William J. *Poetry and Poetics of Amiri Baraka: The Jazz Aesthetic*. Columbia: University of Missouri Press, 1985.

Hart, Madelyn Elaine. "Analysis of the Rhetoric of LeRoi Jones (Imamu Amiri Baraka) in His Campaign to Promote Cultural Black Nationalism." Master's thesis, North Texas State University, 1976.

Hatcher, John. *From the Auroral Darkness: The Life and Poetry of Robert Hayden*. Oxford: George Ronald, 1984.

Havely, Nicholas R. *Dante*. Oxford: Blackwell, 2007.

———. "Francesca Observed: Painting and Illustration, c. 1790–1840." Braida and Calè 95–108.

———. "Introduction: Dante's Afterlife, 1321–1997." *Dante's Modern Afterlife* 1–14.

———. "'An Italian Writer against the Pope'? Dante in Reformation England, c. 1560–c. 1640." *Dante Metamorphoses: Episodes in a Literary Afterlife*. Ed. Eric G. Haywood. Dublin: Four Courts Press, 2003. 127–49.

———. "'Prosperous People' and 'The Real Hell' in Gloria Naylor's *Linden Hills*." *Dante's Modern Afterlife* 211–22.

———. "Receiving Dante: From Florence to Hollywood." *Cambridge Quarterly* 35.2 (2006): 196–203.

———, ed. *Dante's Modern Afterlife: Reception and Response from Blake to Heaney*. New York: St. Martin's Press, 1998.

Havely, Nicholas R. and Aida Audeh, eds. *Dante in the Long Nineteenth Century: Nationality, Identity, and Appropriation*. Oxford: Oxford University Press, 2011.

Hayden, Robert, ed. and intro. *Kaleidoscope: Poems by American Negro Poets*. New York: Harcourt, Brace & World, 1967.

Hays, Sue Brown. *Go Down, Death*. New York: Scribner's, 1946.

Henry, Paul. *The Life and Times of John Calvin, the Great Reformer*. Trans. Henry Stebbing. 2 vols. New York: Robert Carter, 1851.

Hensman, Mary. *Dante Map*. London: David Nutt, 1892. British Library 11420.cc.14, and John Rylands University Library, Manchester, R17263.

Hinkley, Edyth. *Mazzini: The Story of a Great Italian*. 1924. Port Washington, N.Y.: Kennikat Press, 1970.

Hogan, William. "The System of LeRoi Jones." *San Francisco Chronicle* Nov. 23, 1965: n.p.

Homans, Margaret. "The Woman in the Cave." Gates, *Gloria Naylor* 152–81.

Horne, Robert. *An Answeare Made by Rob. Bishoppe of Wynchester, to a Book entitled, The Declaration of Suche Scruples . . . as M. John Feckenham . . . delivered unto the L. Bishop of Winchester. . . .* London: Henry Wykes, 1566.

Hudson, Theodore R. *From LeRoi Jones to Amiri Baraka: The Literary Works*. Durham, N.C.: Duke University Press, 1973.

———. *A LeRoi Jones (Amiri Baraka) Bibliography . . .* Washington, D.C.: privately printed, 1971.

Iannucci, Amilcare A. "Dante, Television, and Education." *Quaderni d'italianistica* 10 (1989): 1–33.

Ierardo, Domenico. *Dante nostro contemporaneo*. Abano Terme: Piovan, 1987.

Isabella, Maurizio. "Exile and Nationalism: The Case of the *Risorgimento*." *European History Quarterly* 36.4 (2006): 493–520.

Jackson, Esther Merle. "The American Negro and the Image of the Absurd." *Phylon* 13 (1962): 359–71. Rpt. in *Richard Wright: A Collection of Essays*. Ed. Richard Macksey and Frank E. Moorer. Englewood Cliffs, N.J.: Prentice Hall, 1984. 129–38.

Jackson, Kathryn. "LeRoi Jones and the New Black Writers of the Sixties." *Freedomways* 9.3 (1969): 232–47.

Jackson, Lawrence. *Ralph Ellison: Emergence of Genius*. New York: Wiley, 2002.

Jewel, John. *A Defence of the Apologie of the Churche of England . . .* London: Henry Wykes, 1567.

Johnson, Barbara. "Writing." *Critical Terms for Literary Study*. Ed. Frank Lentricchia and Thomas McLaughlin. Chicago: University of Chicago Press, 1990. 39–49.

Johnson, James Weldon. *God's Trombones: Seven Negro Sermons in Verse*. 1927. New York: Viking Press, 1973.

Johnson, Ronna S., and Maria Damon. "The Skipped Beats." *Chronicle of Higher Education* (Oct. 1, 1999): B4–6.

Jones, Edward Smythe. *The Sylvan Cabin*. Intro. William Stanley Braithwaite. Boston: Sherman and French, 1911.

Jones, G. William. *Black Cinema Treasures: Lost and Found*. Denton: University of North Texas Press, 1991.

———. "Spencer Williams." *Handbook of Texas Online*. Accessed Jan. 11, 2009. <http://www.tshaonline.org/handbook/online/articles/WW/fwiah_print .html>.

Jones, Hettie. *How I Became Hettie Jones.* New York: Dutton, 1990.

Jones, LeRoi. See Baraka, Amiri.

Kapai, Leela. "Ray, Henrietta Cordelia." *Afro-American Writers before the Harlem Renaissance.* Ed. Trudier Harris. Vol. 50 of *Dictionary of Literary Biography.* Detroit: Gale, 1986. 744–45.

Katz, Wendy Jean. *Regionalism and Reform: Art and Class Formation in Antebellum Cincinnati.* Columbus: Ohio State University Press, 2002.

Kelley, Margot Anne, ed. *Gloria Naylor's Early Novels.* Gainesville: University Press of Florida, 1999.

Kellogg, Elizabeth R. "Joseph Dorfeuille and the Western Museum." *Journal of the Cincinnati Society of Natural History* 22 (1945): 8–13.

Kennedy, William J. *Authorizing Petrarch.* Ithaca: Cornell University Press, 1994.

Kerlin, Robert T. *Negro Poets and Their Poems.* Washington, D.C.: Associated Publishers, 1923.

King, R. W. *The Translator of Dante: The Life of Henry Francis Cary (1772–1884).* London: Martin Secker, 1925.

Kirschke, Amy Helene. *Aaron Douglas: Art, Race, and the Harlem Renaissance.* Jackson: University Press of Mississippi, 1999.

Kisch, John, and Edward Mapp. *A Separate Cinema: Fifty Years of Black-Cast Posters.* Intro. Spike Lee. New York: Farrar, Straus and Giroux, 1992.

Klotman, Phyllis. *Frame by Frame: A Black Filmography.* Bloomington: Indiana University Press, 1979.

Knight, Arthur, and Kit Knight. *The Beat Vision: A Primary Sourcebook.* New York: Paragon House, 1987.

Kotz, Mary Lynn. *Rauschenberg: Art and Life.* New York: Abrams, 1990.

Krim, Seymour, ed. *The Beats. A Gold Medal Anthology.* Greenwich, Conn.: Fawcett Books, 1963.

Kubitschek, Missy Dean. *Toni Morrison: A Critical Companion.* Westport, Conn.: Greenwood Press, 1998.

Kuhns, Oscar. *Dante and the English Poets from Chaucer to Tennyson.* New York: Holt, 1904.

———. "Dante as a Tonic for To-day." *The Dial* 23.269 (Sept. 1, 1897): 110.

Lansing, Richard, ed. and intro. *Dante's Afterlife: The Influence and Reception of the "Commedia."* Vol. 8 of *Dante: The Critical Complex.* New York and London: Routledge, 2003.

La Piana, Angelina. *Dante's American Pilgrimage: A Historical Survey of Dante Studies in the United States 1800–1944.* New Haven: Yale University Press, 1948.

Lears, T. J. Jackson. *No Place of Grace: Antimodernism and the Transformation of American Culture 1880–1920.* New York: Pantheon, 1981.

Lee, Spike. "Black Films: The Studios Have It All Wrong." *New York Times,* May 2, 1999, sec. 2A, p. 23.

————. "Second Annual AMC Film Preservation Festival." *American Movie Classics Magazine* 77 (Oct. 1994): 4–5.

Letters on American Slavery. Boston: American Anti-Slavery Society, 1860.

Levi, Primo. *If This Is a Man* and *The Truce.* Trans. Stuart Woolf. London: Abacus, 1987.

Levin, David. "Baldwin's Autobiographical Essays: The Problem of Negro Identity." *Black and White in American Culture: An Anthology from "The Massachusetts Review."* Amherst: University of Massachusetts Press, 1969. 372–79.

Levine, Lawrence W. *Highbrow/Lowbrow: The Emergence of Cultural Hierarchy in America.* Cambridge, Mass.: Harvard University Press, 1988.

Lewis, David Levering. *W. E. B. Du Bois: Biography of a Race, 1868–1919.* New York: Henry Holt, 1994.

Locke, Alain. "The Legacy of the Ancestral Arts." Locke, *The New Negro* 254–70.

————. "The New Negro." Locke, *The New Negro* 3–16.

————, ed. *The New Negro.* 1925. With a new preface by Robert Hayden. New York: Atheneum, 1970.

Loftis, N. J. *Black Anima.* New York: Liveright, 1973.

Looney, Dennis. "The Beginnings of Humanistic Oratory: Petrarch's *Coronation Oration.*" *Petrarch: A Critical Guide to the Complete Works.* Ed. Victoria Kirkham and Armando Maggi. Chicago: University of Chicago Press, 2009. 131–40.

————. *Compromising the Classics: Romance Epic Narrative in Renaissance Italian Narrative.* Detroit: Wayne State University Press, 1996.

————. "Epoch-making Letters: Hiram Powers in the Gabinetto Vieusseux." *The Politics of Writing Relations: American Scholars in Italian Archives.* Ed. Deanna Shemek and Michael Wyatt. Florence: Leo S. Olschki, 2008. 139–63.

————. "'Flame-coloured Letters and Bugaboo Phraseology': Hiram Powers, Frances Trollope and Dante in Frontier Cincinnati." *Hiram Powers a Firenze: Atti del Convegno di studi nel Bicentenario della nascita (1805–2005).* Ed. Caterina Del Vivo. Florence: Leo S. Olschki, 2007. 135–52.

————. "The Poetics of Exile in LeRoi Jones's *The System of Dante's Hell.*" *Exil. Transhistorische und transnationale Perspektiven.* Ed. H. Koopman. Paderborn: Mentis, 2001. 271–79.

————. Review of *The Dante Encyclopedia.* Ed. Richard Lansing. *Speculum* 78.3 (2003): 934–36.

————. Review of *Dante on View.* Ed. Antonella Braida and Luisa Calè. *caa.reviews,* Nov. 12, 2008, DOI: 10.3202/caa.reviews.2008.113. <http://caa.reviews.org/reviewers/949>.

————. Review of *Dante's Modern Afterlife*. Ed. Nick Havely. *Speculum* 76.3 (2001): 733–34.

————. "Spencer Williams and Dante: An African American Filmmaker at the Gates of Hell." *Dante, Cinema, and Television*. Ed. Amilcare Iannucci. Toronto: University of Toronto Press, 2004. 129–42.

Lowance, Mason, ed. and intro. *Against Slavery: An Abolitionist Reader*. New York: Penguin, 2000.

Lowenthal, David. *George Perkins Marsh: Prophet of Conservation*. Seattle: University of Washington Press, 2000.

————. *George Perkins Marsh: Versatile Vermonter*. New York: Columbia University Press, 1958.

Mackey, Nathaniel. "The Changing Same: Black Music in the Poetry of Amiri Baraka." Benston, *Imamu Amiri Baraka* 119–34.

Marraro, Howard. "Dante negli Stati Uniti." *Dante nel mondo*. Ed. Vittore Branca and Ettore Caccia. Florence: Leo S. Olschki, 1965. 433–559.

Marazzi, Martino. "Preistoria e storia di 'afro-americano.'" *Studi di lessicografia italiana* 24 (2007): 249–64.

Matteo, Sante, ed. *ItaliAfrica: Bridging Continents and Cultures*. Stony Brook, N.Y.: Forum Italicum Publishing, 2001.

Matteo, Sante, and Stefano Bellucci, eds. *Africa Italia. Due continenti si avvicinano.* Santarcangelo di Romagna, Italy: Fara Editore, 1999.

Mathews, J. Chesley. "An Historical Overview of American Writers' Interest in Dante (to about 1900)." Paolucci, *Dante's Influence* 12–21.

Mauro, Walter. *Storia dei neri d'America.* Rome: Newton, 1997.

Mazzini, Giuseppe. *Joseph Mazzini: His Life, Writings, and Political Principles*. Intro. William Lloyd Garrison. New York: Hurd and Houghton, 1872.

————. *The Living Thoughts of Mazzini*. Intro. Ignazio Silone. 1939. Westport, Conn.: Greenwood Press, 1972.

————. *Scritti letterari*. 2 vols. Milan: Bietti, 1933.

McCabe, John C. "The Homeward Bound." *Southern Literary Messenger* 20.3 (March 1854): 187–88.

McDermot, George. "Dante's Theory of Papal Politics." *Catholic World* 65 (1897): 356–65.

McHenry, Elizabeth. *Forgotten Readers: Recovering the Lost History of African American Literary Societies.* Durham, N.C.: Duke University Press, 2002.

McKay, Claude. *The Passion of Claude McKay*. Ed. Wayne Cooper. New York: Schocken Books, 1973.

McKay, Nellie Y., ed. *Critical Essays on Toni Morrison*. Boston: G. K. Hall, 1988.

McKay, Nellie Y., and Kathryn Earle, eds. *Approaches to Teaching the Novels of Toni Morrison.* New York: MLA, 1997.

McLaughlin, Martin. "Petrarch: Between Two Ages, between Two Languages." Barański and McLaughlin 23–38.

McMurtry, Larry. "Grove." *Houston Post* Nov. 28, 1965: n.p.

Milbank, Alison. *Dante and the Victorians.* Manchester: Manchester University Press, 1998.

Miller, D. Quentin. "'Making a Place for Fear': Toni Morrison's First Redefinition of Dante's Hell in *Sula.*" *English Language Notes* 37.3 (2000): 68–75.

Miller, James, ed. *Dante and the Unorthodox: The Aesthetics of Transgression.* Waterloo, Ont.: Wilfrid Laurier University Press, 2005.

Milton, John. *Poems.* Ed. Peter Washington. Everyman's Library Pocket Poets. London: David Campbell for Random House, 1996.

Minganti, Franco. "Tre o quattro sfumature di nero. Il cinema afroamericano." *Storia del cinema mondiale.* Vol. 2 of *Gli Stati Uniti.* Ed. Gian Piero Brunetta. 3 vols. Turin: Einaudi, 2000. 1309–76.

Montgomery, Maxine Lavon. *The Apocalypse in African-American Fiction.* Gainesville: University of Florida Press, 1996.

Moore, John Noell. "Myth, Fairy Tale, Epic, and Romance: Narrative as Re-Vision in *Linden Hills.*" *Callaloo* 23.4 (2000): 1410–29.

Moorehead, Elizabeth A. "Henrietta Cordelia Ray (1849?–1916)." *Nineteenth-Century American Women Writers.* Ed. Denise D. Knight and Emmanuel S. Nelson. Westport, Conn.: Greenwood Press, 1997. 343–46.

Morrison, Toni. *The Bluest Eye.* 1970. New York: Plume, 1993.

———. "A Conversation: Gloria Naylor and Toni Morrison." *Conversations with Toni Morrison.* Ed. Danille Taylor-Guthrie. Jackson: University Press of Mississippi, 1994. 188–217.

———. *Playing in the Dark: Whiteness and the Literary Imagination.* 1992. New York: Vintage Books, 1993.

Moses, Wilson Jeremiah. *Afrotopia: The Roots of African American Popular History.* Cambridge: Cambridge University Press, 1998.

Mossell, N. F. "The Colored Woman in Verse." *AME Church Review* 2 (1885–86): 60–67.

———. *Work of the Afro-American Woman.* Ed. Joanne Braxton. The Schomburg Library of Nineteenth-Century Black Women Writers. New York: Oxford University Press, 1988.

Mumford, Lewis. *The Golden Day: A Study in American Literature and Culture.* New York: Boni and Liveright, 1926.

Naylor, Gloria. *Bailey's Cafe*. New York: Harcourt Brace Jovanovich, 1992.

————. "An Interview with Gloria Naylor." With Charles H. Powell. *Callaloo* 20.1 (1997): 179–92.

————. *Linden Hills*. 1985. New York: Penguin Books, 1986.

————. *Mama Day*. New York: Vintage, 1993.

————. *Men of Brewster Place*. New York: Hyperion, 1998.

————. *Women of Brewster Place*. New York: Viking Penguin, 1982.

Naylor, Gloria, and Toni Morrison. "A Conversation: Gloria Naylor and Toni Morrison." *Southern Review* 21.3 (1985): 567–93. Rpt. in Morrison, *Conversations with Toni Morrison*.

"Negroes in Rome." *Our World* (Sept. 1961): 26–39.

Neville-Sington, Pamela. *Fanny Trollope: The Life and Adventures of a Clever Woman*. New York: Viking, 1997.

Newman, Ivey White, and Walter Clinton Jackson, eds. *An Anthology of Verse by American Negroes*. Intro. James Hardy Dillard. Durham, N.C.: Trinity College Press, 1924.

Nielsen, Aldon L. "Fugitive Fictions: Amiri Baraka." *African American Review* (Summer–Fall 2003): 1–11.

————. *Writing between the Lines: Race and Intertextuality*. Athens: University of Georgia Press, 1994.

North, Michael. *The Dialect of Modernism: Race, Language, and Twentieth-Century Literature*. New York: Oxford University Press, 1994.

North Star. Rochester, N.Y., 1847–51. Available in Accessible Archives, *African American Newspapers: The 19th Century*. <http://www.accessible.com>.

The Norton Anthology of African American Literature. Ed. Henry Louis Gates, Jr., and Nellie Y. McKay. New York: Norton, 1997.

O'Brien, John. "Racial Nightmares and the Search for Self: An Explication of LeRoi Jones' 'A Chase (Alighieri's Dream).'" *Negro American Literature Forum* 7 (1973): 89–90.

Oelsner, Hermann. *The Influence of Dante on Modern Thought*. London: Unwin, 1895.

Omi, Michael, and Howard Winant. "Racial Formation in the United States." *The Idea of Race*. Ed. Robert Bernasconi and Tommy L. Lott. Indianapolis: Hackett, 2000. 181–213.

Oration Delivered by Frederick Douglass at the Unveiling of the Freedmen's Monument in Memory of Abraham Lincoln. In Lincoln Park, Washington, D.C. April 14, 1876. Rpt. New York: Pathway Press, 1940.

"Out of Touch." *Newsweek* Nov. 22, 1965.

Paolucci, Anne, ed. *Dante's Influence on American Writers 1776–1976.* New York: Griffon House, 1977.

Pearl, Matthew. *The Dante Club.* 2003. London: Vintage, 2004.

Pellegrini, Anthony L. "American Dante Bibliography for 1965." *Dante Studies* 84 (1966): 73–113.

Penn, I. Garland. *The Afro-American Press and Its Editors.* 1891. Rpt. New York: Arno Press and the New York Times, 1969.

Pennington-Jones, Paulette. "From Brother LeRoi Jones through *The System of Dante's Hell* to Imamu Ameer Baraka." *Journal of Black Studies* 4.2 (1973): 195–214.

———, ed. *Amiri Baraka: Bibliography, Biography, Playography.* London: TQ Publications, 1978.

Phillips, Carl. *Cortège.* St. Paul, Minn.: Graywolf Press, 1995.

———. *From the Devotions.* St. Paul, Minn.: Graywolf Press, 1998.

Phillips, Wendell. "Lincoln's Election." *Speeches, Lectures, and Letters.* Boston: Lee and Shepard, 1894. 294–318.

Podhoretz, Norman. "The Know-Nothing Bohemians." Krim 111–24.

"A Poet among the Poets." Review of *Among My Books,* by James Russell Lowell. *Catholic World* 23.133 (April 1876): 14–21.

Portelli, Alessandro. *La linea del colore: Saggi sulla cultura afroamericana.* Rome: Manifestolibri, 1994.

Posnock, Ross. *Color and Culture: Black Writers and the Making of the Modern Intellectual.* Cambridge: Harvard University Press, 1998.

Powell, Richard J. *Black Art and Culture in the 20th Century.* London: Thames and Hudson, 1997.

Prescott, Peter. "Books." *Women's Wear Daily* Nov. 26, 1965: n.p.

Price, Kenneth M. *To Walt Whitman, America.* Chapel Hill: University of North Carolina Press, 2004.

Purcell, Richard Erroll. "Ralph Ellison and the American Pursuit of Humanism." Diss. University of Pittsburgh, 2008.

Quondam, Amedeo. *Petrarca, l'italiano dimenticato.* Milan: Rizzoli, 2004.

Raboteau, Albert J. "African Americans, Exodus, and the American Israel." *Down by the Riverside: Readings in African American Religion.* Ed. Larry G. Murphy. New York: New York University Press, 2000. 20–25. Based on excerpts from his *Fire in the Bones.* Boston: Beacon Press, 1995.

Rampersad, Arnold. *Ralph Ellison: A Biography.* New York: Knopf, 2007.

Randall, Dudley. *A Litany of Friends.* Detroit: Lotus Press, 1983.

Rankine, Patrice D. *Ulysses in Black: Ralph Ellison, Classicism, and African American Literature.* Madison: University of Wisconsin Press, 2006.

Ray, Charles Bennett, Theodore S. Wright, and Dr. J. M'Cune Smith. *An Address to the Three Thousand Colored Citizens of New York, Who are the owners of one hundred and twenty thousand acres of land, in the State of New York, given to them by Gerrit Smith, Esq. of Peterboro. September 1, 1846.* New York: n.p., 1846.

Ray, Henrietta Cordelia. "Dante." *American Methodist Episcopal Church Review* 1.3 (1885): 251.

———. *Poems.* New York: Grafton Press, 1910. Rpt. *Collected Black Women's Poetry.* Ed. Joan R. Sherman. The Schomburg Library of Nineteenth-Century Black Women Writers. Vol. 3. New York: Oxford University Press, 1988.

Ray, Henrietta Cordelia, and F. T. Ray. *Sketch of the Life of Rev. Charles B. Ray.* New York: J. J. Little, 1887.

Redding, Saunders. "Pretentiousness." *The Crisis* (Jan. 1966): 56–57.

Reynolds, Donald Martin. *Hiram Powers and His Ideal Sculpture.* New York: Garland, 1977.

Roe, John. "Foreseeing and Foreknowing: Dante's 'Ugolino' and the Eton College Ode of Thomas Gray." Havely, *Dante's Modern Afterlife* 17–30.

Ronnick, Michelle Valerie. "Vergil in the Black American Experience." *A Companion to Vergil's "Aeneid" and Its Tradition.* Blackwell Companions to the Ancient World. Ed. Joseph Farrell and Michael C. J. Putnam. Oxford: Wiley-Blackwell, 2010. 376–90.

Roosevelt, Theodore. "Dante and the Bowery." *History as Literature.* New York: Scribner's, 1913.

Rossi, Joseph. *The Image of America in Mazzini's Writings.* Madison: University of Wisconsin Press, 1954.

Rubenstein, Roberta. "Pariahs and Community." In Gates and Appiah, *Toni Morrison* 126–58.

Rudman, Harry W. *Italian Nationalism and English Letters: Figures of the Risorgimento and Victorian Men of Letters.* New York: AMS Press, 1966.

Said, Edward. *Culture and Imperialism.* New York: Vintage Books, 1993.

———. *Orientalism.* New York: Vintage Books, 1979.

———. *Reflections on Exile and Other Essays.* Cambridge: Harvard University Press, 2000.

Samuel, Irene. *Dante and Milton: The* Commedia *and* Paradise Lost. Ithaca: Cornell University Press, 1966.

Sandiford, Keith. "Gothic and Intertextual Constructions in *Linden Hills.*" In Gates and Appiah, *Gloria Naylor* 195–214.

Sanguineti, Edoardo. *Dante reazionario.* Rome: Editori Riuniti, 1992.

Santini, Luigi. *The Protestant Cemetery of Florence Called "The English Cemetery."* Florence: K. S. Printing, 1981.

Sarti, Roland. *Mazzini: A Life for the Religion of Politics.* Westport, Conn.: Praeger, 1997.

Saunders, James Robert. "The Ornamentation of Old Ideas: Naylor's First Three Novels." In Gates and Appiah, *Gloria Naylor* 249–62.

Savage, Kirk. *Standing Soldiers, Kneeling Slaves: Race, War, and Monument in Nineteenth-Century America.* Princeton: Princeton University Press, 1997.

Schildgen, Brenda Deen. *Dante and the Orient.* Urbana: University of Illinois Press, 2002.

Schneck, Stephen. "LeRoi Jones or Poetics & Policemen or, Trying Heart, Bleeding Heart." *Ramparts* (June 29, 1968): 14–19.

Schockley, Anne Allen. *Afro-American Women Writers 1746–1933.* Boston: G. K. Hall, 1988.

Scott, Darieck Bruce. "Closet Case: Readings of the Black Male Figure in Twentieth Century African-American Literature (Frantz Fanon, James Weldon Johnson, Richard Wright, Amiri Baraka, Toni Morrison)." Diss. Stanford University, 1999.

Serafin, Steven R., ed. "Amiri Baraka." *Modern Black Writers: Supplement.* New York: Continuum, 1995. 69–77.

Seward, Adrienne. *Spencer Williams.* The New American Film and Video Series 46. New York: Whitney Museum of American Art, 1988.

Shapiro, Marianne. "Addendum: Christological Language in *Inferno* 33." *Dante Studies* 94 (1976): 141–43.

Sherman, Joan R. *African-American Poetry of the Nineteenth Century: An Anthology.* Urbana: University of Illinois Press, 1992.

———. *Invisible Poets: Afro-Americans of the Nineteenth Century.* 1974. Urbana: University of Illinois Press, 1989.

Singleton, Charles S. "In Exitu Israel de Aegypto." *Dante: A Collection of Critical Essays.* Ed. John Freccero. Englewood Cliffs, N.J.: Prentice Hall, 1965. 102–21.

———. "The Irreducible Dove." *Comparative Literature* 9 (1957): 124–35.

Slade, Carole, ed. *Approaches to Teaching Dante's "Divine Comedy."* New York: Modern Language Association, 1982.

Slide, Anthony. *The New Historical Dictionary of the American Film Industry.* Lanham, Md.: Scarecrow Press, 1998.

Smalley, Donald. "Introduction: Mrs. Trollope in America." Trollope, *Domestic Manners of the Americans.* New York: Vintage Books, 1949. vii–lxxvi.

Smethurst, James Edward. *The Black Arts Movement: Literary Nationalism in the 1960s and 1970s.* Chapel Hill: University of North Carolina Press, 2005.

Smith, Denis Mack. *Mazzini.* New Haven: Yale University Press, 1994.

Smith, Graham. *The Stone of Dante and Later Florentine Celebrations of the Poet.* Florence: Leo S. Olschki, 2000.

Snead, James. *White Screens/Black Images: Hollywood from the Dark Side.* Ed. Colin MacCabe and Cornel West. New York: Routledge, 1994.

Sollors, Werner. *Amiri Baraka/LeRoi Jones: The Quest for a "Populist Modernism."* New York: Columbia University Press, 1978.

Solzhenitzyn, Aleksandr. *The First Circle.* Trans. Thomas P. Whitney. New York: Harper and Row, 1968.

Soon, One Morning: New Writing by American Negroes, 1940–1962. Ed. Herbert Hill. New York: Knopf, 1963.

Soyinka, Wole, ed. and intro. *Poems of Black Africa.* New York: Hill and Wang, 1975.

Spillers, Hortense J. "Ellison's 'Usable Past': Toward a Theory of Myth." *Black and White and in Color: Essays on American Literature and Culture.* Chicago: University of Chicago Press, 2003. 65–80.

Spivak, Gayatri Chakravorty. *Death of a Discipline.* New York: Columbia University Press, 2003.

Stapleton, Thomas. *A Counterblast to M. Horne's Vayne Blast against M. Feckenham.* Louvain: Johannes Foulerus, 1566. Rpt. in *English Recusant Literature, 1558–1640.* Vol. 311. Ed. D. M. Rogers. London-Ilkley: Scholar Press, 1976.

Stauffer, John. *The Black Hearts of Men: Radical Abolitionists and the Transformation of Race.* Cambridge: Harvard University Press, 2002.

Steele, Meili. *Theorizing Textual Subjects: Agency and Oppression.* Cambridge: Cambridge University Press, 1997.

Stepto, Robert. *From Behind the Veil.* Urbana: University of Illinois Press, 1979.

Stewart, Jacqueline Najuma. *Migrating to the Movies: Cinema and Black Urban Modernity.* Berkeley: University of California Press, 2005.

Stiller, Richard. *Commune on the Frontier: The Story of Frances Wright.* New York: Crowell, 1972.

Straub, Julia. *Victorian Muse: The Afterlife of Dante's Beatrice in Nineteenth-Century Literature.* New York: Continuum, 2009.

Sumner, Charles. *His Complete Works.* Intro. George Frisbie Hoar. New York: Negro Universities Press, 1900.

———. *A Memorial of Abraham Lincoln, lately President of the United States.* Boston: City Council, 1865.

———. *The Selected Letters of Charles Sumner.* Ed. Beverly Wilson Palmer. 2 vols. Boston: Northeastern University Press, 1990.

Tambling, Jeremy. "Dante and Blake: Allegorizing the Event." In Havely, *Dante's Modern Afterlife* 33–48.

Tate, Greg. "Smiley the Redeemer." *Village Voice* Jan. 10, 1989: 61.

Terry, Arthur LeMont. "Genre and Divine Causality in the Religious Films of Spencer Williams, Jr." Diss. Regent University, 1995.

Thatcher, B. B. "Sketch of a Self-Made Sculptor." *The Knickerbocker* 5.4 (April 1835): 270–76.

Thompson, Andrew. "Dante, the *Risorgimento,* and the British: The Italian Background." Rpt. in *Dante: The Critical Complex.* Ed. Richard Lansing. Vol. 8. New York: Routledge, 2003. 92–120.

Thompson, Julius E. *Dudley Randall, Broadside Press, and the Black Arts Movement in Detroit, 1960–1995.* Jefferson, N.C.: McFarland, 1999.

Tolson, Melvin B. *Libretto for the Republic of Liberia.* New York: Twayne, 1953.

Toomer, Jean. *Cane.* Ed. Darwin T. Turner. New York: Norton, 1988.

————. *The Letters of Jean Toomer, 1919–1924.* Ed. Mark Whalan. Knoxville: University of Tennessee Press, 2006.

Touré, Askia M. *From the Pyramids to the Projects: Poems of Genocide and Resistance!* Trenton: Africa World Press, 1990.

Townsend, George Alfred. *The Life, Crime, and Capture of John Wilkes Booth . . .* New York: Dick and Fitzgerald, 1865.

Toynbee, Paget. *Dante in English Literature.* 2 vols. London: Methuen, 1909.

————. "John Foxe and the *editio princeps* of Dante's *De Monarchia.*" *Athenaeum* (April 14, 1906): 450–51.

Trauth, Mary Philip. *Italo-American Diplomatic Relations, 1861–1882: The Mission of George Perkins Marsh to the Kingdom of Italy.* Washington, D.C.: Catholic University of America Press, 1958.

Trollope, Frances. *Domestic Manners of the Americans.* Ed. Richard Mullen. Oxford and New York: Oxford University Press, 1984. "Introduction." Ix–xxxi.

————. *Domestic Manners of the Americans.* Ed. Donald Smalley. New York: Vintage Books, 1949. Rpt. Gloucester, Mass.: Peter Smith, 1974. Vii–lxxvi.

————. *A Visit to Italy.* 2 vols. London: Richard Bentley, 1842.

Trollope, Thomas Adolphus. "Some Recollections of Hiram Powers." *Lippincott's Magazine* 15 (1875): 205–15.

————. *What I Remember.* New York: Harper, 1888.

Tucker, Louis Leonard. " 'Ohio Show-Shop': The Western Museum of Cincinnati 1820–1867." *A Cabinet of Curiosities: Five Episodes in the Evolution of American Museums.* Intro. Walter Muir Whitehill. Charlottesville: University Press of Virginia, 1967.

Turner, James. *The Liberal Education of Charles Eliot Norton.* Baltimore: Johns Hopkins University Press, 1999.

————. *Without God, without Creed: The Origins of Unbelief in America.* Baltimore: Johns Hopkins University Press, 1985.

Underwood, Thomas A. *Allen Tate: Orphan of the South*. Princeton: Princeton University Press, 2000.

United States State Department. *The Assassination of Abraham Lincoln . . .* Washington, D.C.: Government Printing Office, 1866.

Vellon, Peter. "Black, White, or In Between? How America Saw Early Italian Immigrants." *Ambassador* 46 (2000): 10–13.

Verduin, Kathleen. "Dante in America: The First Hundred Years." *Reading Books: Essays on the Material Text and Literature in America*. Ed. Michele Moylan and Lane Stiles. Amherst: University of Massachusetts Press, 1996. 16–51.

———. "Dante's *Inferno*, Jonathan Edwards, and New England Calvinism." *Dante Studies* 123 (2005): 133–61.

Vickery, Olga W. "The *Inferno* of the Moderns." *The Shaken Realist: Essays in Modern Literature in Honor of Frederick J. Hoffman*. Ed. Melvin J. Friedman and John B. Vickery. Baton Rouge: Louisiana State University Press, 1970. 147–67.

Viscusi, Robert. *Max Beerbohm, or the Dandy Dante*. Baltimore: Johns Hopkins University Press, 1986.

Wallace, David. "Dante in England." *Dante for the New Millennium*. Ed. Teodolinda Barolini and H. Wayne Storey. New York: Fordham University Press, 2003. 422–34.

———. "Dante in English." *The Cambridge Companion to Dante*. Ed. Rachel Jacoff. Cambridge: Cambridge University Press, 1993. 237–58.

Walters, Tracey L. *African American Literature and the Classicist Tradition: Black Women Writers from Wheatley to Morrison*. New York: Palgrave Macmillan, 2007.

Ward, Catherine. "Gloria Naylor's *Linden Hills*: A Modern *Inferno*." *Contemporary Literature* 28 (Spring 1987): 67–81. Rpt. in Gates and Appiah, *Gloria Naylor* 182–94.

Ward, Jerry Washington, Jr. "N. J. Loftis' *Black Anima*: A Problem in Aesthetics." *Journal of Black Studies* 7.2 (1976): 195–209.

Warren, Kenneth W. "Race and Ethnicity." *Introduction to Scholarship in Modern Languages and Literatures*. Ed. David G. Nicholls. 3rd ed. New York: MLA, 2007.

Warren, Robert Penn. *Who Speaks for the Negro?* New York: Random House, 1965.

Washington, Booker T. *My Larger Education: Being Chapters from My Experience*. Garden City, N.Y.: Doubleday, 1911. *Documenting the American South*. Accessed Sept. 5, 2009. <http://docsouth.unc.edu/fpn/washeducation/washing.html>.

Washington, Booker T., and Robert E. Park. *The Man Farthest Down: A Record of Observation and Study in Europe*. 1912. Rpt. with intro. by St. Clair Drake. New Brunswick/London: Transaction Books, 1984.

Watkins, Mel. "The Circular Driveways of Hell." *New York Times Book Review* March 3, 1985: 11.

Watson, Steven. *The Birth of the Beat Generation: Visionaries, Rebels, and Hipsters, 1944–1960.* New York: Pantheon, 1995.

Watts, Jerry Gafio. *Amiri Baraka: The Politics and Art of a Black Intellectual.* New York: New York University Press, 2001.

Weisenfeld, Judith. *Hollywood Be Thy Name: African American Religion in American Film, 1929–1949.* Berkeley: University of California Press, 2007.

Welle, John P. "Dante in the Cinematic Mode: An Historical Survey of Dante Movies." *Dante's* Inferno: *The Indiana Critical Edition.* Ed. Mark Musa. Bloomington: Indiana University Press, 1995. 381–95.

Westminster Review 75.147 (Jan.–April 1861). New York: Leonard Scott, 1861.

Whitt, Margaret Earley. *Understanding Gloria Naylor.* Columbia: University of South Carolina Press, 1999.

Wicks, Margaret C. W. *The Italian Exiles in London, 1816–1848.* Manchester: Manchester University Press, 1937. Rpt. Freeport, N.Y.: Books for Libraries Press, 1968.

Wicksteed, Philip H. *Dante: Six Sermons.* 1879. London: Elkin Mathews, 1905.

Wilkins, Ernest Hatch. "Petrarch's *Coronation Oration.*" *Studies in the Life and Works of Petrarch.* Cambridge: Medieval Academy of America, 1955. 300–14. Originally published in *PMLA* 68 (1953): 1242–50.

Williams, Spencer, dir. *The Blood of Jesus.* Sack Amusement Enterprises, 1941.

———, dir. *Go Down, Death!* Sack Amusement Enterprises, 1944.

Wilson, F. P. "A Supplement to Toynbee's *Dante in English Literature.*" *Italian Studies* 3 (1946): 50–64.

Withrow, H. W. "The Ladies of Port Royal." *The Ladies' Repository: A Monthly Periodical, Devoted to Literature, Arts, and Religion* 4.2 (Aug. 1869): 129–34.

Wolff, Geoffrey A. "A Suit Borrowed from Dante Looks Funny on LeRoi Jones." *Washington Post* Nov. 20, 1965: A18.

Wolseley, Roland E. *The Black Press, U.S.A.* Ames: Iowa State University Press, 1990.

Work, M. N. "The Life of Charles B. Ray." *Journal of Negro History* 4.4 (1919): 361–71.

Wright, Richard. *Black Boy.* New York: Harper and Brothers, 1945.

———. "The Man Who Lived Underground." *Eight Men.* 1940. Cleveland: World Publishing, 1961. 27–92.

———. *Native Son.* New York: Harper and Brothers, 1940.

———. *12 Million Black Voices.* Photo direction by Edward Rosskam. 1941. New York: Thunder's Mouth Press, 1988.

Wunder, Richard P. *Hiram Powers: Vermont Sculptor, 1805–1873.* 2 vols. Newark: University of Delaware Press, 1991.

Young, Al. *Straight No Chaser.* Berkeley: Creative Arts Book Co., 1994.

Zafar, Rafia. "Capturing the Captivity: African Americans among the Puritans." *Melus* 17.2 (1991–92): 19–35.

———. *We Wear the Mask: African Americans Write American Literature, 1760–1870.* New York: Columbia University Press, 1997.

Ziolkowski, Jan M. "Introduction." Special issue, *Dante and Islam. Dante Studies* 125 (2007): 1–34.

INDEX

DENNIS LOONEY

is professor of Italian at the University of Pittsburgh.